Georges Bataille

C000104072

Georges Bataille (1897–1962) was a philosopher, writer, and literary critic whose work has had a significant impact across disciplines as diverse as philosophy, sociology, economics, art history, and literary criticism, as well as influencing key figures in contemporary European philosophy such as Jacques Derrida and Michel Foucault.

In *Georges Bataille: Key Concepts* an international team of contributors provide an accessible examination of Bataille's work. The chapters in the first section of the book study the social, political, artistic, and philosophical contexts that shaped Bataille's thought, while those in the second section cover a series of key areas of his writings, including art, eroticism, evil, religion, sacrifice, and sovereignty.

This book is an invaluable guide for students from across the Humanities and Social Sciences coming to Bataille's work for the first time.

Mark Hewson teaches at the Melbourne School of Continental Philosophy and at the University of Melbourne, Australia. He is the author of *Blanchot and Literary Criticism* (2011), and of articles on Wordsworth, Mallarmé, and the history of literary criticism.

Marcus Coelen is an affiliate of the Institute for Cultural Inquiry, Berlin, and a practicing psychoanalyst. He is the author of a study on Proust and the problem of aesthetic judgment in the *Recherche*, and several translations and editions in German of texts by Maurice Blanchot. He is a co-editor of the book series *Neue Subjektile*.

Key Concepts

Georges Bataille

Key Concepts

Edited by
Mark Hewson and Marcus Coelen

Routledge
Taylor & Francis Group

LONDON AND NEW YORK

First published 2016
by Routledge
2 Park Square, Milton Park, Abingdon, Oxon OX14 4RN

and by Routledge
711 Third Avenue, New York, NY 10017

Routledge is an imprint of the Taylor & Francis Group, an informa business

British Library Cataloguing in Publication Data
A catalogue record for this book is available from the British Library

Library of Congress Cataloging in Publication Data
Georges Bataille : key concepts / edited by Mark Hewson and Marcus Coelen. – 1 [edition].
pages cm. – (Key concepts)
Includes bibliographical references and index.
1. Bataille, Georges, 1897-1962. I. Hewson, Mark, editor.
B2430.B33954G463 2016
194–dc23
2015025365

ISBN: 978-1-138-90855-0 (hbk)
ISBN: 978-1-138-90856-7 (pbk)
ISBN: 978-1-315-65736-3 (ebk)

Typeset in Times New Roman
by Taylor & Francis Books

Contents

Contributors

Giulia Agostini is assistant professor at Heidelberg University where she obtained her PhD with a thesis on Pierre Klossowski. From 2012–2014 she was a Marie-Curie fellow at Versailles University. Since October 2014 she has been visiting scholar at Sorbonne–Paris IV. She is currently preparing a book on "After Literature. Leopardi, Mallarmé, Zambrano."

Elisabeth Arnould-Bloomfield is Associate Professor of French and Comparative Literatures at the University of Colorado, Boulder. She is the author of *Bataille, La terreur et les lettres* (2009) and has published articles and book chapters on Bataille, Ponge, Proust, Pierre Michon, Marie NDiaye and others. She is currently researching contemporary representations of animals and is at work on a manuscript entitled *"Negative Zoologies, Death and Suffering in Twentieth- and Twenty-first Centuries Animal Representations."*

Tiina Arppe is a Senior Research Fellow at the Department of Social Research, University of Helsinki. She is a specialist in French social theory and has written about Rousseau, Durkheim, Mauss, Bataille and Baudrillard among others. Her publications include *Affectivity and the Social Bond: Transcendence, Economy and Violence in French Social Theory* (2014), "Sacred Violence: Girard, Bataille and the Vicissitudes of Human Desire" (*Distinktion* 19/2009) and "Sorcerer's Apprentices and the Will to Figuration: The Ambiguous Heritage of the Collège de Sociologie" (*Theory, Culture and Society* 26(4), 2009). She has also translated several French theorists into Finnish, including texts of Derrida, Bataille, Baudrillard, Kristeva and Bourdieu.

Marcus Coelen is an affiliate of ICI Berlin and a practicing psychoanalyst. He held positions in Romance Philology and Comparative

Literature at the universities of Hamburg, Zürich and Munich (LMU) and has taught in Israel and Brazil. Among his publications are a study on Proust and the problem of (aesthetic) judgment in the *Recherche* (*Angemaßte Notwendigkeiten. Lektüren Proust*, 2007), several translations and editions in German of texts by Maurice Blanchot (*Politische Schriften 1958–1993*, 2008; *Das Neutrale. Texte und Fragmente zur Philosophie*, 2010; *Vergehen*, 2012) and a constellation around the "primal scene" (*Die andere Urszene. Texte von Maurice Blanchot*, Philippe Lacoue-Labarthe et al., 2009). He is a co-editor of the book series *Neue Subjektile* with Turia+Kant, Vienna and Berlin.

Simonetta Falasca-Zamponi is a professor of sociology at the University of California, Santa Barbara and the author, among other publications, of *Fascist Spectacle: The Aesthetics of Power in Mussolini's Italy* (1997) and *Rethinking the Political: The Sacred, Aesthetic Politics, and the Collège de Sociologie* (2011). She is also the editor of Georges Bataille's unpublished lecture at the Collège, *La sociologie sacrée du monde contemporain* (2004).

Patrick ffrench is Professor of French at King's College London, where he specialises in 20th-century French literature and thought, especially the legacies of French theory post-1945 and the work of Georges Bataille. He is the author of *The Time of Theory: A History of* Tel Quel (1996), *The Cut: Reading Bataille's Story of the Eye* (2000) and *After Bataille: Sacrifice, Exposure, Community* (2007). He is also co-editor and co-translator of *The Tel Quel Reader* (Routledge 1999). He is currently working on the question of bodily movement in French literature and thought from the late 19th century to the present.

Marina Galletti is Professor of French Literature at the University of Rome III. She is the author of *La comunità impossibile di Georges Bataille*. She edited and introduced *L'Apprenti Sorcier. Textes, lettres et documents (1932–1939)* (La Différence, Paris), a collection of documents pertaining to Georges Bataille's work in the 1930s and also collaborated on the Pléiade edition of the *Romans et récits* of Georges Bataille. She is presently working on a new English version of *L'Apprenti Sorcier*, focussing on Bataille's activities with Acéphale.

Nadine Hartmann is a doctoral candidate at the Bauhaus University Weimar. She is currently working on her Ph.D. thesis on epistemological challenges in Georges Bataille's "Summa Atheologica." She has published articles on the theoretical writings of Bataille, Freud, and Lacan. Her research interests include psychoanalysis, feminist philosophy, continental philosophy of the 20th/21st century, and art theory.

Mark Hewson teaches at the MSCP and at the University of Melbourne. He is the author of *Blanchot and Literary Criticism* (2011), and of articles on Wordsworth, Mallarmé and the history of literary criticism.

Andrew Hussey OBE is Professor of Cultural History, School of Advanced Study, University of London. He is Director of the Centre for Post-Colonial Studies, University of London. He has written extensively in French and English on Georges Bataille and Guy Debord. His latest book is called *The French Intifada* (2014). He is currently working on a book called *The Art of Heroin: A Cultural History of the Hardest Drug*.

Stuart Kendall is a writer, editor, and translator working at the intersections of modern and contemporary poetics, visual culture, and design. He is the author of a biography of Georges Bataille and translator of six volumes of Bataille's work including *Inner Experience, Guilty,* and *On Nietzsche.* He is Associate Professor of Design in the graduate design program at the California College of the Arts.

Claire Nioche studied philosophy at the Ecole Normale Supérieure and at the Université Paris Sorbonne, France. She is currently a postdoctoral fellow at the Institute for Cultural Inquiry (ICI, Berlin, Germany). Among her publications are a series of articles on literature (Maurice Blanchot, Claude Simon), contemporary philosophy and psychoanalysis (Deleuze, Derrida, Freud, Lacan).

Gerhard Poppenberg is Professor of Romance Languages at the University of Heidelberg. He is the author of *Ins Ungebundene. Über Literatur nach Blanchot* (1993) and of *Die Antinomie des Gesetzes. Der Orestmythos in der Antike und der Moderne* (Matthes and Seitz, 2013), a study on modern versions of the Orestes myth, which is soon to appear in English translation. His current research project concerns the theory of figural language.

Michèle Richman is Professor of French Studies at the University of Pennsylvania. Publications include *Reading Georges Bataille: Beyond the Gift* (1982) and *Sacred Revolutions: Durkheim and the College de Sociologie* (2002), as well as articles, chapters, encyclopedia entries, and book introductions devoted to Barthes, Bataille, Durkheim, Lahire, Leiris, Mauss, and Nitsch. Her current research project examines the impact of prehistory on French Modernism.

Abbreviations

A	*L'Apprenti sorcier: Du Cercle Communiste Démocratique à Acéphale* (1999).
AS 1	*The Accursed Share*, Vol. 1 (1988).
AS 2	*The Accursed Share*, Vols 2 and 3 (1991).
BN	*Blue of Noon* (1986).
CH	*The Cradle of Humanity: Prehistoric Art and Culture* (2009).
CL	*Correspondence: Georges Bataille Michel Leiris* (2008).
CS	*The College of Sociology 1937–39* (1988).
D	*Documents: Doctrines, Archéologie, Beaux-Arts, Ethnographie* (1991).
E	*Eroticism: Death and Sensuality* (1986).
EW	*Georges Bataille: Essential Writings* (1998).
G	*Guilty* (2011).
HDS	"Hegel, Death and Sacrifice" (1990).
L	*Choix de lettres, 1917–1962* (1997).
LBA	*Lascaux or the birth of art* (1955).
LE	*Literature and Evil* (1985).
M	*Manet* (1983).
MM	*My Mother, Madame Edwarda, The Dead Man* (2012).
O	*October, 36*: "Georges Bataille: Writings on Laughter, Sacrifice, Nietzsche, Un-Knowing" (1986).
OC	*Oeuvres Complètes* (1970–1988).
ON	*On Nietzsche* (2004)
RR	*Romans et récits* (2004).
SE	*The Story of the Eye* (2001).
SS	*La sociologie sacrée du monde contemporain* (2004).
TE	*The Tears of Eros* (2001).
TR	*Theory of Religion* (1992).

US	*Unfinished System of Non-Knowledge* (2004).
VE	*Visions of Excess. Selected Writings 1927–1939* (1985).
WS	*Absence of Myth: Writings on Surrealism* (2006).

Note

Where possible, citations are taken from existing English translations. Modifications are indicated in the text.

Introduction

Mark Hewson and Marcus Coelen

In recent years, the number of works published on Georges Bataille, as well as the variety of contexts in which his work is invoked, has markedly increased. It could be argued that the last 15 years have marked a new stage in the reception of his work. In Bataille's lifetime, he did not have a prominence comparable with the most influential intellectuals, even in France, and certainly not internationally. He only began to be recognized by a wider public, towards the end of his life. In 1957, five years before his death, he published three books (*Eroticism, Literature and Evil*, and the novel, *Blue of Noon*), which prompted some discussion in the intellectual press, and one television interview. However, while Bataille was close to the centre of the Parisian intellectual world throughout his life, and from 1946, was the founding editor of the much admired journal *Critique*, his status as one of the figures of reference in modern thought has been acquired posthumously.

In the years after Bataille's death (in 1962), homages and review articles were published by a number of the writers who shaped the intellectual landscape in France in the 1960s – including Roland Barthes, Michel Foucault, and Jacques Derrida – and the journal *Tel Quel* gave him a privileged position in their revised canon of literary modernity. The elevation in his status was consolidated in 1970, with the commencement of the publication of all of his writings by Gallimard, a treatment reserved for the most important authors. The 12 volumes of the *Oeuvres Complètes*, which were progressively released over the next 18 years, are among the most impressive works in the philology of modern literature, and profoundly changed the image of Bataille. Drawn from the mass of papers left behind by Bataille at his death, these volumes collect works previously out of print, as well as drafts and notes from all periods of his life, and include several more or less complete unpublished works. The notes to each volume give additional material, notes and variants, information on the intended publication, even a list of the books he borrowed from the library.

Bataille's work is very diverse in terms of the intellectual areas which it enters into. It includes contributions to philosophy, sociology, economics, prehistory, literary criticism, and several other domains, as well as novels, stories, poetry and some works that are very difficult to classify. Nonetheless, the impression that one comes to have in studying it is not so much one of abundant diversity, but rather of the remarkable consistency and single-mindedness of a thought which never loses sight of its own objectives. This sense of an underlying purposefulness cannot be missed when the texts assume their place within this collected edition. Bataille appears no longer primarily as the author of individual works, but as the initiator of a thought that is maintained throughout a life, and of a mode of writing whose address, tone and gesture is discernible in scholarly exposition and in literary narratives, in contributions to sociology, theology or pornography. This cohesiveness makes very great, perhaps impossible demands on the reader, since it seems to demand cognizance of the textual labyrinth that, as we now see, lies behind the most famous and striking works. The result is that Bataille has rapidly become the terrain of specialists, especially in France, and so entering into his work becomes all the more difficult at the very point at which it begins to have an impact on debates which, by their contemporary and evolving nature, cannot be entirely subject to the rigors of specialization.

This introduction is intended for the reader seeking an orientation in the terrain of Bataille's work. For this purpose, the chronological approach is perhaps the most useful, even if it remains at the level of heuristic indications. Any kind of division of Bataille's work into phases only has limited validity precisely because of its consistency, which shows itself in the fact that very often what comes later is already present in some form in the earlier works. It is possible, however, to trace an itinerary in an external way, by reference to the distinct intellectual and material contexts of Bataille's writing during his life. The literary writings are a little less amenable to this approach, and they will feature less in this overview: the reader is referred to the essay by Patrick ffrench in this volume.[1]

The 1920s – Surrealism and *Documents*

As Marina Galletti shows in her text in this volume, Bataille's intellectual career is deeply marked by his contact with surrealism, despite his conflictual relationship with André Breton. On the formal level his

1929 novella, *The Story of the Eye*, could be counted among the most successful products of literary surrealism; its mixture of realistic and hallucinatory representation is similar to that in surrealist art and poetry and its volatile eroticism is a confrontation for normalized social values just as are the surrealist manifestos. The techniques of surrealism are also apparent in the less well-known, but no less extreme and accomplished text "The Solar Anus", a poetic cosmology and a love poem, written in 1927 and published in 1931. Taken as a whole, his early writings appear as an alternative realization of the surrealist impulse and, as such, invite a renewed understanding of the meaning of this movement. This only became apparent with the publication (in 1970) of the first two volumes of the *Oeuvres Complètes* (compiled by Denis Hollier), which bring together all the work which Bataille had produced during these years. The re-publication of these essays, most of which had remained in a dispersed state after their initial publication in literary and art journals, in one volume, and the addition of many important unpublished texts from the same period (collected in the second volume of the *Oeuvres Complètes*) was perhaps the most immediate factor in Bataille's revaluation. A similar effect was produced in English with the collection, *Visions of Excess*, published in 1985, a translation into English (by Allan Stoekl) of a selection from these two volumes; and then by the publication, the following year, of a further selection of translations (by Annette Michelson), mostly from the same period of Bataille's production, in *October*, the art theory journal which has played an animating role in the dissemination of his thought in the U.S.

In particular, these re-publications have turned attention towards *Documents*, the journal which Bataille edited between 1929 and 1931. The title signals the peculiar effect that is attained by the objective presentation of images and artefacts, if they are presented without reference to the horizon of beauty or aesthetic value (Hollier 1992). The articles present and discuss contemporary works of art, but also photographs, objects drawn from popular culture and from everyday life, from archaeology and from ethnography. The journal includes entries for a "critical dictionary", brief texts, by Bataille and his collaborators, reflecting on the charge of significance to be found in certain objects in the natural or human world: the eye, the big toe, the flower, the factory, the abattoir. If there has been a new stage in Bataille's reception in recent years, as his work has emerged from the margins and become an endemic reference, this shift took place first of all in art theory. As Michèle Richman notes in her essay in this volume, artists and art-historians have recognized the resonance of *Documents* with their own recent preoccupations with the materiality of artistic works and the dissolution of the boundary between high and low art. Georges Didi-Hubermann (1995) devoted a major book (still not translated into English) to a close reading of *Documents*, positioning it as a key text for interpreting the modern transformation of aesthetic categories away from the notions of beauty and taste. Yve-Alain Bois and Rosalind Krauss's *Formless: A User's Guide* (1996), an exhibition catalogue and set of essays developing out of their work with *October*, also takes Bataille's work as key to modern art; their texts appropriate the terms and concepts of *Documents*, arguing that Bataille's categories of the formless and the "low" correspond to something essential in modernist innovations that is missed in the formal and aesthetic terms in which it has been recognized and acclaimed. The interest for Bataille in art-history and art-theory has been reflected by a series of recent publications in English which have made a much more complete picture of Bataille's work during the 1920s available in English – although there is still no integral translation of *Documents*. The *Encyclopedia Acephalica* (1996) translates and collects the articles making up the critical dictionary which appeared in *Documents*. *Undercover Surrealism* (2006), edited by Dawn Ades and Simon Baker, a catalogue from an exhibition at the Tate Gallery in London, seeks to give a new perspective on surrealism, taking *Documents* and Bataille's work as a point of departure; it includes many illustrations from *Documents*, essays on Bataille and surrealism, and some new translations. A translation of Bataille's correspondence with Michel Leiris has also appeared (2008), which includes the retrospective reflections of each on their participation in surrealism, and an important discussion of *Documents* by Leiris.

While it has been art history and art theory that has brought these early writings into discussion in recent years, Bataille's early writings are not solely, or even primarily, a reflection on art and its modern transformations. At least two further dimensions need to be noted. In terms of their material content and range of examples, Bataille's writings are characterized by their frequent reference to research in ethnography and the history of religion. With his closest early associates, Michel Leiris and the ethnographer, Alfred Métraux, Bataille studied the work of Émile Durkheim, Robert Hertz and Marcel Mauss in the 1920s, and the writings of this school remain a central reference in his political and social thought, as Simonetta Falasca-Zamponi underlines in her article in this volume. Throughout his writings, Bataille supports his analyses by reference to ancient religion, mythology and ritual, prehistory and archaeology; in *Documents*, there are articles on Gnosticism, and its antecedents in ancient religion, on "Primitive Art", and on the practice of religious sacrifice.

The second element that would have to be introduced here is the initial philosophical thought of Bataille, which comes from the theorization of the effect of *Documents*. He imagines a "heterology", a scientific reflection on the heterogeneous, on that which is abnormal or disturbing and its relation to the normal, to the homogeneous. This thought is first developed in order to elaborate Bataille's sense of his difference from surrealism: the first major text on this question is "The Use Value of D.A.F Sade", unpublished in his lifetime (in English, in *Visions of Excess*); the second volume of the *Oeuvres Complètes* includes a dossier of unpublished reflections on heterology.

Already, with this rapid indication of the concerns that come together in Bataille's early writings, it is possible to recognize the tensions that have shaped their reception. These have to do, not so much with the diversity of this work itself, as with the diversity of the disciplinary and discursive contexts in which it has been taken up. For Bataille's admirers in the 1960s in France, including Foucault and Derrida, it was the elements of a philosophical thought in Bataille – especially the theory of the heterological – which resonated with their own critical reflection on the "law of the same" and on the coercion of the normal regime in both discourse and social and political institutions. The interest in Bataille's writing as an original theorization and realization of the surrealist impulse, as we have noted, has come above all from art history and art theory. It is true that the interest of art theory for Bataille has often approached his work through the mediation of the thought of the 1960s – but this has not necessarily been the most successful aspect of his appropriation. On the contrary, when this has happened, in art theory as elsewhere, Bataille's thought has often been dissolved into a generalized post-structuralism or post-modernism, which does not represent its real concerns, as has been convincingly argued in several critical studies of Bataille (Richardson 1994; Connor 2000; Hussey 2000). This "post-structuralist" vision of Bataille, which for a certain time dominated his reception, has been attenuated as a result of his work being taken more seriously in sociology, ethnography and history of religions. It has become more common to see his work included within a discourse whose frame of reference comes not from the legacy of 1960s deconstruction, but from the concerns of these disciplines (Falasca-Zamponi, 2011; Pawlett, 2013; Arppe, 2014). The result is that the reception of Bataille tends to diverge according to the directions of each inquiry: for art history, it is the realization that he gives to transformations in aesthetics that demands to be interpreted: for the philosophers, his insight into discourse as a regime of homogeneity, excluding the heterogeneous, needs to be developed and formalized; for anthropology, it is a matter of testing or modifying his social and historical insights. It is only to be expected, of course, that each study takes from Bataille what is important for their own inquiry; but the diversity of these directions poses the question as to whether it is possible to identify something like a central axis of his thought that first enables him to move between such diverse areas of inquiry.

The 1930s – Contre-Attaque and Acéphale

The direction of Bataille's work shifts from around 1931, as *Documents* folds, and he begins to write for *La Critique Sociale* (1933–1934), a journal devoted to critical analysis of the contemporary political situation, founded by Boris Souvarine, a dissident communist and the translator of Lenin and Trotsky into French. While this shift is conditioned by his new intellectual circle, it is also motivated by changes in the political situation. The situation for Bataille is essentially that confronted by the avant-gardes more generally, who can no longer simply direct their energies against the bourgeoisie and establishment culture, but have to respond to the emergence of fascism. Surrealism also passes through a fundamental crisis at this time, as it attempts to recognize the validity of communism, without simply becoming subject to its authority (Nadeau, 1978).

Bataille published two key essays in *La Critique Sociale*: "The Notion of Expenditure" (1933) and "The Psychological Structure of Fascism" (1933–1934). These texts address directly questions of the economy and the state in a way that his earlier writings had not. *Documents* may have seemed to its readers to be an exercise in provocation, but the strategies that it deploys – the identification of the heterological moment, the comparison with archaic societies – now show themselves capable of functioning with a similar subversive effect when applied to political objects. "The Notion of Expenditure" challenges a fundamental assumption that Marxism shares with the capitalist political economy – the notion that humanity is essentially productive and that all value therefore has its measure in production and conservation. Drawing on Marcel Mauss's anthropological study of gift giving, Bataille argues for the centrality of expenditure in all forms of society. The various forms of unproductive expenditure – monuments, festivals, spectacles, gifts, parties, luxuries – make up an original category of economic activity, one which cannot be analysed or evaluated in terms of utilitarian value or the profit motive. The excitement and the passions to which expenditure gives rise reveal that it is always perceived as the most important economic activity, although for the most part, this judgment is not openly professed when it comes to stating social values and priorities.

With this essay, Bataille introduces an inquiry that he will continue to develop for 15 years, and which will reach its provisional completion with *The Accursed Share* (1949). As Stuart Kendall underlines in his essay on this topic here, the question takes on a new aspect in consequence of changes in the economy that have supervened since Bataille was writing. These developments by no means invalidate the theory. It remains an open question, however, how Bataille's notion of expenditure should be integrated into critical reflection on an economy shaped by the global movement of capital and tending towards ecological disaster. This has been the leading question in a number of critical discussions of Bataille, including Baudrillard (1993), Goux (1990), Noys (2000) and Stoekl (2007).

"The Psychological Structure of Fascism" offers both a general theory of society and class-structure and a historical analysis of the political forces in play in Europe in the 1930s, in order to understand the psychological conditions that favour fascism. Bataille recognizes Marxist economic and social theory as the precondition for its own political thought, but seeks to make up for the inability of Marxist theory to explain the success of fascism in its own terms. In view of the length and intricacy of "The Psychological Structure of Fascism", we will turn to the manifesto for *Contre-Attaque*, a short-lived political organization founded by Bataille in 1935 in order to give a sketch of the argument. The formation of this group marks a new shift in the external conditions of Bataille's work. He now becomes an activist and an organizer, a role he will continue to play up until the beginning of the war. During this period, most of his texts specifically address the concerns of the intellectual and political groups of which he is the instigator. Contre-Attaque brings together members of the surrealist group led by André Breton and the communist group organized around Boris Souvarine, with both of which Bataille had been associated. It is an attempt to form a new political organization that would channel the revolutionary impulses of both of these groups and that could intervene in the increasingly volatile political situation of France; the significance of this situation as a condition for Bataille's work is discussed in this volume in the essay by Andrew Hussey. The manifesto of Contre-Attaque (available in Richardson and Fijalkowski, 2001) illustrates very concretely the conformity and the deviation of Bataille's thought from the revolutionary left of *La Critique Sociale*. The text declares the group's commitment to opposing capitalism, nationalism and nationalist militarism. It openly calls for armed revolt, the re-distribution of wealth, and the establishment of a "dictatorship of the people". Towards the end of the document, however, with the thirteenth of the numbered points of the manifesto, one sees a marked shift away from the language of the revolutionary left as it declares the necessity "to make use of the fundamental aspiration of men to affective exaltation and to fanaticism" (OC I, 382). For Bataille, fascism's strength has been its ability to offer the sense of collective belonging which has atrophied in the individualist ideology of liberal democracy. Its appeal to the affective dimension gives it an advantage over communism, whose claims are rational – a scientific analysis of the production process and an appeal to a consciousness of the universal interest. Bataille, in the name of Contre-Attaque, declares the necessity of appropriating this power of the affects for the left. What this meant in concrete terms remained at this point undefined, but this willingness to engage with fascism on its own terrain has invited suspicions – first voiced by the surrealists, with malicious intent, but often repeated in subsequent historical reflections – that Bataille's thought crosses the line into the domain it seeks to neutralize. There can be no doubt about the injustice of this accusation on the biographical level: Bataille was one of the first in France to develop an in-depth critical analysis of fascism, and he continued to actively oppose it up until the beginning of the war, with a purposeful energy which had few equals in the intellectual world of the time. Nonetheless it is true that the direction of Bataille's political thought has very often provoked misgivings in his critics, and has rarely received even qualified assent. The political ideas he developed at this time are, however, often taken up in attempts to understand the intertwining of politics and affectivity in the history of this period. This possibility is discussed by ffrench (2007), and it is central to the recent books by Falasca-Zamponi (2011) and Arppe (2014).

The personal and ideological oppositions between the various factions that Bataille had brought together in Contre-Attaque soon led to the dissolution of the movement. In 1936, Bataille announced the principles of a new social movement in "The Sacred Conspiracy", the opening text of the journal entitled *Acéphale*. This group, largely composed of Bataille's allies within Contre-Attaque, continues the revolutionary opposition to existing society of the former group, but now manifests this opposition in the form of a separate and secret community, rather than in public agitation. The history of this social experiment has long been surrounded with a nimbus of mystery and legend, and the precise nature of the activities will likely remain a subject of speculation. It may be, however, that the rumours of strange rituals (which some have largely dismissed, however: see Bischof, 2010), have distracted attention from the thought, which is documented in the texts published in the journal Acéphale (1936–1939), as well as other texts published by Bataille at the time, most of which are available in English (in *Visions of Excess* and *October* 36, or in the third section of *Inner Experience*). With the publication in French of *L'Apprenti Sorcier* (edited by Marina Galletti, 1999), which collects letters and documents by Bataille and other participants of Contre-Attaque and Acéphale, it becomes possible to recognize the coherence of the writings of this period, which were not gathered together by Bataille, and remained dispersed in different publications (as indeed they still are today).[2]

The formation of Acéphale is conceived as a displacement away from the more immediate political concerns of Contre-Attaque – which are henceforth disparaged – and towards what the writings of the group often call a "religious" activity (Falasca-Zamponi, 2011, 144–165). It is worth entering into a little more detail on some of these texts, since at this point, Bataille begins to formulate his social and political position in terms of the most fundamental questions. Let us here begin with the movement of the text "What I have to say" – a position paper from April 1937, delivered to a meeting of Acéphale, and collected in *L'Apprenti Sorcier*. As a communication to the group, rather than a publication, the text does not have the brilliance of "finish" of many of Bataille's texts. But perhaps just because it is given in these circumstances, it has a kind of simplicity and directness which the texts of the post-war years which come closer to a synthetic statement (such as "Method of Meditation", for example) certainly do not seek to attain.

The text begins with a denunciation of the mode of living of present day society, and in particular, of the individual, as the taken for granted point of orientation of our understanding of the world. The dominant preoccupation with the specific goals of the individual is seen as the root of the contemporary spiritual malaise, and more than this, as a fundamental ontological delusion, by which the question of existence as a whole is dissimulated (A, 324–325). This denunciation of the priority of the individual (often referred to as "the isolated being") figures centrally in Bataille's writings from this time: it is most fully developed in "The Labyrinth" and "Communication", texts belonging to this same period, and later included in the third section of *Inner Experience* (1941). Politics, Bataille writes in the text with which we are here concerned, has at least the merit that it turns our attention away from our own particular interests, and poses the question of society as a whole. But the goals envisaged in a political program are only an inadequate representation of a more "essential aspiration" (A, 326), which concerns our position in the midst of the totality of the real. It is this relation to reality as a whole (*la realité en son ensemble*) which is suppressed in a social existence that is organized around the individual self. Reality is characterized in this text by "its avarice and its continual aggressions against man" – its "aggressivity" (A, 327–328). This terminology is perhaps modelled on Nietzsche, the key philosophical reference of the Acéphale group, who conceptualizes the will to power as a violence and an exploitation, characteristic of nature itself (c.f. Haar, 1996, chapter 6). The term "aggressivity" is not retained by Bataille, but the same perception is expressed by the term "violence", a central category in his later texts.

The power of the individual point of view has advanced so far, Bataille suggests, that it has become difficult even to envisage any alternative mode of being. It is only with the development of ethnography and the history of ancient religions that a point of view becomes available from which to recognize the limits of our own horizon. These disciplines give us the image of a society in which "violence was not separated from the humanity who lived with it", a society which did not simply recoil from violence, but responded to it "with all the complexity of its affective movements":

> The dance of human life would now come closer to violence, now distance itself from it in terror, as if its attitudes were composed in view of a compromise with violence itself.
>
> (A, 328)

With the metaphor of the "dance" here, Bataille has in mind the alternation of periods of profane and sacred time. Archaic humanity enters into complicity with the violence of existence by participating in the exaltation and the violence of the festival and the sacrifice; but this complicity is strictly limited to the period of time marked out for it, and outside of this time, social life moves in the profane element of work, in which it assures its preservation and holds itself apart from violence. One should note the illustrative value given to sacrifice in this argument. As Elisabeth Arnaud-Bloomfield underlines in her essay in this volume, the question of sacrifice is present in texts written throughout Bataille's career, and he nominates the interpretation of this quasi-universal practice in ancient human societies as the key question for philosophical anthropology.

Bataille goes on to argue that the great universal religions are characterized by a more simple affective structure, one that is shaped by their terror of violence, in which they deny themselves any part. This is above all the case with Christianity, which justifies "reality as a whole" by its theodicy, and attributes violence to the fault of man. Socialism perpetuates the Christian heritage, Bataille argues: it looks forward to a revolution, and is prepared to countenance its violence, but only on the understanding that it is a necessary stage on the path to a final eradication of violence. Like Christianity, it refuses to recognize that violence is constitutional in humanity (A, 330). It is notable that the rhetoric and the terminology of Marxism, which still serves to some extent as a framework for the articles for *La Critique Sociale* and the tracts of Contre-Attaque, recedes from view in the texts of Acéphale, as Bataille begins to formulate his own position. The rejection of socialism in these terms opens on to the debate with communism in his later writings, especially in the projected third volume of *The Accursed Share* entitled *Sovereignty* (1951–1953, though not published in Bataille's lifetime).

In "Propositions", published in Acéphale in 1937, the same themes – the individual and the totality, religion and violence – are developed in relation to contemporary Europe. Modern economic history, Bataille writes, has been dominated by the immense effort to discover and appropriate the wealth of the earth. The great success of this endeavour, however, has led to the two world wars (both of which Bataille lived through, it should be noted). The "fire and iron" drawn from out of the earth have been turned into weapons with which men have slaughtered each other. It is necessary that we draw the lesson from this sequence:

> It is the misunderstanding of the Earth, the star on which he lives, the ignorance of the nature of riches, in other words, of the incandescence enclosed within this star that has made for man an existence at the mercy of the merchandise he produces, the largest part of which is devoted to death. As long as men forget the true nature of terrestrial life, which demands ecstatic drunkenness and splendour, nature can only come to the attention of accountants and economists of all parties by abandoning them to the most complete results of their accounting and their economics.
>
> Men do not know how to freely enjoy the products of the Earth freely and with prodigality. The Earth and her products only lavish and liberate themselves in order to destroy
>
> (VE, 201)

The violence and aggressivity of reality as a whole reappears in this text in mythic form as "the Earth", imagined as a power of prodigal and indifferent generation, constantly creating new beings only to destroy them. The affective structure of modern society is characterized by avarice rather than terror; it is governed by the calculations of the accountants rather than the laws of the priests. The Earth has come to be understood as a store of riches, which can be accumulated in the forms of property and possessions. Modern humanity dedicates itself to the generation of wealth, and then finds itself in a reified, factitious world, "at the mercy of the goods we produce". What is required then is another mode of living, one that would not "forget the true nature of earthly riches". Just as archaic man, in the sacrifice and the festival, allowed himself a complicity with the violence of the totality, so also modern humanity has to respond to the "incandescence" of the Earth with "ecstasy and drunkenness". But here "ecstasy and drunkenness" is only given in overcoming the anguish at destruction that underlies the inert affect of continual work and accumulation; it is a joy that is inseparable from "an exalted acceptance of tragic destruction" (A, 476). In the last issue of Acéphale, Bataille proposes a manual of meditation – "The Practice of Joy before Death" (VE, 235–239).

Reading through the documents collected in *L'Apprenti Sorcier*, it is apparent that the sense in which the Acéphale group want to take over the term "religion" to designate their own activity remains subject to an ongoing discussion – and it does not seem that definitive clarification had been attained before the dissolution of the group in 1939, following internal dissensions. Certainly, one can see a family resemblance to the rhetoric of religious discourse in Bataille's texts when they denounce the narrowness and the inertia of the atomized individual, and call for an awakening to concerns that are more essential and shared by all. The tone is at times almost prophetic, and its intensity and seriousness is at odds with the received image of Bataille as an avant-garde *provocateur*. The position paper "What I have to say" concludes by proposing early Christian communities as the model for the experiment of Acéphale. Bataille adds at once that this comparison is only used for lack of a more suitable example, and that it is regrettable, given that Acéphale takes the "death of God" as its founding principle. But it holds true in the sense that Acéphale is an intense and restrictive community, founded on "a common and rigorous affirmation", whose vocation is to prepare the ground for an awakening of the consciousness of community more generally (A, 334).

From the end of 1937, the role of dissemination is assigned to the College of Sociology, which Bataille together with Michel Leiris and Roger Caillois founded during this period, and which came to replace the journal of Acéphale as the public face of the group's activities. The College of Sociology draws on the work of the French sociological school – and especially their work on archaic religion – in order to reflect upon the means and the practices that make community present and active to its members. The question is how the collective dimension can be reinvigorated, once the mythological and religious beliefs that sustained the existence of the community have died out or atrophied. With both the College of Sociology and Acéphale, Bataille weighs the prospects of myth and ritual under present-day conditions, although his movement in this direction remains tentative and exploratory. One can see some of the leading themes and motifs in his subsequent writings as responding to the question of community under modern conditions – especially in all that relates to the theme of "communication", a word that he uses in a terminological sense to designate all the forms by which the individual moves out of a state of enclosure in its own isolated existence and opens on to others: its privileged example is laughter, which Bataille conceives of as strictly analogous to sacrifice (the one who is laughed at is the victim): one can see the question of "communication" at work in a whole series of motifs in Bataille's subsequent texts, including contagion, complicity or friendship.

With the dissolution of Acéphale, the experiment in community was at an end. One cannot assess its success, since the group refused in principle to give itself a precise goal, but it may be telling that Bataille did not take up any comparable activities during or after the war. The texts and activities of Bataille in the inter-war years have had an afterlife in the philosophical discussion of recent years, however, beginning with Jean-Luc Nancy's book, *The Inoperative Community* (1991, first published as an essay in French in 1983, and then in book form in 1986). Rather than being a study of Bataille as such, this book takes his work as a point of departure for a philosophical articulation of the question of community. It is Bataille, more than any other thinker, Nancy suggests, who reveals the importance of this question in the background of the political oppositions between democracy, fascism and communism during the 1920s and 1930s. The notion of the "inoperative community" (*La communauté désoeuvrée*) that gives Nancy's book its title builds upon the distinction by which Acéphale separates itself from other forms of social and political organization. Acéphale is a community in the strongest possible sense in that it is based solely on the shared fact of existence, as opposed to any corporation formed with a view to cooperation towards a common goal, including, ultimately, the goal of self-preservation (cf. A 367, 482). Like Bataille, Nancy argues for the need to think community as constitutive of human existence, prior to evaluating its various forms in terms of their material or moral advantages. It must be said, however, that Nancy's text is very different in its language and atmosphere from the texts of Bataille. Where

Bataille draws on the French sociological school for his own speculative construction of the individual and the community (in texts such as "The Labyrinth"), Nancy's thought proceeds much more from Heidegger (and in particular, his analysis of being-with (*Mitsein*) in *Being and Time*). In order to renew the concept of community, Nancy argues, it is necessary first of all to recognize its effacement or distortion by the metaphysics of subjectivity. Modern philosophical thought conceives of the collective dimension of human existence in terms of the rationality common to all human subjects or the rights and the equality of political and legal subjects. Indeed, Nancy argues that Bataille's own conception of community and his notion of sovereignty are still tributary to conceptions of freedom stemming from this metaphysics, and this critique of Bataille lays the ground for an alternative exposition of the communal dimension as founded in the "sharing" (*le partage*) of existence.

Nancy's book has given impetus to a more gradual shift in the reception of Bataille, as the proximity of his work to modern social thought and to its playing out in the political alternatives of the 20th century has been recognized. From within Bataille's work too, Nancy's study has inflected the direction of research, since it poses the question of to what extent, and under what forms, the question of community remains present in his later writing.[3]

1939–1945 – the *Atheological Summa*

The period leading up to the war was one of feverish collective and public activity for Bataille. From 1936, he was the editor and principal contributor to the journal Acéphale, and the animator of the secret society of the same name; and then, from 1937 to 1939, he was the driving force behind the College of Sociology. To an even greater extent than *Documents*, this activity had been lost from sight until the recent resurgence of interest in Bataille's work. The re-discovery of some of the texts from this period, notably the collation of the lectures from the College of Sociology by Denis Hollier, and the partial re-constitution of the Acéphale experiment affects the reading of his entire work. To begin with, it allows one to read the books written during the war – *Inner Experience* (1941), *Guilty* (1943) and *On Nietzsche* (1944) – with an eye for the traces of the intellectual itinerary that precedes them, and to consider to what extent they are its continuation under new circumstances. "Friendship", the first chapter of *Guilty*, opens at the beginning of the war. Here Bataille speaks of his withdrawal from society and his exhaustion by overwork (referring to the College of Sociology, no doubt). Now he will let himself go to his caprices, he writes, but he will also "speak without detour" (G, 9).

The books composed during the war follow out this decision, even if they are in fact highly elliptical, and more difficult to find one's way into than most of Bataille's preceding writings. "Without detour" here means, first of all, without the interposition of a specific theme, without an expositional framework, without an address to a more or less defined public. Each of these books narrate something like a spiritual quest. "In the last two years", Bataille writes, "I had been able to make progress in inner experience. In this sense, at the very least, the states described by the mystics had ceased to be closed to me" (IE, 95). The three books recount his experiences of such states, and explicate their significance. *Inner Experience* tells of a series of moments from his earlier life that appeared to him as something close to mystical illuminations – one remembered from his adolescence during a period in a seminary, one as a student in Paris, two further from his travels in the 1930s; and it describes his own more recent and more conscious experiments in inducing ecstatic states in himself. The third section presents extracts from texts he had written during the 1930s, accompanied with a retro-spective narrative (in italics), recounting his itinerary, including the adventure of Acéphale – but in an elliptical way that would be largely impenetrable if one did not already have some awareness of the history to which he is referring. *Guilty* and *On Nietzsche* are located in the present, for the largest part taking the form of a series of dated sequences, developing the thought and the practice of "inner experi-ence", against the background of the war. In the latter, Bataille considers his reading of Nietzsche as part of this experience: in her essay in this volume, Giulia Agostini studies the terms – fidelity, friendship, complicity – in which Bataille formulates his relation to the writer to whom he feels the closest affinity.

At first sight, these texts – referred to collectively as the *Atheological Summa*, following plans for a publication that Bataille did not finalize in his lifetime – appear to belong within the genre of autobiography. This impression is only justified, however, in the sense that the very open-ended character of this genre allows it to give a form to what remains essentially a work of thought. Of these three texts, it is *Inner Experience* which does the most to indicate the conceptual articula-tions. The opening section presents "a sketch for an introduction to inner experience" and "principles and methods" for a community that would be founded on this experience. The book does not have the systematic construction that such didactic language might lead one to expect; but on its erratic path, Bataille specifies conditions, defines and differentiates concepts, and positions himself in relation to other religious and philosophical systems. Even the disorder of his presentation, he claims, is commanded by the rigour of the thought (EI, 118).

The elements of the exposition are centred above all on the sense and the limits of Bataille's affinity with the mystics, in whose writings he recognizes descriptions that converge with his own experience of ecstatic states. As Gerhard Poppenberg shows in this volume, Bataille constantly draws on the language and the schemes of the Christian mystics in order to narrate an experience of the absence of God. As in Nietzsche, the first consequence of the constatation of divine absence is the recognition of how deeply theological assumptions are embedded in our understanding of ourselves and our position in the world. In many ways, it is as if the belief in God appears more important to those who renounce it than to those who remain in tranquil adherence. The revelation of the Scriptures, Bataille writes, gave the Christian world the conviction that it knew what it was essential to know, and that it did not need to know what it in fact did not know. Without this conviction, he writes, we remain a "question without issue" (IE, 31). Modern rationality and scientific knowledge have not fully acknowledged this absence of exit or term; they have merely imitated the authority of religion, and in this sense, remain theological in their foundations. The only way to free oneself from the belief in God, then, is through a confrontation with non-knowledge.

The discourse on the absence of God and of non-knowledge in Bataille cannot be equated with what one generally refers to as atheism or scepticism. These intellectual positions appeal to a fundamental principle, which can be represented by a reasoning, which can be more or less skilfully defended, and which can be reflected in an attitude towards the world and a character. The argumentation necessary to sustain a position has little place in the *Atheological Summa*. The encounter with non-knowledge and contingency here proceeds, not by logical arguments, but by "sensible experience" (IE, 39) – which in this context means emotional experience, in which non-knowledge becomes present as a felt reality – states of anguish, despair, horror, even feelings of ignorance and stupidity. These experiences are clearly all negative: nonetheless, it is not a matter of pessimism, any more than it is of atheism or scepticism. Bataille wants to persuade us that anguish is also "a chance" (IE, 40) – but if we want to take it, we have to pursue it to its end, to "the extreme of the possible", in which there remains no other option than "supplication" (EI, 41). To this end, it is necessary to avoid the temptation of inertia, the evasion into "the workable attitude", which he denounces as a degradation and a betrayal. Bataille tells us that he has to provoke himself against his own tendency to slip back into an anodyne acceptance of life within a limited but familiar world, and that his ambition is to provoke others to the same effect. The aspiration to attain the "extreme of the possible", the apotheosis of non-meaning, he underlines, demands to be shared and communicated with others. One sees then that the work is not conceived as an exploration of extreme states for their own sake. Where the traditional pastoral role of philosophy is to dissipate anxiety by offering wisdom, this text – like certain forms of religious discourse – sets out to teach despair, demanding that one recognize and identify with the condition of non-knowledge that it describes. To enter into "the night" is the condition for the decision in which "the destiny of the humanity to come is at stake" (EI, 33 trans. mod.). If it can be brought to recognize its "entire destitution" (IE, 52), humanity is in a position to transform itself. It can no longer turn away from itself, in taking itself to be the man that was made in the image of God, and can coincide with its own being, such as it truly is. By this line of thought, which is not marked or underlined in the construction of the work to the extent that one might expect, *Inner Experience* continues the "activism" that is very clear in the texts written for the journal Acéphale.

Unlike many of Bataille's writings, the works of the *Atheological Summa* attained a degree of recognition from an early stage. Maurice Blanchot wrote a highly laudatory review on the release of *Inner Experience*, and Jean-Paul Sartre wrote a very critical assessment, which by its very length however (over three consecutive issues of the journal *Cahiers du Sud*, in its initial publication) implied a recognition of its importance (Blanchot 2001; Sartre 2010). There are also several excellent studies available in English focusing on these works, in particular on their relation to mystic and religious traditions (Hussey 2000; Connor 2000; Hollywood 2002). Nonetheless, the texts of the *Atheological Summa* have been a little less frequently invoked in the recent explosion of interest in his work, as if they constituted a domain apart from the rest of his work, an impression which is understandable but misleading. The situation will perhaps change with the greater accessibility of these works as a result of the recent updated and revised translations by Stuart Kendall, which also include the notes and variants contained in the *Oeuvres Complètes*.

1945–1962 *Critique. The Accursed Share, Lascaux, Manet, Literature and Evil, Eroticism, The Tears of Eros*

In the "Preface" to *Inner Experience*, Bataille tells of the circumstances of the composition of this work (IE, 6). His theorizing had reached a point at which it dazzled him, he writes, and he felt he had solved all the enigmas (he is probably referring to his work on *La Limite de l'Utile*, the first draft of *The Accursed Share*, of which one important chapter, entitled "Sacrifices", is included in the collection of translations published in *October*: O, 61–74). Feeling a malaise at this success, however, he broke off the work, and wrote "The torture", the central chapter of *Inner Experience* (and the novella *Madame Edwarda*, which he viewed as inseparable from this chapter).

He had not forgotten the solution he had arrived at, however, and one can see his post-war writings as its patient and lucid elaboration, after the intense and often obscure explorations of the *Atheological Summa*. The period between the end of the war and his death in 1962 is one of extraordinary intellectual productivity. During this time, Bataille published a sequence of important theoretical and historical works: *The Accursed Share* (first published in 1949), the novel *L'Abbé C* (1950), *Lascaux or the Birth of Art* (a study on the prehistoric art in the caves of Lascaux) (1955), *Manet* (1955), *Eroticism* (1957) and *Literature and Evil* (1957), as well as writing several further almost complete works, which he left unpublished: *Theory of Religion*, and two further volumes of the *Accursed Share* (the *History of Eroticism*, which is a first version of *Eroticism* – but sufficiently different to have merited its translation into English; and *Sovereignty*).

At least part of this productivity can be attributed to a new institutional situation – his position as editor at *Critique*, a journal founded immediately after the war. This journal had the aim of reviewing intellectual production in all fields for a non-specialist audience; and in Bataille's writings during these years, he develops his ideas in dialogue with multiple fields of knowledge, as well as with the literary production and the political questions of the day. In addition to the books we have just mentioned, Bataille published a considerable number of essays in *Critique* and other journals during the post-war period. These articles make up the last two volumes of the *Oeuvres Complètes* (XI and XII), which come to well over a thousand pages. Where the major book length works from this period have been available in translation in English for some time, the material in these volumes has only been recently and partially translated. Many of these essays are identifiably related to work on the major books Bataille published during the period, but they nonetheless contribute independent and original perspectives on the same topics. A number of recent collections in English draw on this material: *The Absence of Myth: Writings on Surrealism* (1994), translated and edited by Michael Richardson combines some texts from the 1920s with essays from the post-war phase, during which, as Richardson points out, Bataille's writings on the surrealist movement would have easily provided the material for a book if he had taken the time to assemble it; *The Unfinished System of Non-Knowledge* (2004), translated by Stuart and Michelle Kendall, is made up of texts intended for a definitive version of the *Atheological Summa*, and a series of lectures on "non-knowledge" given by Bataille in the early 1950s; and *The Cradle of Humanity* (2009), translated and introduced by Stuart Kendall, collects essays on prehistory, related to Bataille's work on the caves of Lascaux. Some other texts from this period have been translated individually, although there remains a considerable amount that is not available in English; even if the shorter review pieces were to be cut, there is still material for at least another book, made up of very high quality and very "finished" essays.

After the "activist" and the "mystical" phases of the 1930s and the war, Bataille's post-war writings stand in a much closer relation to the discourse of knowledge and philosophy. The books and the essays published during this period are characterized by a remarkable self-possession, and are learned and judicious, even humane, contrary to the received ideas. Whether the subject-matter is politics, sociology, the history of religion, ethics, or literature, Bataille takes the topic on its own terms and, in the process of exposition and clarification, gravitates towards his fundamental concerns. What in earlier phases was present in the form of images, fragments, intuitions rather than ideas, is now elaborated in the direction of conceptual exposition. Due to the relative accessibility of these texts, as well as the proximity of their subject-matter to the questions of contemporary social thought, it has been these works – above all, *The Accursed Share* and *Eroticism* – which have been most discussed in research and theory in recent years. The essays in the second part of this volume, dedicated to specific concepts, generally take the texts from this period as their primary frame of reference (the exception is the idea of a "heterology" which, as Marcus Coelen observes, was developed alongside the texts in *Documents*, but disappears, at least in name, from the later works).

The shift in the mode of Bataille's writing between the "mystic" texts of the war-years and the post-war books and articles could perhaps be formulated in terms of a shift from the pursuit of an ultimate non-knowledge ("the night") to an interest in the specific and local non-knowledges to be found in the domain of our familiar social and cognitive reality. Most of the essays in the second part of this volume – among them, Nadine Hartmann on eroticism, Claire Nioche on sovereignty, Tiina Arppe on evil – turn around the paradox of Bataille's concepts, which seek to circumscribe an experience that remains by definition inaccessible to discourse. This characteristic of Bataille's reflections is not necessarily a barrier to the assimilation of his work into scholarly discourse. The sciences have to secure their domain in becoming conscious of their limits, and Bataille's lucid exploration of the point of demarcation between what belongs to knowledge and discourse and what escapes it in the realm of eroticism, sovereignty, inner experience or even prehistory is one of the aspects of his work by which he most directly speaks to contemporary theoretical reflection. What continues to hold his work at a distance from this discourse is its ethical and at times its religious dimension. The post-war writings do not have the same explicitly "activist" rhetoric of Acéphale, but the convictions that underlay this rhetoric have by no means disappeared. *The Accursed Share* can serve as an example. In comparison with "The Notion of Expenditure", the 1933 essay whose theses it takes up and elaborates, this work gives to a much greater extent the appearance of a work of scholarship and research. The rhetoric of revolutionary politics in the earlier essay has disappeared and the thesis on the determining role of the surplus in political economy is substantiated by reference to historical and anthropological work on the Aztecs, the Native Americans, Islamic societies, Tibet, the Europe of the Middle Ages, the Reformation and modern industrial capitalism. The insightfulness of these analyses is sufficient to have attracted the interest of anthropologists, historians of religion and sociologists; scholars have even shown a surprising willingness to take up the wild biophysical speculations on "general economy" as a means of theorizing the global economy. There remains, however, an element that places real difficulties before an assimilation into the work of the disciplines. If one works through the entire argument of any of these texts of Bataille, it becomes evident that they speak from a definite ethical position; while this position is often somewhat muted in the movement of the argument, when it emerges, it strikes a completely different note, one that seems incompatible with the value-neutrality of research. Thus, for example, in the section of *The Accursed Share* entitled "The bourgeois world", Bataille argues that while the Marxist analysis of the economy represents an incontestable advance, it does not resolve the need for humanity to find itself, to rediscover its truth (AS 1, 129–142). This demand speaks through all the works of this period: the exposition of the historical, social and psychological analysis moves towards the point at which it calls for an inner decision. The *Theory of Religion*, for example, concludes by inviting its readers to assume the "sovereign self-consciousness that no longer turns away from itself" (TR, 111). In noting the presence of the ethical-religious commitment of Bataille, one can only signal the need for a fundamental debate with his works on the philosophical level, something which remains beyond the scope of this introductory work. To the extent that his concepts continue to prove themselves useful to the work of the disciplines, this task will surely remain on the agenda.

Notes

1 For Bataille's intellectual biography, one can consult the treatment by Stuart Kendall, which is succinct and readable. The first major French biography, by Michel Surya, has also been translated into English. This work is more detailed and a valuable resource – although its high degree of dramatization is not likely to help the cause of Bataille's inclusion in general intellectual discussion.
2 One could imagine a book composed of the texts by Bataille during the period covered by Galletti's collection – that is to say, in between his work for *La Critique Sociale* and the composition of *Inner Experience* and *Guilty*. This would include "Sacrifices", "The Labyrinth" and "Communication", all of which were incorporated into *Inner Experience*; the texts translated by Allan Stoekl for the third section of *Visions of Excess* (which includes most of the texts written for Acéphale); "Van Gogh and Prometheus", "Sacrifices" and "Celestial Bodies", translated in *October*, as well as a small number of untranslated texts – notably the "Manual of the Anti-Christian", an incomplete philosophical text from the same period, included in the second volume of the *Oeuvres Complètes*.
3 This question is taken up in the response given by Maurice Blanchot to Nancy's book in *The Unavowable Community* (1988, in French in 1983).

References

Ades, Dawn and Baker, Simon, eds. 2006. *Undercover Surrealism*. Cambridge MA: MIT Press.

Arppe, Tiina. 2014. *Affectivity and the Social Bond – Transcendence, Economy and Violence in French Social Theory*. London: Ashgate.

Baudrillard, Jean. 1993. *Symbolic Exchange and Death*. Translated by Ian Hamilton. London and Thousand Oaks: Sage.

Bischof, Rita. 2010. *Tragisches Lachen: die Geschichte von Acéphale*. Berlin: Matthes und Seitz.

Blanchot, Maurice 1988. *The Unavowable Community*. Translated by Pierre Joris. Barrytown, NY: Station Hill.

Blanchot, Maurice. 2001. *Faux Pas*. Translated by Charlotte Mandell. Stanford: Stanford UP.

Bois, Yve-Alain and Krauss, Rosalind. 1997. *Formless: A User's Guide*. Cambridge MA: MIT Press.

Brotchie, Alastair, ed. 1996. *Encyclopædia Acephalica: Comprising The Critical Dictionary & Related Texts; The Encyclopædia Da Costa*. London: Atlas Press.

Connor, Peter Tracey. 2000. *Georges Bataille and the Mysticism of Sin*. Baltimore/London: Johns Hopkins University Press.

Didi-Hubermann, Georges. 1995. *La Ressemblance Informe ou le gai savoir visuel selon Georges Bataille.* Paris: Macula.

Falasca-Zamponi, Simonetta. 2011. *Rethinking the Political: the Sacred, Aesthetic Politics and the Collège de Sociologie.* Montréal: McGill-Queen's University Press.

ffrench, Patrick. 2007. *After Bataille: Sacrifice, Exposure, Community.* London: Legenda.

Goux, Jean-Joseph. 1990. "General Economics and Postmodern Capitalism." *Yale French Studies* 78: 206–224.

Haar, Michel. 1996. *Nietzsche and Metaphysics.* Translated by Michael Gendre. Albany: SUNY Press.

Hollier, Denis. 1992. "The Use Value of the Impossible." Translated by Liesl Ollman. *October* 60: 3–24.

Hollywood, Amy. 2002. *Sexual Ecstasy: Mysticism, Sexual Difference and the Demands of History.* Chicago: University of Chicago Press.

Hussey, Andrew. 2000. *The Inner Scar. The Mysticism of Georges Bataille.* Amsterdam (Atlanta): Rodopi.

Nadeau, Maurice. 1978. *The History of Surrealism.* Translated by Richard Howard. London: Penguin.

Nancy, Jean-Luc. 1991. *The Inoperative Community.* Translated by Peter Connor et al. Minneapolis: University of Minnesota Press.

Noys, Benjamin. 2000. *Georges Bataille: A Critical Introduction.* London: Pluto.

Pawlett, William. 2013. *Violence, Society and Radical Theory: Bataille, Baudrillard and Contemporary Society.* London: Ashgate.

Richardson, Michael. 1994. *Georges Bataille.* London: Routledge.

Richardson, Michael and Krzystof Fijalkowski, eds. 2001. *Surrealism against the Current: Tracts and Declarations.* London: Pluto.

Sartre, Jean-Paul. 2010. *Situations I.* Translated by Chris Turner. London: Seagull.

Stoekl, Allan. 2007. *Bataille's Peak: Energy, Religion and Post-Sustainability.* Minneapolis: University of Minnesota Press.

Surya, Michel. 2010. *Georges Bataille: an Intellectual Biography.* Translated by Krzysztof Fijalkowski and Michael Richardson. London: Verso.

Part I
Contexts

1   Surrealism

Marina Galletti

> If there is a possibility that humanity can be torn out of itself, it lies
> with surrealism and nothing else
>
> (WS, 51)

In an interview with Madeleine Chapsal, a few months before his
death, Georges Bataille stated: "My relations with surrealism have
been of a certain absurdity, but probably no more so than anything else
in my life [...] I could better express my relations with surrealism by
speaking of an idea which came to me [...] of writing a book which
would bear on the first page of the cover *Surrealism is Dead* and on the
other side, *Long Live Surrealism*" (EW, 221).

For the purpose of exposition, one can organize Bataille's relations
with surrealism into three phases, corresponding to three distinct historical moments: the period between the wars; the Occupation of France;
and the post-war period. In the first place, however, this schema shows
that Bataille's intellectual itinerary is marked by a constant confrontation
with surrealism. One can say that this history begins with the sense of
exclusion felt by Bataille at the moment of Michel Leiris' adhesion to
surrealism, which marked a rupture in their friendship and the end of
the projects which had brought them together. They had envisaged a
movement to be named *Yes*, which was supposed to be superior to Dada
"because it would avoid the puerility of provoking through systematic
negation" (CL, 8); and also an Orphic and Nietzschean society which
Leiris had suggested calling *Judas*. At a certain moment, Bataille felt
himself compelled to convert to the convictions of Leiris who, although
younger, was invested with the authority of an initiate. In a posthumous
autobiographical text, "Surrealism from Day to Day", Bataille writes:
"my timidity, my stupidity and my distrust of my own judgment were
so great that I resolved to think what Leiris said with such absolute conviction" (WS, 37). Encouraged by Leiris, Bataille participated in the

surrealist review, *The Surrealist Revolution* of 1926, contributing a translation into modern French of the "Fatrasies", a group of poems from the 13th century, preceded with a brief note from the translator associating them with a "burst of laughter" (OC I, 103). This anonymous publication was to be "the only gesture of Bataille's indicating any kind of public or written participation in surrealism", as Jean-Louis Houdebine writes, in an article discussing the conditions – suspect at the very least – of this publication, which does not give the reader information on the function, the addressee or the context (Houdebine, 1973, 157). The *fatrasie* is a poetic genre composed of freely juxtaposed sayings and proverbs, with an absurd or incoherent content. The overt nonsense of such texts brings them close to the spirit of Dada; and Bataille in fact associates his first steps in surrealism with this movement: "One of my difficulties, at the beginning, with surrealism, was that I was much more Dada than the surrealists, or rather, I was still Dada, whereas they were no longer" (EW, 222).

This beginning was followed by an explosion of conflict between Bataille and André Breton, the leader of the surrealist group. It was Breton who initiated hostilities in the "Second Manifesto of Surrealism", denouncing Bataille for planning to form an anti-surrealist group, denouncing also the journal *Documents* (of which Bataille was the editor and the animating force), which Breton saw as the organ of the dissident group. The group that had been criticized in the "Second Manifesto" responded with the pamphlet entitled "A Corpse". The idea was proposed by Robert Desnos and supported by Georges-Henri Rivière, but it was Bataille who put together this violent denunciation. The pamphlet takes over the form and the title of an earlier pamphlet, put out by the surrealists themselves at the moment of the funeral of Anatole France. Bataille also contributed to the volume with a text entitled "The castrated lion". Houdebine remarks that this text "is not simply a series of insults, unlike most of the other contributions to the tract, but condenses in pointed form the arguments developed by Bataille in a number of other texts which remained unpublished at this time, notably 'The Use-Value of D.A.F. Sade' and 'The Old Mole and the Prefix "Sur" in the words *Surhomme* and Surrealist'" (Houdebine, 1973, 157–158).

We will come back to these two posthumously published writings; they need to be read in the context of the combative atmosphere of the time, which culminates in a veritable brawl, the "Maldoror Affair". In his denunciation of the dissidents in the "Second Manifesto of Surrealism", Breton writes: "As final proof, I shall merely note in passing the unspeakable idea they had to use as a sign for a 'nightclub' in

Montparnasse, the customary haunt of their nocturnal exploits, the only name which, since time began, constituted a pure challenge to everything stupid, base and loathsome of earth: Maldoror" (Breton, 1969, 167).[1] On the night of 14 February 1930, the surrealists ransacked the establishment.

For the moment, we will confine ourselves to noting that, in considering the intellectual relations between Breton and Bataille, one cannot ignore all that muddies their personal relations from before their first encounter. This basic incompatibility will be softened by time, without entirely being effaced. On Bataille's side, it is a matter of an intolerance which he cannot conceal, a feeling of being reduced to silence by the prestige of Breton, the master of the surrealists. On Breton's side, it is rather the violent refusal of one whom he sees as an obscure "obsessive", the author of the scandalous tale *W.C*; but, as Bataille recognizes himself, it was also "a sense of unease next to a man who was so disturbed by him, who could never breathe freely in front of him and who lacked both innocence and resolution" (WS, 42). The fictional production of the two authors throws this persistent incompatibility into relief.

The two men overcame their differences in the 1930s in order to form Contre-Attaque, the "Union of intellectual revolutionaries", which was constituted in the margin of the French Popular Front, with the aim of opposing the rise of fascism. Even if this attempt ultimately led to a renewed rupture, its theoretical presupposition – the elaboration of a science of totalitarianism or a sacred sociology, based in a problematics emerging from surrealism – continues to figure in the intellectual movements that Bataille led later in the 1930s, the College of Sociology and the secret society, Acéphale. In describing this latter, Bataille writes: "I had decided, if not to found a religion, at least to move in this general direction. What I had learnt from the history of religions had exalted me. Moreover, it seemed to me that the surrealist atmosphere, in the margins of which I had been living, was ripe with this singular possibility" (OC VI, 369).[2]

The second phase can be located at the beginning of the war and under the Occupation. Bataille contributed to a poetry review called *Messages*, which was created by Jean Lescure in 1942, in order to give expression to an idea of poetry as an instrument of tacit resistance to Nazism and the Vichy government, as well as opposition to the politics of the French communist party (Lescure, 1998). In this forum, Bataille was the subject of a violent attack by *Main à Plume*, a group which, while Breton was in exile in America, continued to work for the intellectual position taken by surrealism during the pre-war period. The attack was now extended to Bataille's book, *Inner Experience*. It was focused on a passage in which Bataille criticizes the surrealist theme of the poetic utilization of the dream, citing a text by Jean-François Chabrun, who had developed this theme within the context of *La Main à Plume* (IE, 53). The response explicitly situates itself as a continuation of Breton's attacks on Bataille in "The Second Manifesto of Surrealism"; but in accord with the transition of *La Main à Plume* from Trotskyism to Stalinism, it also takes on a political dimension. In the same year, Bataille, on the suggestion of Lescure, formulated a project for a book of aphorisms to be entitled *Becoming Orestes or the Exercise in Meditation*. This set of aphorisms was conceived as a "vehement protest against the equivocation of poetry" (C, 192). It can be interpreted as a reply to the accusations of mysticism made by the *Main à Plume* group in the 1943 tract, *Nom de Dieu*. It is also the first version of the text that came to be entitled "The Oresteia". Here, Bataille interrogates the status of poetry which can constitute a form of expenditure, or as he writes in *Inner Experience*, "as a sacrifice in which the words are victims"; but which is more often only an abdication, "a minor sacrifice, an illusory transgression", as Jacqueline Risset writes (Risset, 1999, 222). This is a crucial question which Bataille will continue to reformulate until the end of his life, and it leads him to annex "The Oresteia" first to *The Hatred of Poetry* (1947) and then to *The Impossible* (1962). Houdebine, noting that a fragment of *The Oresteia* bears the title "Abstract History of Surrealism", underlines how Bataille's interrogation of poetry presupposes his conflicted relation to surrealism, since it was surrealism which linked poetry to revolt and to the transformation of the world (Houdebine, 1973, 158).

In fact, this interrogation unfolds in two stages. In 1942, in his response to the "Inquiry on Poetry" organized by *Main à Plume*, Bataille states that where knowledge "leads from the known to the unknown", poetry "leads from the unknown to the known." In *Inner Experience*, this affirmation becomes the key to his reading of Proust as well as of surrealism. Then, in "The Oresteia", he states that poetry "can neither put in question nor put in action this world to which I am bound". In "Method of Meditation", a text published in 1947, and closely linked to *The Hatred of Poetry*, it becomes clear that the point is made in opposition to surrealism:

> In the end, poetry is only an *evocation*; poetry only changes the order of the words and *cannot change the world*. The sentiment of poetry is linked to the nostalgia to change more than the order of words, *the established order*. But the idea of a revolution *starting* with poetry leads to that of poetry *in service of* a revolution

> (IE, 196).

In the third phase, corresponding to the post-war period, Bataille reaffirms his irreducible opposition to the movement of Breton, but abandons the polemical tone of the past. This position is already represented in the brief 1945 article, "The Surrealist Revolution" (a review of Jules Monnerot's book, *La Poésie Moderne et le Sacré*). Here Bataille writes:

> No matter what its defects or rigidity may have been, surrealism has given from the beginning a certain consistency to the "morality of revolt" and its most important contribution – important even, perhaps, in the political realm – is to have remained, in matters of morality, a revolution.
>
> (WS, 53)

Above all, in "Method of Meditation", in face of the ascendancy of existentialism, Bataille proclaims his adhesion to surrealism for the first time, writing: "I situate my efforts beyond but alongside surrealism" (IE, 167).

Bataille's new stance is explained by his enthusiasm for the little periodical *Third Convoy*, which appeared after the war. This journal placed itself "under the flag of surrealism", as Michel Fardoulis-Lagrange specified (in conversation with me); its goal, however, he writes, was to "bring out the natural character of a rupture that surrealism had represented from the beginning, in seeking to link it to the movement to intelligence, rather than to magic" (cf. Blanc, 1998, 191). The revolt of surrealism was to be re-organized and interiorized, beginning with a rejection of its weaknesses, not only the aestheticism of automatic writing, but also surrealism's "golden-age complex", as Marcel Lecomte calls it (Blanc, 1998, 122) – that is, its tendency to give priority to forms of thought associated with the past, such as esotericism, and to make them into the key for a re-appropriation of human destiny. In his first contribution to *Third Convoy*, Bataille writes: "Whenever the occasion has arisen, I have opposed surrealism. And I would now like to affirm it from within as the demand to which I have submitted and as the dissatisfaction that I exemplify" (WS, 49). Bataille proposes to reject the "surrealism of works" (that is, surrealism inasmuch as it is oriented purely towards the production of literary and artistic works) as well as its "conspicuous and even gaudy" aspect (WS, 68 trans. mod.). Instead he proposes to follow Rimbaud on another path, one not taken by surrealism, where the priority shifts from the accomplishment of works of art to the experience on to which their creation opens – the experience of "being", or of "the depth of things" (*le fond des choses*): "at this point there begins the debate of existence in the night" (*dès lors com-mençait le débat de l'être dans la nuit*) (WS, 50). Bataille gives us an orientation for understanding this language in his text on André Masson, where he speaks of "an interior debate" which "has meaning only experienced in the depth of one night, with the same sense of being overwhelmed that, in the past, the Christian experienced before the idea of God" (WS, 178–179 trans. mod.). It is with this prospect in view that Bataille announces "the great surrealism" that is still to come (WS, 51).

One can say then that in the period after the war Bataille resumes the position of the "old enemy within", in order to initiate an over-coming of surrealism, through a paradoxical combination of Dada and mysticism. In the interview with Madeleine Chapsal, Bataille remarks: "Certainly it is necessary for me to go to the extreme limit, to what one would perhaps call mysticism, and that I have tried to designate through St John of the Cross. When I say to the limit, I mean to two extremes; can you imagine a greater contrast than that of someone who affirms at the same time dada and is affected by the biography of St John of the Cross" (EW, 222).

It is not possible here to take into account the numerous texts writ-ten in the post-war period on the subject of surrealism, most of which appeared in the journal *Critique*. We can see the orientation of these writings if we turn to the re-definition of surrealism proposed by Bataille in his first major homage to Breton, written in 1946, the text "Surrealism and its difference with existentialism". This re-definition turns around three points. The first and the most important is the character of totality that is proper to the movement, which separates it from the ordinary notion of a literary school. Surrealism, Bataille affirms, is above all, a "moral demand" (WS 58, trans. mod.); it is centred on an ecstatic apprehension of the instant, and it demands the conversion of being into being into the instant (WS, 66); as such, the decision that links Breton to surrealism also engages our "common destiny" (WS, 61). Secondly, however, surrealism nonetheless remains a literary and artistic school, based on the principle of automatic writ-ing. Like the dream, automatic writing is a modality of thought that functions outside of the conscious control of reason, and it can be understood as a form of "poetic thinking". And thirdly, the term sur-realism signifies a collective organization, making each member into an "impersonal necessity" (WS, 60).

In this regard, one should note Bataille's insistence, in his articles from the post-war period, on the contribution of those who, well before the constitution of the surrealist group, attest to "the historical existence of an orientation of minds" (WS, 55); as well as those who, like Henri Pastoureau or Jean Maquet, are oriented towards an extremist surrealism, thus allowing for "the extreme rigour and passion of those who wanted to take the human adventure to its limit through Christianity" (WS, 128), transcending Christianity in the direction of a "hyperchristianity" (Nietzsche's term); or those who, like the painter André Masson and the poets Jacques Prévert and René Char, are close to surrealism, but "remain at a distance from a movement which has the disadvantages of a crowd" (WS, 68); or the writer Raymond Queneau, a "renegade from surrealism". The existence of such figures at the margins of the group "does not bear witness at all to the inauthenticity of surrealism: rather, it reveals its background and far-reaching consequences" (WS, 68). The same is true of Antonin Artaud, whose *Letters from Rodez* "are like the last gleams of the setting of shipwrecked surrealism" (WS, 45).

After this diachronic itinerary, we can now indicate the path of Bataille's dissolution of the canonical sense of surrealism. To this end, it will be necessary to turn back to the moment of the polemic with Breton. In *Documents*, the conflict appears in the form of Bataille's affirmation of the low and of its ethical figure, evil, as an "active principle", and by an erosion of the surrealists' idealism and their devotion to the marvellous.[3] Beyond these two basic principles, there are two further points by which Bataille separates himself from the surrealists:

1. The denunciation of the Icarus complex. This complex accounts for the degeneration of surrealism, which comes about with the reconversion of the low into the high, and the emergence of "castration reflexes". Bataille writes: "In December 1929, M. Breton did not hesitate to make himself ridiculous by writing that 'the simplest surrealist act consists of dashing down into the street, pistol in hand, and firing blindly, as fast as you can pull the trigger, into the crowd' [...] That such an image should present itself so insistently to his view proves decisively the importance of castration reflexes in his pathology: such an extreme provocation seeks to draw immediate and brutal punishment" (VE, 39).

2. The aspiration to found a new science, to be called heterology (or at times, agiology or scatology), based on the notion of the alien or heterogeneous body, in other words, on all that is inaccessible to scientific knowledge. The practical development of this science implies the reversal of the established order, following a model given by the most abject and transgressive practices of Sade's characters. The adoption of this model, however, requires the rejection of the surrealists' adoption of Sade, as one of their own historical antecedents. Bataille affirms:

"The behaviour of Sade's admirers resembles that of primitive subjects in relation to their king, whom they adore and loathe, and whom they cover with honours and narrowly confine" (VE, 92). The surrealists, Bataille argues, give a "use-value" to Sade by exalting his spirit of revolt and toning down the most heterogeneous aspects of his thinking. Their reception of Sade exhibits the two elementary functions of any psycho-physical or social organization: appropriation and excretion. In order to break with this "use-value", heterology reveals a more complex process of "excretion" at work in Sade's world, one that affirms the sacred value invested in the object of exclusion, by the very fact of this expulsion. Heterology implies a double reversal. The classificatory system dividing the human world into sacred and profane, and identifying the sacred with the "high" and the profane with the "low", is replaced with a more complex scheme, one that is capable of applying the categories of French sociology (which were worked out in reference to archaic societies) to the contemporary world. The term "the sacred" is given back the double signification implicit in the Latin word *sacer*, at once high and low, pure and impure, right and left: "The notion of the (heterogeneous) foreign body permits one to note the elementary subjective identity between types of excrement (sperm, menstrual blood, urine, faecal matter) and everything that can be seen as sacred, divine or marvellous" (VE, 94). On the other hand, it is also necessary to recognize the transformation introduced into the domain of the sacred by the revealed religions, which progressively homogenize the sacred, identifying it wholly with the "high" pole: "God rapidly and almost entirely loses his terrifying features [...] in order to become, at the final stage of degradation, the simple (paternal) sign of universal homogeneity" (VE, 96).

At a deeper level, the aim of this critique is to bring out the central role of unproductive expenditure, or *loss* in all economic processes, against the censoring effects practiced by institutionalized religions, effects which have only been reinforced by Marxism and capitalism: "Without a profound complicity with natural forces such as violent death, gushing blood, sudden catastrophes and the horrible cries of pain that accompany them, terrifying ruptures of what had seemed to be immutable, the fall into stinking filth of what had been elevated – without a sadistic understanding of an incontestably thundering and torrential nature, there could be no revolutionaries, there could only be a revolting utopian sentimentality" (VE, 101).

If we return now to the post-war period, when Bataille was concerned to defend Breton against the attacks of Sartre, it is essential to consider the lecture "The Surrealist Religion", given by Bataille in 1948, since it resumes and expands ideas advanced in all of the articles published during this period on the topic of surrealism. Following the argument of "Surrealism and its difference with existentialism", Bataille underlines that the surrealists' conception of their activity exceeds the literary and artistic field. Rather than being a purely literary group, surrealism is closer to an initiatic sect, as Maurice Nadeau had argued, or to a church, or again, in the more narrowly sociological terms of Jules Monnerot, to a "set", "a contingent union, without obligation or sanction", similar to a secret society (Monnerot 1945, 72–73). Picking up on these suggestions, Bataille suggests that surrealism can be understood as a religion, although one that by its poetic interest in myth and ritual, is opposed to Christianity, with its ambiguous amalgam of the sacred and rationality.

This lecture also returns to Breton's provocative equation of surrealism with the act of shooting at random into a crowd in the "Second Manifesto of Surrealism". This image is now no longer associated with the Icarus complex, as it had been in the 1930s; instead, it is associated with a tradition of the islands of Malaysia, the *amok*, a term designating the act by which an individual, possessed of a sudden fury, runs into a crowd with a knife, killing everyone he can, until he is himself killed. The amok now comes to represent the impossible surrealist imperative of archaic man, that is, the man of the sacred, free from modern humanity's subjection to technology and work; it becomes, in other words, the figure for the "will to the impossible" that is at the origin of surrealism. The change of attitude towards this image of Breton's is in accord with the new reading Bataille gives to the opening lines of the "Second Manifesto of Surrealism". Here Breton writes: "Surrealism is not interested in giving very serious consideration to anything that happens outside of itself, under the guise of art, or even anti-art, of philosophy or anti-philosophy – in short, in anything not aimed at the annihilation of being into a diamond, all blind and interior, which is no more the soul of ice than that of fire" (Breton, 1969, 124). In Bataille's pre-war text on surrealism ("The 'Old Mole' and the prefix *sur* in the words *surhomme* and Surrealist"), these lines had been stigmatized as the expression of what he saw as the Icarian syndrome. In "Surrealism and its difference from Existentialism", by contrast, the same passage comes to exemplify what Bataille now identifies as the essential contribution of surrealism, the morality of the instant: that is, "an immediate consumption, openly mocking the consequences" (WS, 59). This morality corresponds to a desire "to be totally" which, in its refusal of reason and any kind of subordination to goals, "cannot differ from ecstasy" – a mystic experience, then, but one freed from the ulterior concerns of the mystics of the past (WS, 66).

This "religious" dimension was already present in automatic writing, at least at the level of its theory, since it was conceived as an act of rupture with the profane world and a "destruction [...] of the personality" and of the utilitarian imperatives of reason (WS, 76). The essence of surrealism is thus identified with the negation of material interest – which explains, one can note, its anti-capitalism and its adhesion to Marxism. This conclusion leads Bataille to specify two crucial limitations to Breton's enterprise: first, its inability to satisfy contemporary humanity's need for the sacred by the creation of real myths and rites; and second, Breton's reluctance to place himself in the service of the revolution, and the equivocal character of his position with regard to the communist revolutionary party. In consequence, in an article on Camus' text, *The Rebel*, Bataille will denounce Breton's attitude as the "quietism of the shipwrecked".

Let us leave aside the fraught relations of surrealism and Marxism for the moment, in order to focus on the impossibility of the surrealist religion to adhere to the dimension of the sacred, of myth and ritual. Bataille's opposition to surrealism is premised on the necessity to link the "depersonalization" accomplished by automatic writing to the modern lucid consciousness and the intellect. This is the sense of what Bataille sees as the only real myth accessible today, namely "the absence of myth". The term does not merely designate a negative situation; it designates "the suppression of particularity" in myth, and as such, it announces the most accomplished form of myth, one that is "infinitely more exalting than myths in the past, which were bound up with everyday life" (WS, 81).

The notion of the "absence of myth" is linked for Bataille to a new notion of community, which is to be its accomplishment. The foundation of this new form of community – which Bataille calls "the absence of community" – requires the expulsion of the community outside of the field of reality and history. This decision marks the abandonment of the function of social renewal that Bataille had invested in the secret society of Acéphale, between the wars. The new form of community aims to free itself from the ambiguity of the religious communities of the past. These have remained caught in the contradiction between their attempt to overcome the limits of the individual by the constitution of a "collective individual", on the one hand; and the obstacle that is created by their own structure as closed groups, on the other. The new conception of community is also opposed to the tendency of the surrealist religion, with its "contempt for the experiments of the intellect" (WS, 50 trans. mod.). Such contempt now appears as a kind of complacency: automatic writing is the expression of a thought which is "freed from the world" and which "can neither serve action nor form a totality" (WS, 180). It is illustrated by the relapse of surrealism into past forms of thought such as magic. The fascination of the surrealists for the ancient non-moral religions reveals a certain awareness of the obscure depths from which these religions draw their power, but it distracts them from the task of modern humanity, "which is not to recover what is lost without possibility of recovery" (WS, 64). The same complacency is illustrated by the willingness of surrealism to allow its commitment to insubordination to be co-opted by the facilities of aesthetic pleasure. For Bataille: "perfect disorder [*dérèglement*] (abandon to the absence of limits) is the rule of an absence of community" (WS, 96). But this movement to abandon all the limits remains tied to consciousness and intellect:

> The state of passion, the state of release [*déchainement*] which was unconscious in the primitive mind, can become lucid to the extent that the limit imposed by [...] the community, as it closed in on itself, must be transgressed by consciousness. It is not possible to have limits between men in consciousness; moreover consciousness, the lucidity of consciousness, necessarily re-establishes the impossibility of a limit between humanity itself and the rest of the world. What must disappear, as a result of consciousness becoming more and more lucid, is the possibility of distinguishing man from the rest of the world.
>
> (WS, 82 trans. mod.)[4]

Ultimately, the formula "the absence of community" names a community which "exists, but in the form of absence", as Bruno Moroncini writes (2001, 80). Following the failure of the Acéphale group, Bataille imagines a purified community, one that does not share the material interest of the rites of primitive communities, nor the political impotence to which surrealism was condemned by its nostalgia for myth. It represents "the form of a community emancipated from the tyranny of capital" (Moroncini, 2001, 80), one consciously given over to consumption [*consumation*] and wastage, having rediscovered its accord with the principle of prodigality proper to the cosmos. This prodigality – the "festival of the stars" – is repressed, not only by liberal regimes, devoted to the unlimited growth of the forces of production, but also by the communist world, in which sovereignty is renounced, resulting in the amplification of the material interest that it set out to destroy.

Far from reflecting the eclipse of the political, the absence of community sketches out a politics freed from class-based revolution, a notion which was still central at the moment of Bataille and Breton's movement Contre-Attaque, but which appeared obsolescent in the context of the cold war. In the place of this conception, Bataille comes back to the economic foundation that is constitutive for community, namely, the use of riches; in other words, to the possibility, in the face of industrial over-production, that society could recognize the need for the dissipation without profit of its surplus wealth. The "revolution", such as Bataille conceives it in the post-war period, concerns the possibility of a transition from the restricted economy of capitalist society, dominated by the principle of utility, to the "general economy", modelled on the solar economy, and founded on the recognition of unproductive expenditure as a process central to all societies. Already in the 1930s, this question was at the centre of Bataille's polemic with Breton. In the climate of the cold war, it leads him to envisage the Marshall plan, which converts the surplus of the United States into *expenditure*, in the form of economic aid to Europe, as a possible means of overcoming the rule of individual profit proper to bourgeois capitalism. Thus Bataille can reverse the formula of Clausewitz, and propose the economy as the *political* site of the continuation of war by other means.

Translated by Mark Hewson. This essay appeared in an earlier version in French in: Catherine Maubon, ed. 2009. *Tradizione et contestatione: Canon et Anti-Canon*. Florence: Alinea.

Notes

1 On Bataille's attitude towards Lautréamont, see Galletti (2013).
2 On the College of Sociology and Acéphale, see Hollier (1988) and Galletti (2008) 57–112.
3 See the article "Base Materialism and Gnosticism" (VE, 45–52).
4 On the transition from the "Sacred Conspiracy" of Acéphale to the absence of community and hence to the atheological community of *Literature and Evil*, see Galletti, 2008.

References

Blanc, Philippe, ed. 1998. *Troisième convoi*. Tours: Farrago.
Breton, André. 1969. *Manifestoes of Surrealism*. Translated by Richard Seaver and Helen R. Lane. Ann Arbor: University of Michigan Press.
Galletti, Marina. 2008. *La Comunita Impossibile di Georges Bataille*. Turin: Kaplan.
Galletti, Marina. 2013. "Le chapitre manquant de La Littérature et le mal: Lautréamont. " *Georges Bataille, cinquante ans après*. Edited by Gilles Ernst and Jean-François Louette. Nantes: Editions nouvelles Cécile Defaut.

Hollier, Denis, ed. 1988. *The College of Sociology*. Minneapolis: University of Minnesota Press.

Houdebine, Jean-Louis. 1973. "L'ennemi du dedans." *Bataille*. Edited by Philippe Sollers. Paris: Union Générale d'Éditions.

Lescure, Jean. 1998. *Poésie et liberté. Histoire de "Messages", 1939–1946*. Paris: Editions de l'Imec.

Monnerot, Jules. 1945. *La Poésie Moderne et le Sacré*. Paris: Gallimard, 1945.

Moroncini, Bruno. 2001. *La communità e l'invenzione*. Naples: Cronopi.

Risset, Jacqueline. 1999. "La Question de la Poèsie: Les Enfants dans la Maison" in *Bataille-Leiris: L'intenable assentiment au monde*, edited by Francis Marmande. Paris: Belin.

2   Sociology and Ethnography

Simonetta Falasca-Zamponi

To many French intellectuals of the 1920s and 1930s the sociologist Émile Durkheim (1858–1917) remained a divisive figure both as proponent of a positivist sociology and a secular morality and for his role in the reform of state education. Having rescued sociology from its status of Cinderella science at the turn of the twentieth century, Durkheim had helped it climb the ranks of academic legitimacy by arguing for its unique ability to explain and research social phenomena. As sociology became a fundamental component of French school curricula and pedagogical training, however, it suffered from its newly acquired position of dominance to the point that Durkheim found himself the target of attacks from both the right and left (Clark, 1973). In this scenario that negatively identified sociology with the status quo and presented Durkheim as guilty of sectarianism, tyrannical thought, conservatism and reductive scientism, it is no doubt surprising that such an iconoclastic figure as Georges Bataille embraced Durkheim and relied on him for his own investigation of modern sociality. A "pornographic" author, poet, mystic and essayist, albeit an austere librarian too, Bataille seemed the least plausible of candidates to be supporting Durkheim and his sociology. And yet Durkheim, along with other members of his school, became the leading figures in Bataille's long lasting concern with sociological matters. What drove Bataille to Durkheim? And why did Bataille embrace sociology?

One of the most prominent features of Durkheim's theory is the idea that society can only be held together by common beliefs, an ensemble of shared values. In the past, traditional social ties and religions fulfilled the task of maintaining cohesion within a group; Durkheim amply discussed the strong solidarity present among pre-industrial populations. In the modern epoch dominated by the scientific spirit and individualism, however, what elements could guarantee the integrity of the collectivity, Durkheim asked. Absent the faith that sustained traditional communities, was society destined to collapse? Durkheim firmly believed that it was possible to replace traditional moralities based on religious faith with a morality based on science; as long as people agreed on the values they upheld, their consensus ensured the strength of the social bond. Once beliefs are shared, he claimed, they gain a life of their own and impose themselves on the collectivity, for they express a power that does not derive from individual ideas but in contrast originates from an external force: society. As the result of the group's shared beliefs, society acquires a sort of transcendence, a superior status, an almost religious character that makes it independent (*sui generis*) of its members, grander and more important than the sum of its parts. While individuals die, societies live on.

For Durkheim, society was the ultimate sacred; it anointed the group's beliefs and practices and made them overlap with religion. When we worship the gods, he stated, we worship ourselves – the unity of the group. His study, *The Elementary Forms of Religious Life* (1913) was meant to demonstrate this process by looking at the origins of the religious spirit. Through the case of totemism as the most primitive religion practiced by Australian aboriginal groups organized in clans, Durkheim claimed that religion is a hypostatization of society, its cypher. The venerated totem-god that the Australians celebrate during collective rituals and ceremonies expresses the group's awareness of its own unity, the group's sanctity.

Bataille was entranced by Durkheim's notion of the sacred as what holds a society together. As he proclaimed in 1937, he was interested in all human activities that "have a communifying value" and "are the *creators* of unity," and he considered sacred "everything in human existence that is *communifying*" (CS 74). For Bataille, Durkheim showed how to detect the presence of the sacred in society and pointed to sociology as able to identify the new morality necessary to forge social bonds and build strong communities in the contemporary world. The concept of the sacred, as formulated by Durkheim, linked Bataille to sociology and led him to develop original analyses of modern society; to Bataille, modernity seemed to lack a genuine sacred, the communitarian spirit necessary to accomplish true existence.

How did Bataille come to appreciate Durkheim? Bataille was an avid reader and working as a librarian at the Bibliothèque nationale in Paris certainly provided him with even more opportunities to satisfy his intellectual curiosity. From the records of his borrowings at the Bibliothèque, we know that he consulted Durkheim's *Elementary Forms* several times between 1931 and 1933 (OC XII, 549–621). Beginning in 1930, he also borrowed books by several members and affiliates of the

Durkheimian circle, including Marcel Mauss, Henri Hubert, Marcel Granet, Célestin Bouglé, Georges Davy, and the Durkheimian journal, *L'Année sociologique.* Whether he had come across these works earlier, it is hard to establish. We know without a doubt that he began to cite Durkheim's *Elementary Forms* in his 1933 essay "The Psychological Structure of Fascism." In 1930 he referred to Hubert and Mauss in his essay "Sacrificial Mutilations," while his 1933 article "The Notion of Expenditure" was highly indebted, at least in terms of inspiration, to Mauss's *The Gift.* In 1933–34 Bataille also cooperated in the preparation of a sociology course organized by the review *Masses.* Then in 1937, at the peak of his involvement with sociology, Bataille together with Roger Caillois and Michel Leiris founded the *Collège de sociologie*, a study group that appealed to sociological science in order to explore and illuminate issues concerned with the sacred. The *Collège* explicitly stated that it studied "sacred sociology," which it defined as the realm that included all human activities with a communifying value.

Bataille had selectively picked his inspirational sources for studying the sacred from an array of available thinkers. One of the reasons that particularly attracted him to the Durkheimians was their perceptive focus on "primitive" societies. Mauss, Hubert, Davy, Granet, as well as Durkheim, all engaged in ethnographic research, even if from the armchair. Because of this anthropological emphasis, they had been able to generate a deeper understanding of the life of groups as compared to the individualistic behavior typical of modern societies. By studying the conditions of social communities before the impact of modernity, the Durkheimians showed the spectrum of human potential in places and times untouched by the industrialized era, and they demonstrated the role of affective emotional states in the creation and strengthening of the social bond. Bataille benefited from the complementarity of sociology and ethnography displayed by the Durkheimians. In exploring the sacred, the College of Sociology was geared towards "rediscovering the primordial longings and conflicts of the individual condition transposed to the social dimension" (CS, 10).

In his writings of the late 1920s and throughout the 1930s, Bataille was interested in assessing ways to revive a society that, characterized by the logic of productivity and fully subscribed to a market economy, seemed to have lost the sense of what gives value to existence. The historical phenomenon of fascism, which had emerged in full force in Italy at the time, made Bataille's intellectual mission even more urgent. With its cults and rituals, fascism had shown a return to affective movements that complicated the analysis of modern societies. Were not the latter supposed to be characterized by the triumph of reason and the end of myths? How could one interpret this apparent incongruity? Bataille believed that findings on primitive societies could help assess the modern world's emotional needs that were trampled on by interest-based behavior. Ethnography, as deployed by the Durkheimian school and others, played a critical role in this operation.

Ethnography's appeal to Bataille emerges from the journal *Documents*, which was published between 1929 and 1931 under Bataille's leadership. A critical response to Surrealism, *Documents* was first conceived as an art magazine, but progressively moved to placing a larger emphasis on ethnographic material. The journal was many things at the same time, yet its originality chiefly resided in the juxtaposition of art and popular culture, which was prominently featured in its pages, along with an innovative use of photography and a non-conformist approach to beauty. Several of *Documents'* collaborators were ethnographers, including the future co-leader of the *Collège*, Leiris. The director and assistant director of the Parisian *Musée d'ethnographie* (later renamed *Musée de l'Homme*), Paul Rivet and Jean-Pierre Rivière, were on *Documents'* editorial board and wrote several articles for the review.

The revolutionary but also contradictory idea that guided *Documents* was the need to affirm the value of "primitive" cultures even when their material production did not fit classic aesthetic standards. According to the journal, more rigorous knowledge of "other" societies was indispensable to overcome the superficial and exotic approaches that had traditionally vexed the study of "primitive" people. Leiris in particular regarded ethnographic material not as a mere classification of cultures but as means to explore and attain our humanity. As he wrote for the entry on "Civilization," our culture rejects what is savage and in so doing denies our own violence and forfeits our instincts.[1] Art, with its aesthetic ideals and conventions, is in part responsible for this attitude and epitomizes the distance modern bourgeois Europeans have traveled away from emotions and human nature in general. Leiris emphasized the disagreeable – a move that Bataille pushed to the extremes by promoting the repulsive (what he defined as the heterogeneous) against any forms of perfection.

Bataille's early writings, including those in *Documents* and his whole polemic against Surrealism, had been geared toward dismantling idealist categories and hierarchical values. Without wishing to replace one form of idealism with another, Bataille opposed materialism and the formless to reason and harmony in order to challenge major Western philosophical conceptions and, ultimately, the modern ethics of "production." Against capitalism and its utilitarian, ascetic ideals, Bataille invoked the notion of uselessness, or "useless expenditure," which became one of his featured ideas, a trademark of his thought. The concept, especially deployed in "The Notion of Expenditure" (1932), was clearly inspired by the analysis of the potlatch in Mauss's 1925 essay *The Gift* (Mauss, 1990), the only scholarly reference cited in the "Expenditure" article.

For Mauss, the potlatch practiced by tribes of the American Northwest exemplified an economy based on giving – a form of exchange and contract that had a symbolic dimension: it was by participating in the potlatch that social hierarchy was established. A festival lasting the entire winter, the potlatch was characterized by an exchange of gifts between nobles in which the gift-givers tried to outdo their rivals in order to gain prestige and power. The competition was so fierce that it even involved irrational acts of violence, such as the destruction of wealth, when all participants defied each other to give more without expecting anything in return. In the end, the struggle among contenders was not about the appropriation of material wealth but about attaining "the social-symbolic good of prestige" (Karsenti, 1997, 375). Honor derived from the ability to waste wealth and possessions, a slap in the face of utilitarian logic. Violence helped renew sociality, Mauss seemed to suggest, with a nod to Sorel's notion of violence as regeneration.[2]

The Gift had a notable impact on Bataille, whether it inspired him or confirmed his intuitions. "Durkheim's work and even more Mauss's exercised an unquestionable influence on me" – he wrote in his "Notice biographique" (OC VII, 615). And in 1946, in his *Theory of Religion*, he stated that *The Gift* "forms the basis of any understanding of economy as being tied to forms of destruction of the excess of productive activity" (TR 125). For Bataille, irrational impulses are part of human existence, and he regretted that the bourgeoisie's stingy calculations and attachment to accumulation had discarded emotions along with consumption for unproductive ends. Loss, destruction and expenditure came to play a critical role in Bataille's approach to the sacred. Beginning with his 1930 essay "Sacrificial Mutilations," Bataille relied on Hubert and Mauss's work on sacrifice to ruminate about the relationship between what is destroyed – sacrifice – and the sacred. The essay on expenditure specifically related the two: "In the etymological sense of the word, sacrifice is nothing other than the production of *sacred* things" (VE 127).

It is impossible to appreciate Bataille's interest in ethnography and sociology as well as his approach to the sacred without taking into account his negative assessment of established order and what he considered "homogeneous" society – a system founded on production and money where everything useless is excluded. Critical of bourgeois platitude, and convinced of the non-economic essence of human nature, Bataille was attracted by the idea of the social as founded on irrational emotions and a non-identitarian bond. He was thus particularly intrigued yet worried by the resurgence of affective drives in the guise of fascist movements, in particular Mussolini's regime. If the sacred is the other of homogeneous society – what is excluded – when it returns under false premises, as in the case of fascism, it changes into a fake sacred. In other words, if, as Bataille believed, an affective link united Mussolini to his followers, if attraction united the led to their leader, then it became urgent to decipher the emotional forces traversing social relations in order to stop a fake sacred from triumphing.

Understanding the sacred became Bataille's main preoccupation in the 1930s, although it was only after a few years of active political militancy that he resumed researching the constitutive elements of the social bond. Thus in 1936 he founded a secret society, Acéphale, accompanied by a journal also called Acéphale. First issued on 24 June 1936, the journal's subtitle was: "Religion, Sociology, Philosophy." It anticipated some of the themes later to be studied at the Collège.

Acéphale called for a headless community that would mark the end of the dominance of authority and reason in order to re-envision the human condition. Existential motifs characterized the whole Acéphale project and signaled an inward turn in Bataille's intellectual journey. Despite this turn, the original sociological impulse that had guided Bataille to imagine novel ways of conceiving society remained alive in Acéphale; it now combined with "religion," intended not as mystical retreat but as a beacon for achieving a community of heart based on fraternity rather than tradition or blood.[3] This community would be pervaded by a religious spirit and held together by the ritual performance of myths, without however subscribing to an authoritarian model as was the case with fascism. Acéphale advocated an atheological church bound together by communal intoxication, with the "religious" emphasis on the constitution of the social bond.

With Acéphale, Bataille attempted a closer analysis of one aspect of the sacred the Durkheimians had highlighted: myths and rituals. How did myths and rituals work?, he asked. What was their role? Acéphale had been conceived as a sociological study group to answer this question, but it never applied itself to the task. Recognizing that knowledge was necessary to understand the mechanisms guiding our impulses, Bataille called for a "mythological sociology" that would apply insights from ethnological studies of "primitive" societies to modern forms of human existence.[4] If myths were catalysts of communal life, sociology would help gauge the emotional drives that move people; it would then be able to reverse the fate of modern societies now yoked to the dominance of instrumental reason. The time was ripe for the *Collège de sociologie*.

Established in March 1937, the announcement of the Collège's founding appeared in the July 1937 issue of Acéphale, where the Collège stated its commitment to developing a strong research program; as a study group, the Collège would explore all the elements that contributed to building a sacred community. "The precise object of the contemplated activity can take the name of Sacred Sociology, implying the study of all manifestations of social existence where the active presence of the sacred is clear" (CS, 5). A longer version of the statement published a year later concluded by proclaiming: "Three prominent problems dominate this study: the problems of power, of the sacred, and of myths" (CS, 11). The group acknowledged being inspired by Durkheim's *Elementary Forms*. Just as Durkheim had highlighted the role of mythical manifestations in creating and maintaining "primitive" communities, one could unveil the irrational elements at the foundation of the modern collective life that would reinstate the sacred at a time of its supposed demise. To be sure, the Collège did not embrace the whole of Durkheim's work. Nevertheless, it saw in the *Elementary Forms* the spark for initiating a deep examination of the "interplay of instincts and 'myths'" with the ultimate goal of enhancing the formation of true communities in the contemporary world (CS, 10).

The Collège particularly drew lessons from Durkheim and his school on three points: 1. the definition of society; 2. the assessment of the sacred as ambiguous; and 3. the importance given to festivals, rituals and myths for forging the social bond. At the Collège's opening lecture of 20 November 1937, entitled "Sacred Sociology and the Relationship between 'Society,' 'Organism' and 'Being'," Bataille echoed Durkheim's notion of society as more than the sum of its parts when he stated that society is "different from the sum of the elements that compose it" (CS, 74). At the heart of the sacred, Bataille continued, there lay an overall movement that transforms persons from individually oriented economic subjects into a "compound being" (CS, 77). Rejecting the individualist conception of social existence, Bataille eventually defined society as a "field of forces" traversing individuals in spite of their will (SS, 18). The group, as Durkheim had argued, was superior to the individual; associational life could not at all be explained by contractual theory.

How does a community then take shape, the Collège asked. What makes society? Inspired by another student of Durkheim, Robert Hertz, and by his study of the collective representations of death, Bataille theorized that death, and more specifically the horror death provokes in humans, enables the communifying movement. Hertz had pointed to the double valence of the sacred: the sacred could be pure and impure, right and left, attractive and repulsive. Bataille developed an original take on Hertz's theory and envisaged unity as the result of horror: society's origin was linked to disgust (Hertz, 1960). The institution of taboo, present among "primitive" societies, was a proof. As a form of prohibition, taboo marked the division between sacred and profane. By forbidding access to certain objects, people and places, it indicated their sacredness as compared to the profane world of everyday activities, where people and goods freely circulate. Bataille and the Collège evidently expanded the Durkheimians' basic lessons on the sacred and pushed them to their limits by focusing on the dynamic of the duo attraction and repulsion. In connection with this duo, at the inaugural session of the Collège's second cycle, Caillois gave a lecture by the title "The Ambiguity of the Sacred." Leiris had addressed the same topic in his own lecture about the sacred in everyday life earlier in the year, at the 8 January 1938 session.

The Collège was mainly interested in gauging how modern forms of sociality could be transformed into true communities thanks to the force of the sacred. As Durkheim had addressed the role of myths and rituals in the making of the social, so the Collège was intent on examining the mythical and ritualistic activities that would help enact the sacred in modern societies. "Community" was after all a key term for the Collège. Durkheim's identification of the sacred with the social, his argument about the hypostatization of society through religion, his emphasis on the need for social bonds against individualistic interests in modern societies upheld the Collège's conviction that it was possible and indeed paramount to rekindle the communal spirit at a time of supposed desacralization. In the *Elementary Forms*, Durkheim had emphasized the role of practices, besides beliefs, in the making of society. We become aware of the energy elevating us above our everyday life and petty interests, Durkheim claimed, only when we share experiences with others. In the case of the Australian clans, the feeling of being in an assembly – the perception of material and spiritual closeness – provoked an emotion among members that moved them to the point of obliterating their individual selves. The ceremonies held at seasonal meetings during night celebrations provided participants with an electrifying atmosphere that affected their minds and bodies and made them be dominated by emotions. Durkheim's poignant evocation of the *corrobori* ritual vividly portrayed the excitement of the assembled clan – a "collective effervescence." The emotional intensity arising from the gatherings, heightened by screams and words, unified the group and made people feel as part of a bigger, superior whole. Individuals' mental state became so suggestible that they believed external forces were moving them, and they identified those forces with what they saw represented in totems all around them. They did not realize that these forces were connected to society, that it was the collectivity's moral authority that impressed them with excitement and enthusiasm for their totem-gods. They did not recognize that authority was indeed the clan itself but transfigured; the totem merely symbolized society. Durkheim referred to *mana* (or totemic principle) to explain this phenomenon. In the anthropological literature he had consulted, *mana* was defined as a dangerous anonymous force with which things are endowed; it was an impersonal energy hard to describe but that, once believed to possess random objects or persons, made them acquire sacredness and enabled them to exercise authority over others.[5] Group assemblies, as the case of the Australian clans demonstrated, awakened the feeling of *mana* among the participants. For it was the group that was feted while celebrating the gods; rituals supported the coming together of the group in the creation and recreation of society.

The festivals' critical role in evoking the sacred, which Durkheim had so suggestively emphasized in his discussion of the Australian clans, did not escape the Collège. Although Caillois was the most knowledgeable on the topic and delivered a lecture about it, festival was the one practice the Collège saw as able to rekindle and re-enact the sacred in modern societies. The Collège's intent had always been to apply knowledge from archaic formations to modern reality while infusing the latter with that spirit of excitement and participation that would make possible attaining and worshipping the social bond – the guarantor of true existence. The utilitarian world of economic productivity and accumulation only deprived moderns of their human yearnings, Bataille warned. In particular, function defeated existence. With their excess and exaggerations, festivals, in contrast, constituted the antidote to functional movements, the counter altar to servitude, calculation and security. The Collège's formulations strikingly echoed those of the potlatch, where destruction was the *leitmotiv* of the ceremony, against any "rational" consideration of needs or utility. Indeed, whether or not Durkheim would have agreed with the Collège's take on the renewal of modern society, the Collège thought of the sacred as paroxystic and turbulent, an explosive force. This "left" sacred would surpass the administrative world's conservative orientation; expenditure, waste, and the violation of interdictions would all preside over a regenerating, orgiastic sacred. This was a sacred that needed transgression in order to survive, for only destroying and rebuilding allowed renewal. Thus, festivals constituted the social manifestation of the transgressive act, a time when the order of things could be disrupted and the flame of energy lit. Within this context, sacrifice was the ultimate festival – an offering with no return.

In order for rituals to function, however, myths were necessary. As Durkheim had suggested in his definition of religion, beliefs went hand in hand with practices. Bataille agreed with this statement. In "The Sorcerer's Apprentice," a sort of manifesto for the Collège first published in the summer of 1938 in the *Nouvelle Revue Française*, he recommended inventing mythology; myths could then be enacted ritually as the collectivity appropriated them emotionally and physically. "A community that does not succeed in the ritual possession of its myths possesses only a truth that is on the wane," Bataille wrote. "Myth ritually lived reveals no less than true being" (CS, 22). Myths inspired the ritual action of the group and at the same time were inspired by the rituals that allowed the community to recognize itself as such. If the Collège's ultimate goal were to recompose modes of collective existence in modern societies, rituals and myths had a paramount role in this undertaking.

An activist stance was at the heart of the Collège, although it eventually caused its demise. For Bataille, there was no meaning in setting up a study group that painstakingly looked at defining "crucial problems"; it was "an open door to chaos," if it did not also pursue change (CS, 334). By focusing on specialization, on the part as opposed to the whole, science failed to get at the totality of existence. Blindfolded and narrow-minded, science excluded human destiny; sociology risked the same constrictions if it followed scientific rules. The consequences would be particularly negative considering that sociology addressed the emotional-symbolic underpinnings of society. If research assumptions were not modified, if sociology shied away from addressing "burning questions," it would not be different from any other science. "If it is the social phenomenon alone that represents the totality of existence, science being no more than a fragmentary activity, the science that contemplates the social phenomenon cannot achieve its objective if, insofar as it achieves it, it becomes the negation of its principles" (CS, 12). As Bataille made it clear in "The Sorcerer's Apprentice," he embraced sociology only insofar as it took upon itself to confront "life's major decisions" (CS, 224). Sociology could not merely pursue knowledge for knowledge's sake.

At the last session of the Collège, Bataille was faulted for having neglected to abide by the rules of Durkheimian sociology. In a letter he sent to Bataille, Leiris expressed "doubts as to the rigor with which this venture has been conducted" (CS, 354). He continued by saying that "serious offenses against the rules of method established by Durkheim – whose spirit we continually evoke – have been committed many times at the Collège." Leiris also judged the Collège's emphasis on the sacred as demoting Mauss's idea of "total phenomenon" – an asset of modern sociology in his opinion. Not that one needed to do pure sociology, Leiris acknowledged, but if one claimed to be applying the principles of Durkheim, Mauss and Hertz, then either one stuck to their methods or stopped calling themselves "sociologists" (CS, 355). Other differences, especially of an intellectual nature, also separated Bataille from Caillois. Thus the Collège finally ended in July 1939, the sociological experiment over. At the Collège's last meeting, however, Bataille defended his right to rely on sociology and dismissed methodological or formal issues as secondary to what he saw as sociology's potential as disinterested knowledge (CS, 254). As he had stated in "The Sorcerer's Apprentice," sociology allowed one to see through our petty existence and to recognize the value of the sacred. Even several years after the Collège's demise, Bataille maintained the importance of Durkheim's sociology for countering the disintegration of modern society. In a 1946 essay, he confirmed his belief in two tenets of Durkheim's theory: 1. Society is a whole different from the sum of its parts; 2. The sacred is the constitutive element of societies. The two principles together worked to demonstrate humans' deep existence beyond the strict confines of interest, Bataille believed (WS, 103–111). Sociology and Durkheim, in sum, continued to hold valuable lessons for Bataille. As he wrote in 1948, "Émile Durkheim seems to me to be unjustly disparaged nowadays. I take my distance from his doctrine but not without retaining its essential lessons" (TR, 123).

Eventually, Bataille redefined the sacred and advocated considering it as a "concrete totality." He also added that totality implied something that sociology would not be able to account for if it followed a scientific approach. Science could not explain the sentiment we feel at the moment when life ends, that is, our existential anguish, the "totality of being which exceeds the limits of the possible and until death" (OC XII, 129). Although sociology did not accept Bataille's challenge and definitively ignored his call for "CONFRONTATION WITH DESTINY" as the "essence of knowledge" (CS, 334), it is ironic that Bataille was the one who came closest to upholding Durkheim's wildest dream of turning sociology into the science of sciences, the science that truly mattered.

Notes

1   "Civilisation" in *Documents* 4, 1929 (D 221–222).
2   Mauss however rejected Sorel's doctrine of violence.

3 "Nietzschean Chronicle" (VE 202–212).
4 "Ce que nous avons entrepris il y a peu de mois..." (A 367–377).
5 Durkheim adopted Robert Codrington's definition of *mana* (Durkheim 1995, 196–199).

References

Clark, Terry N. 1973. *Prophets and Patrons: The French University and the Emergence of the Social Sciences.* Cambridge: Harvard University Press.

Durkheim, Emile. 1995. *The Elementary Forms of Religious Life,* translated with Introduction by Karen Fields. New York: Free Press.

Hertz, Robert. 1960. *Death and the Right Hand.* London: Cohen and West.

Karsenti, Bruno. 1997. *L'homme total: sociologie, anthropologie et philosophie chez Marcel Mauss.* Paris: Presses Universitaires de France.

Mauss, Marcel. 1990. *The Gift: The Form and Reason for Exchange in Archaic Societies.* New York: W.W. Norton.

3 Fascism and the Politics of the 1930s in France

Andrew Hussey

Throughout the 1930s, Georges Bataille devoted a great deal of attention to the problem of fascism. His opinions were not always consistent. This was partly due to the elusive, ever-shifting way that Bataille thought, and the way in which his language was also highly fluid in meaning according to its context. It is also partly because Bataille's relationship with fascism was in itself problematic; this is not to say that he was a fascist or sympathetic to fascism – although the latter point was central to André Breton's arguments against Bataille when they both briefly collaborated on the anti-fascist journal *Cahiers de Contre-Attaque* in 1935 – but that Bataille's perceptions altered with a political reality that was shifting throughout the decade.

For the first part of the 1930s, he involved himself in overtly political struggles which aimed at deflecting the threat of coming war, as well as establishing specific anti-capitalist and anti-fascist positions. In 1933 and 1934, Bataille was not only actively involved in Boris Souvarine's *Cercle Communiste Démocratique* and the journal *La Critique Sociale*, but was also a member of the group *Masses*, which brought together Jean Dautry, Edouard Lienert, Paul Bénichou and, to a lesser extent, Simone Weil, and which sought to establish a theoretical position on the spontaneous movement of the revolutionary classes (Surya 1992, 227; Marmande 1985, 49–50). At this point Bataille was not only able to collaborate with those, like Breton, who had earlier attacked him, but also to engage with debates on the theory and representation of revolution with members of the revolutionary Left who had emerged from Surrealism or the French Communist Party, or both, and who expressed the primacy of experience over Marxist theory.[1]

The Contre-Attaque movement was effectively divided into two camps, one grouped around Bataille (Ambrosino, Klossowki, Dubief, Chavy), and the other around Breton (Eluard, Péret and Gillet). Bataille was the leader of the group (Surya 2002, 266–267; Short 1968, 144–177). In the first instance, this meant that, as Bataille put it in the first tract which signalled the activities of Contre-Attaque, the opposition to fascism was predicated on the perceived failure of communism (C, 105). In the second instance, it meant that the principal aim of the group – as defined in a text by Bataille and Breton – was to call for a renovation of the language and content of revolutionary violence.

The central premise behind Contre-Attaque, at least for Bataille, was that it was possible to turn the weapons of fascism upon itself. This was a notion which would be reflected in the community of Acéphale – exploring the potential of violence and sacrifice in real paroxystic experience and transferring these concerns to the domain of the social and political. These were ideas which Bataille had already begun to develop in 1935 and 1936, but that he had yet to define as specifically anti-fascist positions. More to the point, at a moment in history when intellectual violence was consistently being translated into real violence, Bataille's pursuit of the extreme emotions which led to this action was hard to explain or justify in a world of real physical confrontation between fascists and left-wing groups on the streets of Paris.

That is also why one of the lingering difficulties in Bataille scholarship is how to explain Bataille's determination to resist the rise of fascism as an "outward" reality in the first part of the decade, and the apparent turn towards inner experience, mysticism and an alleged quietism in the 1940s. The aim of this chapter is not so much to explain this turn – in fact Bataille explains it very well if his texts are read with due attention – but rather to put together an itinerary of events in France and Europe in the 1930s that led many French intellectuals towards fascism, and to consider Bataille's relationship to his era.

Bataille's own intellectual itinerary was of course determined by these same events. His "anguish" – this is the word he himself uses to describe his response to events – is not at all straightforward however. For all that he resists fascism, he is not only disappointed at the failure of socialism, which seems to him to belong to the "old Europe" of the 19th century, but also discerns an element of sensuality in the terrible catastrophe to come. This is why the key motifs of his writing at this point are suicide, necrophilia, guilt, annihilation. In 1934, he attempted to write a book called *Le Fascisme en France*, but abandoned the project as events kept spinning out of control, beyond comprehension (ffrench 2006, 68–69).

In this sense, Bataille intuited the danger close at hand for French society as a whole. The early part of the decade saw the coming together of the twin forces of fascism and anti-semitism. Indeed all of the parties of the Right were unashamedly anti-semitic with a virulence that had not been seen since the height of the Dreyfus affair in the 1890s. The main organ of debate was the journal *La Libre Parole*, a long-discontinued Dreyfusard publication, which was re-launched to a wide and enthusiastic, mainly Catholic readership in 1930. Among its contributors was Georges Bernanos – a former leading light in Charles Maurras's *Action Française*, the key activist movement on the Right – who had turned to a form of melancholy nostalgia for the Middle Ages.

In 1933, Germany fell suddenly under the dark shadow of the Nazi Party. By the end of that year, more than 20,000 Germans had fled to France. By the end of the decade over 55,000 exiles from Germany would pass through the country. Most of these were Jews and the term "refugee" immediately became synonymous with "Jew". The successive governments of the Third Republic grew increasingly fragile as pressure on them grew to defend the French worker and bourgeois against what seemed to be an unstoppable tide of aliens. "Paris has become the New Zion," wrote Paul Morand, novelist and diplomat whose anti-semitism had been forged during a stay in Romania (Josephs 1989, 46–48). The word "invasion" now became common currency even in relatively moderate circles. Another fear was that these new aliens would make an alliance with "resident Jews" – Jews who were already established – in a conspiracy against the country. Two Jews speaking Yiddish near the *Gare de L'Est* were attacked by a mob who claimed that they were praising Hitler. Another pair of Jews were nearly battered to death in Belleville by a working-class crowd who accused them of chanting "Long Live Hitler! Long Live Germany!" in a foreign tongue. When the novelist Louis-Ferdinand Céline, now famous as a bestselling author, produced in 1938 his long anti-Jewish diatribe *Bagatelles pour un massacre*, it was hailed as a great work.

Such nihilistic passions could hardly be held in check by any government and there was a certain sense of inevitability when, in February 1934, they spilled over on to the streets of the capital in days and nights of street-fighting that were the most dangerous moments any government had known since 1871. The background to these developments was an increasing disillusionment with the short-lived government of Camille Chautemps, provoked by the long-running affair known as the Stavisky scandal. Between 1932 and 1933, there were five different governments but little change in the personnel, who were as uniformly cynical as the public they were elected to serve. Serge Stavisky himself was no politician but a financier who was variously alleged to be of Hungarian, Polish or Romanian background, and certainly Jewish (he was in fact the son of a Ukrainian Jewish dentist). He was known to have close links with many prominent figures in the worlds of property, politics and the law and in 1933 came under police investigation for alleged corruption (Passmore 2014).

The rumours and allegations turned out to be true but the police investigation was mired in incompetence and in the press and on the streets it was argued that the police themselves were party to the web of evil woven by the high-living Stavisky. The Chautemps government fell at the end of January 1934, having barely survived two months, to be replaced by a coalition led by Edouard Daladier that proclaimed republican unity. The Parisian public were by now heartily sick of all forms of elected government, however. The stage was set for a dramatic confrontation between forces on the Right and the Left, who both believed that a strong and steady hand was needed to steer France away from conflict with Germany and disaster.

Leading the way on the Right was a loose coalition of *"ligues"* (leagues) none of whom were strictly fascist in the terms set by Mussolini in Italy and who had little in common with the revolutionary ideologues of the Nazi Party in Berlin. The *ligueurs* were indeed an echo of the older Catholic League that had brought so much agitation to Paris during the Wars of Religion. They included the *Camelots du Roi*, fiercely Catholic and Royalist militants associated with *Action Française; la Jeunesse Patriote*, who had a mainly anti-Bolshevik agenda; and *Solidarité Française*, an organization led by the parfumier François Coty, whose members marched around in a neo-fascist outfit of blue shirt and black beret. The most convincing and popular league was the *Croix de Feu*, a group of war veterans led by Colonel Casimir de la Rocque whose only stated aim was to clear out the corruption at the heart of the French Republic in the name of the common soldier.

It was de la Rocque who co-ordinated the other leagues into a march on the National Assembly on 6 February, ostensibly to demonstrate against the weakness and instability of government and its corruption as demonstrated by the Stavisky affair. Stavisky had by now committed suicide – or been "suicided"; no one knew for sure – but his ghost was still causing trouble.

There had been skirmishes between *ligueurs* and the police throughout January, but the police had applied a relatively light touch to groups whose aims they basically shared (the prefect of Paris, Jean Chiappe, was anyway known to be a crony of Stavisky, a fact that enraged left-wingers). There was a mini-riot at the *Gare du Nord* over delays on commuter trains and the press was actively looking for a fight, with headlines such as "End of the Régime" and "Time for the Necessary Purge!" But still the mood on the late afternoon of 6 February, as distinguished and be-medalled veterans led the first waves of *ligueurs* across Place de La Concorde, was relatively calm. For two hours or more, the crowd stood still before a lightly armed line of guards, which was all that stood between them and the seat of power. In the days leading up to the demonstration, the press had shouted wildly about government aggression, predicting tanks, machine guns and squads of savage Negro soldiers, who would be sent to run amok among patriotic Frenchmen. Since nothing of the sort happened, or looked likely to happen, the vacuum had to be filled.

The violence came from another source altogether; this was between the most rabid *ligueurs* and factions from all the Leftists parties who had come to protest at "fascists" launching a potential *coup d'état*. The police lost control: kiosks and buses were overturned, street lamps were turned into weapons, paving stones were ripped up and thrown at the forces of order in the name of human dignity. All of a sudden, as the tune of the *Marseillaise* was replaced by the *Internationale*, for a joyous moment it seemed to the rioters of the Left that an insurrection or even revolution might be on the cards.

There was of course no such thing. Daladier's government resigned the next day, but despite the demonstrations and counter-demonstrations which erupted sporadically across the city, there was no real, generalized will for a violent transformation. In all sixteen people had been killed out of crowd of some 40,000 rioters. Throughout bourgeois Paris, there was as much bemusement as excitement; the real tensions of the city – the class divisions which had not been repaired since the Commune – could not be avoided for much longer.[2]

Amongst those radicalized by the Stavisky riots and their aftermath was the novelist Pierre Drieu La Rochelle, who was then forty years old and after wavering between Left and Right for much of his career so far, decided to dedicate himself irrevocably to the fascist cause. He saw France as "decadent" and had decided that democracy was the enemy of a spiritual and intellectual renewal of France. He was above all concerned at the financial crisis which seemed to be propelling France further and faster into decline, and the falling birth rate. This second anxiety had indeed been a staple cause of concern on the French Right since the late 19th century and was perceived both as a slight on French virility and, no less importantly, a statistic which undermined French claims to be a "Great Power". A long forgotten novel by Marcel Arland, *L'Ordre* (winner of the Prix Goncourt in 1929), gives voice to the anxiety in the tale of "a repentant pseudo-surrealist" whose own sterility is a metaphor for the death of France (Hollier 1994, 920–924).

Drieu's own fascism was "a call to order" in this sense, but was also imbued with a deep mystical strain. He was sympathetic to right-wing

Catholics but his own spirituality was also based on an extreme form of individualism and contempt for the "mediocrity" of democracy. He was a strong pro-European and by 1939 believed that only Nazi Germany could ensure the survival of European values and civilization against the hordes from the East. Like many of his generation he was an admirer of Oswald Spengler, in whose writings he found confirmation of his nostalgia for the unified Christian Europe of the Middle Ages and of the alarming thesis that the West was about to collapse under the weight of its own self-destructive urges, to be finally conquered by "Asiatics". From this point of view, Hitler and Franco were both right to impose on Europe a will to resist and conquer.

Jean-Paul Sartre's conclusion about Drieu's work and legacy was that it is conceived from the "old Heraclitean myth according to which life is born from death" – in other words "whosoever wants to save life shall lose it: the future does not germinate in the wombs of women but in the blood of men". Sartre was right about Drieu, and also about the apocalyptic mysticism which was the defining point of this particularly French form of fascism (Hollier 1994, 918)

Literature aside, however, Paris was quickly running out of political solutions to the permanent sense of crisis that paralysed its governments. In the days after the February riots of 1934, the Left was terrified most of all by the spectre of a Right-Wing coup led by de la Rocque and his "leagues". As a response, the Communist Party called for a united front to fight the menace. Surprisingly, the various factions of the Left were able to make common cause and even declared a general strike later that month. In July, the leader of the Socialist Party, Léon Blum, and the leader of the Communist Party, Maurice Thorez, signed an agreement of political unity. The two groups came together most magnificently in a force of nearly half a million, which gathered at the Bastille on 14 July 1935 as a counter-demonstration to the show of strength by *Croix de Feu* on the *Champs-Elysées* a mile or so away. Under the banner of "The Popular Front", socialists and communists launched a movement with the slogan "Peace, Bread, Freedom".

Their historic moment arrived less than twelve months later when the *Front Populaire* swept to power in the May elections of 1936. Everything changed in France more or less overnight. A maximum working week of forty hours and paid holidays were introduced for the first time in the history of Europe. Workers began to sense at least that they were in control. It was of course no more than an illusion, and it was not long, as inflation and depressed wages began to bite, before the workers' demands were creating real hardship for the workers themselves. The right-wing press, ever alert to the "Red Terror" in Paris, began publishing cartoons of workers raping rich old ladies in the name of "rights". Fear returned as the dominant *leitmotiv* of everyday life. As Franco laid siege to Madrid, it was rumoured that de la Rocque was plotting to take Paris. The anti-semitism that had destroyed Stavisky transferred itself to Blum, a Jew and a vociferous supporter of Dreyfus who – again it was rumoured – was planning to wreck France and take refuge with his co-conspirators, the deadly and hypocritical English. The gutter press was alive with the wildest allegations, which no one dared refute or challenge in case the attacks became worse. The same press also regularly carried dire predictions of a devastating future that would destroy France once and for all.

It was also a common enough position among even so-called patriotic Parisians to declare that they had lost all faith in their own politicians and to welcome the scourge of Hitler as a necessary purge. This indeed was the position of Céline who expressed the commonly held view that catastrophe was preferable to the present state of inglorious humiliation. There were other intellectuals, more nuanced and finely mannered than Céline (including the likes of the influential novelists and critics Robert Brasillach and Lucien Rebatet), who were lining up on the Nazi side for their own complicated reasons, ranging from an aesthetic sympathy with fascism, high-bourgeois anti-semitism or simple leader worship.[3] Bizarrely, the translations of *Mein Kampf*, in circulation in Paris at this time, omitted the sections in which Hitler defines France as Germany's historical enemy by force of geography and destiny. The result of this intellectual blindness was a hardening of positions on Left and Right, a process accelerated by the Spanish Civil War, which erupted in 1936, abolishing all possibility of dialogue between two sides now describing themselves as revolutionaries.

The literary history of France during the 1930s is then really the story of how a generation of French intellectuals turned towards fascism, and ultimately a decade later, towards collaboration. As the case of Drieu La Rochelle indicates, this was less due to a generalized Germanophilia but rather a drift from French nationalism into a pan-European quest for order. The nostalgia for the Middle Ages – particularly virulent in Drieu – is matched in the case of Robert Brasillach by a longing for the certainties of classical antiquity, and a self-confident belief that France, even in its degraded and decadent form, was the rightful heir to the splendours of classical civilization. Both forms of nostalgia played a key role in what Walter Benjamin called the "aestheticizing of politics" – the necessary prelude to a fully-blown fascist posture.

Where did Bataille stand in all of this? In the essay "The Popular Front in the Street", Bataille discerns in the climate of the first half of the 1930s "the atmosphere of a storm [...] the contagious emotion that, from house to house, from suburb to suburb, suddenly turns a hesitating man into a frenzied being" (VE, 162). This was a fairly accurate description of how it felt to be in Paris in the first half of the 1930s. Bataille himself was traumatized by the crisis of 1934. Although crippled by rheumatism, he took part in the riots and kept a political diary reflecting on events. "From every quarter, in a world that will quickly cease to be breathable, the fascist constriction tightens", he wrote (cited in Kendall 2007, 105).

Many of the ideas for the abandoned *Fascisme en France* were already present in the long essay, "The Psychological Structure of Fascism" (1933). In this essay Bataille argued that fascism, in its varied European forms, was not simply a political concept but also a religious movement. He noted that it was on account of this that fascism was the only revolutionary movement which had been able to overcome capitalism. Making a comparison with Islam, Bataille pointed out that fascism was a totality whose political success was predicated on its "heterogeneous" processes – that is to say the "sovereign, destructive passions" which are both spontaneous and mystical, and which ignite religious emotion. In comparison, socialism, and especially the "democracy" which is the materialist manifestation of the idea of socialism, appears "mediocre", even impotent. This is partly why Bataille ends the essay in such a pessimistic way, writing that "revolutionary movements that develop in a democracy are hopeless". This, for Bataille, is the greatest and most unresolvable tension at work in France and Europe (VE, 159).

Accordingly, for Bataille, it is the rise of the irrational which defines the psychological structure of fascism. The irrational is contained within the individual's psyche as well as the collective psyche of society at large. Accordingly, as Bataille turned his attentions to the "outward" problems of history, and in particular, the rise of Hitler and the possibility of a European war, he also understood that war, like politics, was a religious problem. To this extent the world of outward experience, of economic and social struggle, is inextricably related to the problems of "inward" experience; there is no separation in Bataille between the subjective realities of the individual and the objective movement of politics and history.

Bataille's varying positions in relation to fascism are pursued in the essay "Bataille in the Street: The Search for Virility in the 1930s" by Susan Rubin Suleiman (1995). In this essay, Suleiman describes how Bataille's response to the rise of fascism is anguish, which then gives way to a political and sexual powerlessness. She presents as evidence the novel *Blue of Noon*, written by Bataille in 1935, but not'published until 1957. The narrative of this novel is both disoriented and disorient- ing; essentially the main character Troppmann wanders in a suicidal trance across Europe in crisis – each city he visits, London, Vienna, Paris, Barcelona, Trier is a city of historical trauma. Allegedly Bataille did not want to publish the book in the 1930s because he did not think it was "useful" to do so. For Susan Rubin Suleiman and others who have followed her, this is the real turning-point in Bataille's thought; towards the end of the 1930s, as the war, the apocalypse finally approached, he turned his attention to the "inward gaze".

For Suleiman, what *Blue of Noon* reveals is a coming together of mysticism and a generalized disappointment, a literal loss of faith in the "outward" realities of politics and war. To this extent, it does not reveal Bataille as a-political, and certainly not as a fascist sympathizer, nor even a nihilist. It is rather about the impossibility of individual action against historical process. This is why Bataille did not want to publish the book in 1935; not only is the book not "useful" in the struggle against the coming apocalypses, it was a book full of omens and portents; the novel as premonition. In his own post-face to *Blue of Noon*, on its publication in 1957, Bataille wrote:

It has been my aim to express myself clumsily. I do not mean to imply, however, that one burst of fury, or the endurance of suffering, is in itself enough to confer on stories the power of revelation. I have mentioned these things in order to be able to say that the freakish anomalies of *Blue of Noon* originated in an anguish to which I was prey. These anomalies are the ground of *Blue of Noon*; but I was so far from assuming this ground was a guarantee of quality as to refuse to publish the book, which was written in 1935. Friends who were affected by a reading of the manuscript have now urged its publication, and I have decided to leave the matter up to them. I had, however, more or less forgotten its existence.

No later than 1936, I had decided to think no more about it. In the meantime, moreover, the Spanish Civil War had rendered insig- nificant the historical events connected with the novel. Confronted with tragedy itself, why pay any attention to its portents?

(BN, 154)

Since its publication, *Blue of Noon* has been recognized as one of the key texts in French from the 1930s precisely because its mood is alienated, disenchanted, sometimes even demented. To this extent it is not a "useful" book in the sense that it offers no solution, nor even the promise of a solution to the "rising tide of murder" which seems about to engulf Europe. It is indeed hard to imagine a more bitter and bleak scene than the final moment of *Blue of Noon* when Troppmann watches a parade of Nazi youth in Frankfurt. From now on, as Patrick ffrench has suggested, Bataille's writing must necessarily be conditioned by tragedy or black irony (ffrench 2006, 71). That is the significance of this moment of dark illumination – the "anguish to which I was prey". This is acknowledged in the text by Troppmann himself who is gripped by a cruel hilarity in the face of this catastrophe. The novel ends:

> Against this rising tide of murder, far more incisive than life (because blood is more resplendent in death than life), it will be impossible to set anything but trivialities – the comic entreaties of old ladies. All things were surely doomed to conflagration, a mingling of flame and thunder, as pale as burning sulphur when it chokes you. Inordinate laughter was making my head spin. As I found myself confronting this catastrophe, I was filled with the black irony that accompanies the moments of seizure when no one can help screaming. The music ended; the rain had stopped. I slowly returned to the station. The train was assembled. For a while I walked up and down the platform before entering a compartment. The train lost no time in departing.
>
> (BN, 151–152)

Michael Richardson writes that for Bataille fascism is "a perverted and nostalgic form" but one that is successful because, even in a parodic form, it "responds to a deep yearning for an experience of the sacred" (Richardson 1994, 93). Socialism had failed because it had tried to take on capitalism in the domain of economics – precisely the source of capitalist power. Fascism, on the other hand, had revealed the limits of capitalism, and its weakness, by opposing capitalism in the domain of the social, that is to say, the sacred.

In this sense, Bataille had correctly diagnosed the real history of the slide to fascism in France in 1930s. His own journey into mysticism and poetry begins from this starting point – the quest for a sacred of the Left Hand, a religion without God which opposes and transcends fascism. He would later call this position "atheology"; but his philosophical adventure has its source and origin in Bataille's misery at the death of the "Old Europe" of Marx and socialism and the coming apocalypse, ushered in by those French fascists who thought they saw a new dawn rather than fires on the horizon.

Notes

1 The group included for example Maurice Heine, Adolphe Acker, Benjamin Péret, Jean Bernier and Henri Dubief. See the "Cahiers de Contre-attaque" (Nadeau 1967, 452).
2 Amongst the works consulted for this section are Andrew and Ungar (2004); Passmore (2013); Weber (1995), and Zeldin (1980).
3 For accounts of this period see Kaplan (2000); Spotts (2008); Betz and Martens (2004).

References

Andrew, Dudley and Ungar, Steven. 2004. *Popular Front Paris and the Poetics of Culture*. Cambridge MA: Harvard University Press.

Betz, Albrecht and Martens, Stefan. 2004. *Les Intellectuels et l'Occupation: Collaborer, Resister, Partir*. Paris: Autrement.

ffrench, Patrick. 2006. "Dirty Life". In *The Beast at Heaven's Gate, Georges Bataille and the Art of Transgression*, edited by Andrew Hussey, 61–72. Amsterdam: Rodopi.

Hollier, Denis. 1994. "Birthrate and Death-Wish". In *A New History of French Literature*, edited by Denis Hollier, 920–924. Cambridge MA: Harvard University Press.

Josephs, Jeremy. 1989. *Swastika over Paris: the Fate of the French Jews*. London: Bloomsbury.

Kaplan, Alice. 2000. *The Collaborator: The Trial and Execution of Robert Brasillach*. Chicago: University of Chicago Press.

Kendall, Stuart. 2007. *Georges Bataille*. London: Reaction.

Marmande, Francis. 1985. *Georges Bataille Politique*. Lyon: Presses Universitaires de Lyon.

Nadeau, Maurice. 1967. *Histoire du Surréalisme*. Paris: Editions du Seuil.

Passmore, Kevin. 2013. *The Right in France from the Third Republic to Vichy*. Oxford: Oxford University Press.

Passmore, Kevin. 2014. "The Historiography of 'Fascism' in France". *French Historical Studies*, 37, 469–499.

Richardson, Michael. 1994. *Georges Bataille*. London: Routledge.

Short, Robert Stuart. 1968. "Contre-Attaque". In *Entretiens sur le Surréalisme*, edited by Ferdinand Alquié, 144–177. Paris and The Hague: Mouton.

Spotts, Frederic. 2008. *The Shameful Peace: How French Artists and Intellectuals Survived the Nazi Occupation*. New Haven: Yale University Press.

Suleiman, Susan Rubin. 1995. "Bataille in the Street". In *Bataille: Writing the Sacred*, edited by Carolyn Bailey Gill, 27–47. London: Routledge.

Surya, Michel. 1992. *Georges Bataille, La Mort à l'œuvre*. Paris: Gallimard.

Surya, Michel. 2002. *Georges Bataille: an Intellectual Biography*. Translated by Krzysztof Fijalkowski. New York: Verso.

Weber, Eugen. 1995. *The Hollow Years*. London: Norton.

Zeldin, Theodore. 1980. *France 1848–1945*. 3 vols. Oxford: Oxford University Press.

4   Nietzsche

Giulia Agostini

Georges Bataille's encounter with Nietzsche is a decisive one. By his own account, the works of Nietzsche are among his first readings worthy to be mentioned. Dating back to 1923, they are nearly contemporary with his readings of the first volumes of Proust's *In Search of Lost Time*, and followed shortly after by his discovery of Sade in 1926. Nietzsche is quoted and discussed at many stages in Bataille's work, but he is central to Bataille's concern about "experience," and thus to Bataille's *Atheological Summa: Inner Experience* (1943) and *Guilty* (1944), and especially his book *On Nietzsche* (1945), to which must be added Bataille's collection of maxims by Nietzsche entitled *Memorandum* (1945).

To talk about "criticism" with regard to Bataille's writings under the sign of Nietzsche (as a title like *On Nietzsche* might suggest) would be misleading, though. What Bataille has in mind is something radically different from a scholarly discussion of the works of Nietzsche or a biographical account, or even a sort of intellectual biography. He is much rather in search of a "strategy" appropriate to the uniqueness of his thinking as well as to the no less unique appearance of the historical person of Nietzsche.[1] In the late 1930s, Bataille defends the German philosopher against fascism and the contemporary usurpation of his thinking by the Nazis for their own ideology. However, in *On Nietzsche* he also goes beyond this immediate political dimension, and it is by reflecting upon the very *mode* of writing in his work *on* – or rather *with* – Nietzsche that he develops a genuinely novel way of returning to Nietzsche (Hollier 1992, 25–26).

On Nietzsche consists of a "Preface," which itself does not meet the criteria expected of the genre, and two initial chapters introducing "Mr. Nietzsche" and the notions of "Summit and Decline"; but it also contains an apparently incongruous personal journal, including several poems, occupying three quarters of the volume. Thus *On Nietzsche* is characterized by a striking heterogeneity and "imperfection," responding to Nietzsche's own hybrid modes of writing: "My book is in part, from day to day, a narrative of dice thrown – thrown, I must say, with impoverished means" (N, xxiii). It really is as if Bataille starts writing *because of* Nietzsche, yet without even wanting to talk *about* Nietzsche. The relation between Bataille's book and its subject, Nietzsche, is similar then to that between his earlier work, *Guilty*, and the beginning of the war. Choosing this constructive rather than exegetical path, Bataille responds to Nietzsche's demand for "writing with [one's] blood" (N xxi); and he echoes it in avowing that "[he] could only write *with [his] life* this book" (N xxiii). The place of the reader then can be discerned from a maxim of Nietzsche's *Zarathustra* quoted by Bataille at the opening of his *Memorandum*: "Qui écrit en maximes avec du sang ne veut pas être lu mais su par cœur." [The one who writes maxims with his blood does not want to be read, but known by heart] (OC VI, 213).

Bataille feels the necessity of "'being' Nietzsche" in order to read him "authentically" (OC VIII, 476): "My life in Nietzsche's company is a community; my book is this community" (N, 9). This necessity raises what Bataille calls the "essential problem," the problem of "the whole man," linked to the idea of "experience" (N, xxiii): "Only my life, only its ludicrous resources could pursue the quest for the Grail of chance in me. This proved able to respond to Nietzsche's intentions more precisely than power" (N xxiii). The subtitle of his book *On Nietzsche, The Will to Chance*, evokes Nietzsche's idea of the will to power even while suggesting a radical shift away from it. The expression "will to chance" merges ideally with another Nietzschean key notion, the *"amor fati,"* "love of fate" (*The Gay Science*), which Bataille – quite in tune with Nietzsche – defines as "wanting chance" (N, 116). It is in this sense of superposition (*will to power, amor fati*) that Bataille's reading of Nietzsche appears in the mode of the *eternal return of the same* – if the latter is understood as the *return of the same as always different*: "The only motivation justifying the reading of Nietzsche and guaranteeing its sense is to be placed, as he was, without a choice, before the moment of destiny (*l'échéance*)" (OC VIII, 476).

It is thus under the necessarily contingent, Nietzschean sign of "chance" that Bataille responds to Nietzsche. *Chance* here is closely related to *échéance*, a word difficult to directly translate into English, but which has the meaning of "expiration," and something "falling due." This term figures frequently in Bataille, for whom it also refers to the mere fact of something "falling" like a die falling, an image that fascinates Nietzsche's *Zarathustra*, too (N, 141). Both the French *chance* and *échéance* originate in the same Latin etymon *cadentia* "falling": "*Chance* is that which expires, which falls (originally good or bad luck). It is randomness, the *fall* of the die" (N, 68). For Bataille, Nietzsche is the thinker not of the *will to power*, but of the *eternal return*, a notion coinciding in Bataille's view with a *chance* perpetually at the risk of being missed and of turning into *malchance*, "bad luck" (N, 5). Bataille represents this idea as a process of constantly falling, but haplessly missing the "hook," that would keep you from falling further (OC V, 315).

Still, what does Bataille's "community" with Nietzsche mean apart from the certainty that "[w]ith a few exceptions, [his] company on earth is that of Nietzsche..." (N, 3)? What does this *chance community* with Nietzsche, or rather, what do this *communion* and this *communication*, as they are implied in the very idea of *community*, actually consist in? At a first glance, Bataille's understanding of *community* does not seem to surpass the univocity of its ordinary usage, i.e. Nietzsche alone ideally being "solidary" with Bataille simply by "saying *we*" (N, 3). Once Bataille intimates the possibility for community *not to exist*, however, the very question of community becomes equivocal and reveals itself to be of unexpected complexity.

After having introduced the rather banal idea of "solidarity," Bataille continues: "If *community* doesn't exist, Mr. Nietzsche is a philosopher" (N, 3). Thus, when talking about "community as existing" (IE, 33), what Bataille actually means is "virtually" existing (OC V, 436), as he corrects himself in a note to an earlier occurrence of the term. Bataille writes that he burns with "a feeling of anxious faithfulness" towards Nietzsche, and compares this with the burning of the one who wears the "shirt of Nessus" (IE, 33), i.e. a "cloth" covering the body only by adhering to it (and setting it aflame), clothing and nakedness essentially being identical. The image suggests that there really is *nothing* in this community that one can grasp, nothing but "a burning, painful longing that endures in [him] like an unsatisfied desire" (N, xvii). Similarly, his interpretation of the Nietzschean imperative "Be that ocean" from *Zarathustra* points to the same difficulty:

> Such a simple commandment: "Be that ocean", linked to the extremity, makes man at once a multitude and a desert. It is an expression that summarizes and makes precise the sense of community. I know how to respond to Nietzsche's desire speaking of a community having no object but experience (but designating that community, I speak of a "desert")
>
> (IE, 34)

For Bataille, the desire for community, for the "ocean" as a "torrential multitude" expressed in this "simple commandment" turns into the recognition of a "desert" as a metaphor of solitude. If community *does not exist*, though, what is there possibly *remaining* for Bataille and Nietzsche, two "solitaries among solitaries," to have *in common*? Bataille replies: "We can't rely on anything. But only on *ourselves*" (N, 3). And at once another question arises: what does this privation – nothing to be grasped (as in the desperate simile of "Nessus' shirt"), nothing in common, nothing to rely on but *ourselves* – tell us about *philosophy* as Nietzsche the "philosopher" embodies it? *Philosophy*, Bataille seems to suggest, acknowledges the task, takes on the "responsibility fall[ing] *on us*" (N, 3), *our* responsibility to think precisely about this space *suspended in between* the singularities, which in Bataille's exploration of the limits of thought serves as a sort of *background* from which new dimensions may arise. Thus it is precisely in its very *non-existence* that Bataille's "community" with Nietzsche *opens up* the possibility for a *relationship* hitherto "nearly unknown to human destiny" to manifest itself – as he writes not without a touch of pathos (OC V 284); what *remains* is the idea of *friendship* relating the two Nietzschean "solitaries among solitaries," who actually are "in quest of a *friend*" (N, 6), to each other.

What does *friendship* designate, though, apart from the paradoxical "community of those deprived of community?"[2] In an *affirmative* sense, *friendship*, for Bataille no less than Blanchot, his intimate friend and privileged reader, is the name for the relation *between* us, the *in-between* itself ceaselessly *relating between plural singularities*, as though it were the "only measure" (Blanchot 1969, 313), and as it is at work in *conversation* – if one comes to understand the latter as a *plural speech* rather than a dialogue in the everyday meaning of the word. This *plural speech*, as Blanchot describes it with regard to Bataille, is a *plurality* of ever *singular* voices striving for a "unique affirmation," that in a seeming paradox "neither unifies nor lets itself be unified" but is constantly "pointing to a difference more original still," thus "saying the absolutely other" (1969, 319). If Bataille's "conversation" with Nietzsche means that they both are "saying the same," the continuous reflexion of their "sayings" nonetheless differentiates them anew, and reveals still another difference between them – as can be seen, for example, in Bataille's strategy of quoting Nietzsche and "echoing" the words in his own guise at a later stage. It is in this sense that we are witnessing the "speech of the neuter," the "infinite speech," where the "unlimitedness of thought is being played out" (Blanchot 1969, 320).

This idea of *unlimitedness* recurs throughout Bataille's conversation with Nietzsche. It points to Bataille's notion of *non-knowledge* and the *unknown*, both of them being *without limits* by definition. It is the *experience* of the necessarily inaccessible, the incommensurable *unknown*, the *unknowable* – be it called "*inner* (or mystical) *experience*," or given instead the seemingly whimsical, mocking, yet all but unambiguous shorthand name "*impalement*" – upon which Bataille's *Atheological Summa* is grounded.

This can be seen in *Inner Experience*, where Bataille introduces the metaphor of the *blind spot* pertaining to the anatomy of the *eye* as a model for how *understanding* works (IE, 112). "To know means: to relate to the known, to grasp that an unknown thing is the same as another known thing" (IE, 110). Bataille here instead considers the opposed movement "going from the known to the unknown" (IE, 112) to be a more adequate definition of *knowledge*; – *knowledge* then implying the discovery of the *blind spot* within understanding, the "spot" of invisibility ever exceeding what can be known. However, since no stable "position" can be assigned to this "spot" of *blindness* (of *non-knowledge*) continuously accompanying sight (knowledge) like its own "shadow" (Esposito 2006, 119), no tranquillity can follow for existence from its discovery; and not even *ecstasy* – literally that which "stands outside" – can possibly accomplish the exploration of the night of *non-knowledge* in its *unlimitedness*: "Final possibility: that non-knowledge still be knowledge. I would explore the night! But no, the night explores me..." (IE, 112).

This is precisely what *poetry* is about in Bataille's view. Like desire and Nietzschean laughter, it ceaselessly, and inexhaustibly moves towards the *unknown*, imagining, and thus placing one in the first place before the *unknowable*, as can vividly be seen from *metaphor*:

> When the farm girl says "butter" or the stable hand says "horse", they know the butter, the horse. In a sense, the knowledge that they have of these things exhausts the very idea of knowing, since they can make butter or lead a horse at will [...] But poetry, by contrast, leads from the known to the unknown. It can do what the farm girl or the stable hand cannot – introduce a butter horse. In this way, it places us before the unknowable
>
> (IE, 136)

This simple thought experiment, introducing the "butter horse" as a metaphor of the *unknown* performatively shows what Bataille takes to be the strength of *poetry* – appearing as an "agent," or in a deeply Bataillean expression, an "accomplice" of *non-knowledge*, namely its ability of pointing to the *unknowable as unknowable*, and thus opening up the unlimited dimension of *non-knowledge* whence new knowledge may arise. As opposed to this knowledge of poetry, i.e. its *complicity* with *non-knowledge*, the usual, and entirely insufficient notion of knowledge in its movement from the unknown to the known, is falsely reducing to the "same" what is ultimately only the *same as different*, and is establishing a merely apparent, and truly blind relation of unity. When it comes to *non-knowledge*, though, it is evident that we are not only dealing with the inversion of the movement striving for knowledge. The *experience* Bataille has in mind, the experience of *non-knowledge*, the *inner experience defies the very idea of completion, or unity*: like the very "shadow" of knowledge, *non-knowledge* in Bataille's thought is absolutely irreducible to knowledge and figures as an "unknowable absolute" (Esposito 2006, 119). It thus is the *experience* of that which ever lies "beyond complete knowledge" as a graspable "whole," and thus para-doxically *points* to a "relation [...] there where relation is impossible" (Blanchot 1969, 309). Again we encounter the *in-between* that holds open the unlimited *game of thought*, the *in-between* as the infinite movement of the *unknown*: "The unknown [...] cannot serve as an intermediary, since the relation with it – the infinite affirmation – falls outside of all relation" (Blanchot 1969, 320).

It is not surprising, then, that Bataille's attitude towards *poetry* is ambivalent. Despite its strength – it is one of the privileged domains where the unknown is being played out – *poetry* in its inability to escape from the "curse" of representation necessarily fails before that which is essentially *unknowable*; and this means that poetry fails before the *impossible*, too, a term Bataille would introduce with respect to what he had precisely called his *hatred of poetry*.[3] Not only is *The Hatred of Poetry*, published in 1947, nearly contemporary with Bataille's writings on Nietzsche, but it similarly hovers around the idea of the necessity of a "leap." The "freedom" of the leap shows the impossibility of relating to the *unknowable absolute* – and *The Impossible* is then the title given to *The Hatred of Poetry*, when it was republished in 1962.

Now, if it is true that poetry appears as an "accomplice" of *non-knowledge*, it necessarily has to be an "accomplice" of the *impossible*, too. What does this *complicity* mean, though, especially if one bears in mind that one of the volumes of Bataille's Nietzsche project is entitled *Guilty*? It seems worth noting here that Bataille understands *friendship* (in the wake of Nietzsche) as "complicity," qualifying his own *friend-ship* as "complicitous," as we can grasp from his words quoted by Blanchot (1971) as an epigraph to another of his books, *Friendship*: "my complicitous friendship: this is what my temperament brings to other men." This essentially transgressive mode of Bataillean *friendship as complicity*, the *friend as accomplice*, "accompanying" the other *beyond* the limits of existence, *beyond* the known and the knowable, quite literally means that *something* or *someone*, whatever it or he is, is always already "folded together" *with something or someone else*. This in turn implies for Bataille as the *guilty* one to be "jointly guilty" *with* someone else – here *with* Nietzsche, i.e. to be his *accomplice*, his *accomplice in the experience of non-knowledge*, because it is precisely the descent "to the depths" of *non-knowledge*, the solitary exploration of a domain *beyond good and evil*, that is profoundly Nietzschean. This is what Bataille himself realizes when he writes about "go[ing] to the depths" (N, 98), about not hesitating any longer: "Without doubt, I have tended more than Nietzsche towards the night of non-knowledge [...] But I hesitate no longer: Nietzsche himself would be misunderstood if one did not go to this depth" (IE, 33). And these "labours in the dark," the very task of philosophy mentioned earlier on, recalling Nietzsche's *subterrestrial* from the preface to *The Dawn of Day*, "digging, mining, undermining," are also carried on by Bataille, urged by his "love of the unknown" (N 70), his *amor fati*.

Not surprisingly, it is in the section of *Guilty* entitled "The accomplice," in which Bataille's *complicity* with Nietzsche *in the experience of non-knowledge* is developed, as if after his nightly toil, and proceeding on his "own path" in solitude, Bataille were in the very same expectation of his "own morning," his "own rosy dawn," as Nietzsche's "mole." After the account of his "burning experience," walking on a tiresome dark path in the woods at night, Bataille describes his way back as being no more than a "light shadow," complicitous of the "skies opening," and tells of "seeing" the sky all of a sudden being illuminated by a (Nietzschean) dawn rising, "*some dawn*" other than any dawn of day:

> The sky opened up. I saw, I saw [...] But the festival of the sky was pale next to the dawn that was rising. Not exactly in me: I cannot give a location to something that was not more concrete, no less abrupt than the wind. There was the *dawn*, on me, on all sides, I was certain of it [...] I was lost in this dawn.
>
> (OC V 276)

As the *blind spot* of understanding, this *other dawn* Bataille is experiencing here cannot be assigned any position; and like poetry in its ability of pointing to the *unknowable* as irreducibly *unknowable*, it is simply opening up the unlimited dimension of *non-knowledge* whence new knowledge may arise. It thus serves as a *groundless ground*: "[...] love has the power to wrench open the skies. [...] Through the wrenching, I see: as if I was the accomplice of all the nonsense of the world, the empty and free depths appear" (N 60). Like these "free depths" approximating the same experience of *unlimitedness*, the French partitive "*de l'aurore*," literally "*some dawn*," points to the impossibility of ever grasping any "whole," whatever that may be; and it is precisely this *indivisible remainder* infinitely setting free new dimensions – this "rest" being "the chance of the whole man" – that grants him, the "man of *impalement*" to come into existence *again and again*: "Imagine ebb and flow. Admit a deficit. 'We don't have the right to desire a single state, we must desire to *become periodic beings* – like existence'" (N, 130 quoting *The Will to Power*).

It is in this sense that the *inner experience* is itself "the authority" (*auctoritas* initially not only meaning "augmentation," but "creation," and "leading to existence," as shown by Benveniste (1969)), an equation advanced by Blanchot in a conversation Bataille insists on quoting (IE, 104); however, as in the motif of the *other dawn* in its essential incompleteness following the *night of non-knowledge*, and of the rhythmically moving *ebb and flow* – both being images of the *eternal return* defying any sense of a "beginning" – the *limit-experience* actually is *not* an "origin" for thought, but it is "*like* a new origin" (Blanchot 1969, 310). From this, it results for both Bataille and Blanchot that "affirming" the *inner experience* means "contesting" it (IE, 104). The *experience of non-knowledge* is the paradoxical experience that one does *not experience*, but of which one is merely the *accomplice*.

This is where Nietzschean *chance* comes into play again, the *complicity* in the *experience of non-knowledge*, of the *other dawn* entirely depending on "a rare chance" (OC V 275) – i.e. the *randomness* of a "fall," and as if *randomly* "being folded together" with this dice-like fall that "befalls" the accomplice. In the end it is "only chance," that "retains a disarming possibility" (N, 100). Once again, Bataille's *hatred of poetry* turns into its opposite: *poetry*, the *accomplice* of *non-knowledge* inexhaustibly giving voice to the silence of its night, reenters the scene, even if it has all the while been present in the metaphorical guise of the *night of non-knowledge*, and the *other dawn* as figures pointing to the *impossible*. Indeed, for Bataille the *absence* of poetry is no less than the "eclipse of chance" (OC V 320). Expressing the necessity of a *leap* where any relation is impossible, *poetry* thus enacts the *inner experience* as literally doomed to remain *project* (IE, 29); and Bataille's uncertainty about his intimation of "a leap outside of time?" is now transformed into six poems included in the *Journal* of *On Nietzsche*, its number perhaps recalling the six sides of a die, dice actually being "thrown" in the last poem of the series. As the original English title recalling Hamlet "*Time out of joints* [sic]" suggests, these poems take up the idea of the *leap*, which is precisely the *project* of the *experience of non-knowledge*. And it is in the last of these poems hovering around the "*may-be*" of *chance*, "naked chance – remaining free – proudly confined in its infinite randomness" (N 122–23), where all of the motifs we have come across in our reading of Bataille's conversation with Nietzsche seem to converge:

O the dice thrown

from the depths of the tomb

in the fingers of the delicate night

dice from birds of sunlight

leaps from the drunk lark

me like an arrow

out of the night

o transparency of bones

my heart drunk with sunlight

is the shaft of the night.

(N, 81)

Apostrophizing the "dice thrown," the poem presents itself from the beginning as an invocation of the rare chance granting the *experience of non-knowledge*. The "dice thrown," in the double gesture of flying up and falling down, as if necessarily defying and obeying gravity, not only point to the *randomness* of the fall, and the *necessity of contingency*, but also to *infinite finitude*: the "tomb" – in the French *tombe* the verb *tomber* "to fall" is clearly audible – and its "depths" recall the Nietzschean depths as the *groundless ground* of *non-knowledge* that the philosopher (the solitary *subterrestrian*) daringly undertakes to explore while awaiting his *own dawn*, the *authority* of the *experience of the other dawn*. And indeed, both night and dawn are present: the dice are thrown in the "fingers of the delicate night," and the figure of dawn can be glimpsed, as it were, from the evocation of the "birds of sunlight," the leaping "lark" announcing the *chance* of the *other dawn* in its (mute) morning song. And this lark's song (which neither *is* nor *is not* an *aubade* since it is not about any existing dawn of day but about *some dawn other*) figures as a *mise en abyme* of the poem itself, complicitously trying to voice the silence of the *other dawn*, too, a *mise en abyme* of the nightly song of the lyrical I, whose heart is as "drunk with sunlight" as is the lark. These "leaps from the drunk lark" are not only a metaphor of the dice being thrown, of chance as the *authority*, but also of the impossibility of relating with the *unknowable absolute* figured by the blinding visibility of sunlight, the heart of which is the epitome of *invisibility*. Again reflecting the lark leaping as if sent by dawn, the lyrical I is leaping, too, "like an arrow," but towards the sunlight, "out of the night," desiring a relation where any relation is impossible. Echoing the apostrophe of the first verse, the last stanza again begins with an invocation of *chance*, now focusing on its "transparency," if this "transparency" is understood as qualifying the dice made out of bone, thus letting in the "sunlight" of the *other dawn*, which serves as the *invisible background* always accompanying the *visible*, and which is itself pure *transparency*. And it is precisely in its *transparency* that *chance* opposes itself to the *opacity* of *calculation* as the "negation of poetry," and thus the "destruction of chance" (OC V, 320) damned by Bataille. By the very *art* of his poem, and in his *metaphysical* desire of responding to the lark as a "messenger" of the *other dawn*, the lyrical I is not only vertically *projecting* himself – his "heart drunk with sunlight" being "the shaft of the night" – but he is also embodying, as it were, one of Nietzsche's "*little ideals*": staying a "*stranger to reality*," i.e. striving for the *impossible*, "*half an artist, half a bird and metaphysician*" (N 62).

The final metaphor of the "shaft" may certainly recall the ambivalent, and itself *metaphorical* shorthand name of the *inner experience*: "*impalement*" – the French *pal* meaning both "stake" and the "torture of impalement" (*[supplice du] pal*),[4] as well as suggesting the monosyllabic *zen* of Buddhism, which Bataille (like Nietzsche in *The Antichrist*) refers to time and again in opposition to Christian mysticism. However, the metaphor of the "shaft of the night" also seems to hint at a Bataillean *metaphor* from his early anthropology. In its plant-like *verticality* reaching out for the sunlight, and as from the reverse angle of that other ocular metaphor (the *blind spot*), the blind "shaft of the night" recalls the metaphor of the *pineal eye*, a metaphor equally based on an anatomical, albeit vestigial figure, the "pineal gland" (Krell, "Foreword," Gasché 2012, xi). Bataille considered this organ situated in the brain to be a sort of "embryonic" eye at the crown of the head, virtually granting the vision of the incandescent sun as the epitome of impossible knowledge, and thus transgressing the limits of human experience (*Dossier de l'œil pinéal* OC II, 11–47; Gasché 2012). In this distant evocation of the phantasmatic *pineal eye* – the only, but obviously missing organ apt to catch sight, as it were, of the very *invisibility* amidst the extreme visibility of sheer sunlight, to grasp the *impossible* and thus to grant knowledge of the *unknowable*, the "shaft of the night" ever striving for this illumination ultimately reveals the lyrical *I* to consciously be the *lack* of an *eye*. In the tragic awareness, and first of all the expression of its inaptitude, the blind "shaft" as a mere *phantasm* of an eye corresponds to the *inadequacy* of language.

Both the *chance communion* after the "fall of God," announced by Bataille's *atheology* after Nietzsche, and the *chance communication* of his philosophy *as* poetry thus ultimately show the "privileged state" of the *inner experience* to be no more, and no less, than: *first*, the purely *immanent* "impalement" in its utter, yet conscious inadequacy (as the "shaft of the night" desiring the *chance* vision of *invisibility*, the *fall of dice* purely *transparent*); and *second*, the famous Proustian "teacup" celebrating the no less *contingent* and *immanent eucharist* of *poetry* – thus Proust, that other *friend*, at last (and in spite of the doubts expressed in the *Digression on Poetry and Marcel Proust* within the Nietzsche section of *Inner Experience*) recognized by Bataille to be the "sovereign accomplice" (IE, 150) of the inaccessible *unknown*, of ungraspable *nothingness* (N, 54–55). Not surprisingly Bataille's attitude towards Proust – as the one "a little later" than Nietzsche "shar[ing]" the same *experience* – is characterized by an ambivalence similar to his hesitant oscillation between the *hatred of poetry* and *poetry*, rather the *love* of it:

> That privileged state [...] is the only one where we can *if we accept it* completely dispense with the transcendence of the outside. It's true, it's not enough to say: *if we accept it*. We must go further, *if we love it*, if we have the strength to love it.
>
> (N, 134)[5]

This recalls Bataille's idea of *chance* as *the art of loving chance*, and this is what his *will to chance* is all about.

Notes

1   All quotations from *On Nietzsche* are taken from Stuart Kendall's translation (forthcoming in September 2015 through SUNY Press), which he has kindly let us use. The page numbers following the abbreviation N refer to the English translation by Bruce Boone (from 1992) republished by Continuum, 2004. For the passages not available in English we refer to the French *Œuvres complètes* in XII volumes, abbreviated OC.

2   To say it in Bataille's words Blanchot quotes as an epigraph to the first part of *The Unavowable Community*, "Negative Community" (Blanchot 1983).

3 Bataille's *hatred of poetry* corresponds to his *hatred of lies* expressed in *On Nietzsche*, as well as to his despising the *simulacrum* in general (Klossowski 1963).
4 The idea of *torture* present in the French *pal* points to the "Chinese torture" mentioned both in *Inner Experience* and in "The accomplice" (the *accomplice* being essentially linked to the *martyr*, literally "the witness," who also knows), the paragraph of *Guilty* immediately preceding the account of Bataille's "burning experience" culminating in his own Nietzschean *dawn*. It is the same "Torture of the Hundred Pieces" he would come back to almost twenty years later in *The Tears of Eros* (Connor 2000, 2–6, 41).
5 Translation modified.

References

Benveniste, Émile. 1969. *Le Vocabulaire des institutions indo-européennes*, Vol. 2. Paris: Éditions de Minuit.

Blanchot, Maurice. 1969. *L'Entretien infini*. Paris: Gallimard.

Blanchot, Maurice 1971. *L'Amitié*. Paris: Gallimard.

Blanchot, Maurice 1983. *La Communauté inavouable*. Paris: Minuit.

Connor, Peter Tracey. 2000. *Georges Bataille and the Mysticism of Sin*. Baltimore/London: Johns Hopkins University Press.

Esposito, Roberto. 2006. *Communitas. Origine e destino della comunità*. Turin: Einaudi.

Gasché, Rodolphe. 2012. *Georges Bataille. Phenomenology and Phantasmatology*. Translated by Roland Végsö. Foreword by David Farrell Krell. Stanford: Stanford University Press.

Hollier, Denis. 1992. *Against Architecture. The Writings of Georges Bataille*. Translated by Betsy Wing. Cambridge: MIT Press.

Klossowski, Pierre. 1963. "A propos du simulacre dans la communication de Georges Bataille." *Critique* 195–196, 742–750.

Part II

Key Concepts

5   Expenditure

Stuart Kendall

From *The Solar Anus*, written in 1927, to his notes for a final collection of aphorisms, written alongside *The Tears of Eros* in the early 1960s, the problem of expenditure is located at the core of Bataille's thought. It first appears as the "empty notion" (VE, 82) in need of analysis and extrapolation, that haunts and motivates his early exercises in anthropological mytho-poiesis, "The Jesuve" and "The Pineal Eye"; and it then becomes the focal point of some of his most important theoretical and analytic essays and books, above all, "The Notion of Expenditure" and *The Accursed Share*. The motives, strategies, and discursive styles of these writings range widely, to the point of radical discursive heterogeneity, as Bataille shifts from the fringes of the aesthetic avant-garde in the late 1920s to the political avant-garde in the 1930s, and then, in later decades, proposes himself as an ethicist. He appears somewhat embarrassed to admit that he is writing a book of political economy (AS 1, 9) but says nevertheless that he is urgently motivated by "the necessity of giving economic, military, and demographic questions a correct solution, if we are not to give up the hope of maintaining the present civilization" (AS 2, 18).[1] Bataille's sense of urgency in these years follows in large part from post-war global politics and the escalating nuclear arms race, but his thought has only become more compelling in our time, as we confront the challenges produced by local and global economic disparity, demographic explosion, environmental degradation, resource depletion, and climate change.

Bataille states the problem of expenditure succinctly in the early pages of *The Accursed Share*: "It is not necessity but its contrary, 'luxury,' that presents living matter and mankind with their fundamental problems" (AS 1, 12). The "accursed share" is itself this luxury: the share of energy or wealth in excess of what is necessary for the stable maintenance of any organism or system:

The living organism, in a situation determined by the play of energy on the surface of the globe, ordinarily receives more energy than is necessary for maintaining life; the excess energy (wealth) can be used for the growth of a system (e.g. an organism); if the system can no longer grow, or if the excess cannot be completely absorbed in its growth, it must necessarily be lost without profit; it must be spent, willingly or not, gloriously or catastrophically.

(AS 1, 21)

The question posed by this observation is that of expenditure: given the fact of excess energy, the fact of wealth, what will be done with that energy, how will it be spent, gloriously or catastrophically?

To consider the accursed share is to consider the circulation of energy on the surface of the globe. Whether in exchange, transformation, or metamorphosis, this circulation is continuous, relentless, and endless. As a mode of analysis and description, the notion of expenditure proposes that we begin to see all things, all organisms, all systems, from the molecular to the material, from the social to the cosmic, in terms of the allocation, arrangement, and displacement of the energy that they embody. Following Bataille's lead, our task and challenge is to trace the often surprising peregrinations of energy, as inputs and outputs, causes and effects, across the porous borders of what are ultimately only apparently isolated things, apparently independent organisms and systems, in order to prevent the potentially catastrophic misallocation of our own expenditures.

The word energy here is potentially misleading, suggesting as it does only measurable physical energy. While fundamental, this is not the only kind or form of energy that merits attention. Bataille is equally concerned with all forms of luxury and exuberance, physical and psychological. The category of expenditure can be applied to laughter, eating, eroticism, and death, to fashion, architecture, industry, warfare, to religious displays of devotion and to international aid, among many others. His point is that we cannot restrict our view of expenditure either to narrow concerns about utility and functional efficacy – to making the most efficient things – or to any one form of expenditure – as in attempts to make the most efficient fossil fuel burning automobiles, for example. He proposes a more *general* perspective, allowing economic analysis to move from specific narrowly restricted areas of production and consumption to the circulation of energies in general, beyond any single disciplinary frame, any single material resource, or any single type of energy (AS 1, 20). From his point of view, the disposition of physical and psychological resources toward entertainment, military, or religious purposes are of commensurate interest: bursts of laughter may in fact, on this scale, be louder than bombs.

This perspective is not original to Bataille. Nietzsche, for example, used the phrase "general economy of life" to describe his doctrine of will to power as a physio-psychological mechanism of morphogenesis in *Beyond Good and Evil* (Nietzsche 1967a, § 23). The thought also carries the inflection of the French school of social anthropology, specifically that of the work of Marcel Mauss. In *The Gift*, Mauss observed of his orientation and methods: "The facts that we have studied are all [...] *total* social facts or [...] general ones. That is to say that, in certain cases they involve the totality of society and its institutions [...] All these phenomena are at the same time juridical, economic, religious, and even aesthetic and morphological, etc." (Mauss 1990, 78–9). In *The Accursed Share*, Bataille proclaims Mauss as the progenitor of his work: "Let me indicate here that the studies whose results I am publishing here came out of my reading of *The Gift*. To begin with, reflection of potlatch let me to formulate the laws of *general economy*" (AS 1, 193). In an unpublished essay written almost twenty years earlier, Bataille had already linked "the economic analysis of the *potlatch* and the psychoanalysis of monetary facts" to the notion of expenditure (VE, 82), admitting the influence of psychoanalysis alongside Mauss and Nietzsche on this area of his thought. These however are not the only sources for the notion and its application as a tool of description and analysis. In *Justine*, the Marquis de Sade, for example, argued in general economic terms that "the Body Politic should be governed by the same rules that apply to the Body Physical" (de Sade 1965, 690). The search for those rules is reflected in Bataille's elaboration of his notions of expenditure and general economy. All told, the deepest influences on Bataille's work – Nietzsche, Mauss, Sade and later Hegel – all shaped these notions; indeed, these figures appeal to Bataille precisely to the extent that they reflect and exemplify his own concern. Along similar lines, when Bataille discovered William Blake's *The Marriage of Heaven and Hell* in 1937, his sense of recognition was undoubtedly awakened by Blake's observation that "Energy is eternal delight," as well as by the "Proverb of Hell" that he would use as an epigram to *The Accursed Share*: "Exuberance is beauty."

This suggestive range of influences does not, however, make expenditure any easier to accept as a paradoxical but fundamental fact, or to practice in our own lives. The economic, political, and religious systems of the modern world stand in active, even aggressive denial of the significance of luxury and excess in the natural world and in human life. "Under present conditions," Bataille observed, "everything conspires to obscure the basic movement that tends to restore wealth to its function, to gift-giving, to squandering without reciprocation" (AS 1, 38). Rather than being carefully considered, if not celebrated, our modes and mechanisms of expenditure, consumption, and waste are often derided as meaningless, denied to the point of repression, or masked with misdirected social justifications. Whereas the sacrificial rites and religious festivals of the pre-modern world typically gave communal, material form to expenditures, linking them to the passage of time, to cycles of life at the cosmic, seasonal and human scales, in the modern world, these passages through time have become obscured and amorphous, their attendant expenditures unmoored: communal festivals have been replaced by pub crawls through the night. The urges and necessities remain the same, but the social meaning has changed utterly.

All of this in mind, the lack of awareness of the problem of expenditure is not surprising. "The Notion of Expenditure" begins with a wry observation: "Every time the meaning of a discussion depends on the fundamental value of the word *useful* – in other words, every time the essential question touching on the life of human societies is raised... the debate is necessarily warped and the fundamental question is eluded" (VE, 116). Even today many progressive modes of thought – and the social institutions that have grown up around them – struggle to accommodate the facts of general economy.

In the late 1920s and early 1930s, Bataille attempted to articulate his nascent notion in the context of radical Marxist economic and social thought. In essays like "The Critique of the Foundations of the Hegelian Dialectic," co-written with Raymond Queneau, he suggested the need to develop a mode of Marxist dialectical materialism that could account for the actual facts of nature and lived human experience (VE, 113). "Most materialists," he wrote elsewhere, "even though they may have wanted to do away with all spiritual entities, ended up positing an order of things whose hierarchical relations mark it as specifically idealist" (VE, 15). From the beginning of the modern era, scientific rationalists have worked in the shadow of René Descartes to make the resources of nature useful to human purpose, as Descartes proclaimed in his *Discourse on Method* (1985, 142). For even longer, since the very beginning of the Western tradition, philosophers like Plato have explained the world through reference to abstract, ideal forms. For Hegel, as Bataille and Queneau observe: "nature is the *fall* of the idea; it is a negation, at the same time a revolt and an absurdity. Even if he had set aside his idealist prejudices, nothing would have seemed more unreasonable to Hegel than looking for the foundations of the objectivity of dialectical laws in the study of nature" (VE, 107). Engels hoped to resolve this problem but could not sufficiently and convincingly do so: even dialectical materialism remained too idealist for Bataille.

It should be noted that Bataille himself hoped to develop a mode of thought that would be equally applicable to natural systems as to psychological or societal ones. "Given the divorce of the natural point of view and the rational point of view, agreement must be recovered," he wrote (OC VII, 556). The notes and manuscripts for *The Accursed Share* insistently explore this recovery. The first chapter of the abandoned draft of the book is entitled "The galaxy, the sun, and humanity." The relative absence of these materials from the published volumes of *The Accursed Share* can partially be explained by circumstances: Bataille intended to address these topics in a subsequent volume of the series co-written with his friend Georges Ambrosino, a trained and practicing physicist. Bataille mentions this obliquely in a footnote to the preface of *The Accursed Share*: "This book is also in large part the work of Ambrosino... I must hope that he will resume in particular the study he has begun with me of the movements of energy on the surface of the globe" (AS 1, 191). That volume did not materialize.

The physical processes underlying the transformation of energy into and through matter, notably in photosynthesis, are indeed complex. The theoretical models useful in understanding these processes are still in active development by scientists. Many of them were only nascent when Bataille was developing his theories.[2] In our day, even more so than in Bataille's, the hyper-specialization of inquiry in the sciences, social sciences, and the humanities contributes to a lack of communication and common cause across disciplines. In the preface to *The Accursed Share*, Bataille voiced a fear for the fate of the book: "This first essay addresses, from outside the separate disciplines, a problem that still has not been framed as it should be, one that may hold the key to all the problems posed by every discipline concerned with the movement of energy on the earth ... such a book, being of interest to everyone, could well be of interest to no one" (AS 1, 10). When it was finally published, abysmally slow sales proved this fear well founded.

At another level, human biology itself presents significant barriers, physiological and psychological, to the perception and appropriate valorization of excess. Our senses only selectively present phenomena to us, from spectrums of light and sound to objects in space. Our brains then sift and select in order to organize those phenomena into a coherent world. To see the infinite in a grain of sand, as Blake suggested, would be a transformative vision of delirious inspiration but it would also be physically and psychologically debilitating. And yet, obviously, human beings do consistently valorize excesses and luxuries of many kinds on a daily basis: Bataille's problem, our problem, is determining which luxuries and which excesses to valorize at what time, and just exactly how to do so. The challenge is to find ways to think and talk about those expenditures without discharging their capacities for generating the experience that Bataille seeks under the name of sovereignty.

Bataille first mentions the notion of expenditure by name in "The Pineal Eye," an unpublished essay from 1930. In that essay, Bataille proposes a virulent phantasm, a mythical head with a third "pineal" eye at the summit of the skull that "spends without counting." The "great burning head" is, as he puts it, "the image and the disagreeable light of the *notion of expenditure*, beyond the still empty notion, as it is elaborated on the basis of methodical analysis" (VE, 82). He devoted much of the next two decades to this methodical analysis, first in articles like "The Notion of Expenditure," published in *La Critique Sociale* in 1933, and eventually in his major work, *The Accursed Share*, published by Editions de Minuit in 1949. Other short articles and essays aside, Bataille wrote at least five versions of *The Accursed Share*, a fact that may be taken as testimony of the importance of the project to him.

But the notion of expenditure appears in Bataille's work prior to "The Pineal Eye" as well. The "scandalous eruption" of *The Solar Anus*, written in 1927, for example, proclaims the Jesuve, "the filthy parody of the torrid and blinding sun" (VE, 9). *The Solar Anus* offers a delirious and virulent, parodic cosmology founded on a vision of boundless expenditure: "The terrestrial globe is covered with volcanoes, which serve as its anus. Although the globe eats nothing, it often violently ejects the contents of its entrails. Those contents shoot out with a racket and fall back, streaming down the sides of the Jesuve, spreading death and terror everywhere" (VE, 8). Among other possible meanings, the parodic name of the Jesuve conjures an individual self: *je* means I in French; Jesus, a god that died; and Vesuvius, the volcano that buried Pompeii and Herculaneum in 79 CE. *The Solar Anus* thus commingles cosmology and psychology in a mythic figure, over-determined with historical and religious resonance. Like much of Bataille's writing, the piece oscillates between offering a delirious, descriptive account of natural processes and explaining, if not justifying, how human beings might think and act within those processes:

> The erotic revolutionary and volcanic deflagrations antagonize the heavens. As in the case of violent love, they take place beyond the constraints of fecundity. In opposition to celestial fertility there

are terrestrial disasters, the image of terrestrial love without condition, erection without escape and without rule, scandal and terror.

(VE, 8–9)

Locating erotic life "beyond the constraints of fecundity," as Bataille does here, may at first seem strange. Reproduction, the production of more life, is in fact a form of expenditure, family size being a direct physical measure of wealth; but human eroticism also effects consumption through the exuberance of the sexual act itself. "This squandering goes far beyond what would be sufficient for the growth of the species. It appears to be the most that an individual has the strength to accomplish in a given moment" (AS 1, 35). In *Beyond Good and Evil*, Nietzsche made a similar observation about self-preservation: "Physiologists should think before putting down the instinct for self-preservation as the cardinal instinct of an organic being. A living thing seeks above all to *discharge* its strength – life itself is *will to power*; self-preservation is only one of the indirect and more frequent results" (Nietzsche 1967a, § 13). Here as elsewhere the challenge of thinking in general economic terms is laid bare. While eroticism does produce apparently useful results – reproduction – its value and meaning cannot be reduced to those results alone.

To think expenditure is to think in terms of paradox, *both and*. In *The Accursed Share*, even as Bataille attempts to argue on behalf of expenditure in the most explicit and occasionally extreme terms, he also admits that "real life, composed of all sorts of expenditures, knows nothing of purely productive expenditure; in actuality, it knows nothing of purely nonproductive expenditure either" (AS 1, 12). In general terms, the circulation of energies is always multi-determined, in terms of both inputs and outputs, and possibly contradictory or at least paradoxical. Eroticism may produce offspring over the long term but, in the moment, if pursued with abandon, it offers its own pleasures. Eating, to take another example, provides sustaining nourishment but it also provides other sensual and cultural delights. The interpretation of any mode of expenditure as either purely utilitarian – pure production – or purely non-utilitarian – pure consumption, pure excess, pure loss – is as profoundly misguided as it is common.

Already in *The Solar Anus* we see Bataille thinking – and writing – several things simultaneously. His thought turns back upon itself, seeking at once to describe a situation or experience, and to produce that experience within the subject, to simultaneously encompass nature, the body, and the mind. "The Jesuve," he proclaims, "is thus the image of an erotic movement breaking into and entering the mind, giving the ideas contained there the force of a scandalous eruption" (VE, 8 trans. mod.). Much later in a note for *The Accursed Share*, he writes succinctly: "*Matter, mind*, just like *isolated being, communication*, have only one single reality. There are no isolated beings anywhere who do not communicate, nor 'communication' independent from points of isolation" (OC VII, 553). Life presents itself in entities that are independent or isolated only by means of porous, unstable borders, borders that can be easily breached at more or less visible points of entry. The erogenous zones of the human body are only the most obvious example. The separation of these entities is only relative, a fault of perception and the absence of communication. All things are, in fact, as Nietzsche said, "entangled, ensnared, enamored" (Nietzsche 1954, 435). "The verb *to be*," for Bataille, "is the vehicle of amorous frenzy" (VE, 5). "Eros [Desire]," already for Hesiod, is "the most beautiful of the immortal gods, who in every man and every god softens the sinews and overpowers the prudent purpose of the mind" (Hesiod 1953, 56). Matter and mind form an immanent continuum wherein entities circulate energies through couplings, conjunctions, and combinations, in constant, convulsive transformation.

We should, for a moment, remark Bataille's understanding of matter, his notion of base materialism. We have already observed his critique of Marxist dialectical materialism as insufficiently materialist. In writings coincident with his formulation of the notion of expenditure, Bataille offers a forceful articulation of a non-idealist view of matter, a base materialism, "a materialism not implying an ontology, not implying that matter is the thing-in-itself" (VE, 49). "Base matter," he argues, "is external and foreign to ideal human aspirations, and it refuses to allow itself to be reduced to the great ontological machines resulting from these aspirations" (VE, 51). Descartes' proposal that man become the lord and master of nature will never, according to Bataille, fully succeed. At the most fundamental level, matter is a chaotic turbulence, indetermination. In "The Notion of Expenditure," he writes: "matter, in fact, can only be defined as the *non-logical difference* that represents in relation to the *economy* of the universe what *crime* represents in relation to the *law*" (VE, 129). Matter here is manifest as a difference that cannot be circumscribed in advance by logical or linear models of abstract description. This is not however to say that it cannot be described by nonlinear models, as in the theories of emergence in chaos or complexity physics.[3] Bataille formulated his ideas on base materialism during a period of intense reconsideration in advanced physics, roughly coincident with the insights of Niels Bohr on complementarity and Werner Heisenberg on uncertainty in quantum mechanics, among other developments.[4] Bataille followed these developments through readings and conversations with Georges Ambrosino, although refrained from venturing his own thought far into the realm of advanced research in quantum physics and the natural sciences.

Sources for his vision of base matter and the circulation of energy are to be found in Bataille's more direct progenitors. For Heraclitus: "That which always was, and is, and will be everlasting fire, the same for all, the cosmos, made neither by god nor man, replenishes in measure as it burns away" (Heraclitus 2001 § 20). In notes collected in *The Will to Power*, Nietzsche writes:

> This world: a monster of energy, without beginning, without end; a firm, iron magnitude of force that does not grow bigger or smaller, that does not expend itself but only transforms itself; as a whole, of unalterable size, a household without expenses or losses, but likewise without increase or income; enclosed by "nothingness" as by a boundary; not something blurry or wasted, not something endlessly extended, but set in a definite space as a definite force, and not a space that might be "empty" here or there, but rather as force throughout, as a play of forces and waves of forces, at the same time one and many, increasing here and at the same time decreasing there; a sea of forces flowing and rushing together, eternally changing, eternally flooding back, with tremendous years of recurrence, with an ebb and a flood of its forms; out of the simplest forms striving toward the most complex, out of the stillest, most rigid, coldest forms toward the hottest, most turbulent, most self-contradictory, and then again returning home to the simple out of this abundance, out of the play of contradictions back to the joy of concord, still affirming itself in this uniformity of its courses and its years, blessing itself as that which must return eternally, as a becoming that knows no satiety, no disgust, no weariness.
>
> (Nietzsche 1967b, § 1067)

In an early and unpublished essay on the Marquis de Sade, "The Use Value of D.A.F. de Sade," Bataille aligns his thought and all revolutionary thought with a base materialist view of nature, more specifically with Sade's view of a "thundering and torrential nature": "Without a profound complicity with natural forces such as violent death, gushing blood, sudden catastrophes and the horrible cries of pain that accompany them, terrifying ruptures of what had seemed to be immutable, the fall into stinking filth of what had been elevated – without a sadistic understanding of an incontestably thundering and torrential nature, there could be no revolutionaries, there could only be a revolting utopian sentimentality" (VE, 101). Here the adjective "sadistic" does not indicate a fundamental cruelty but rather that the type of understanding proposed by Bataille derives from Sade.

The thought of expenditure is first and foremost a thought of "thundering and torrential nature," of overflowing nature, seething nature, nature exceeding any and all bounds. This vision of nature, in an amorous frenzy of "recklessness, discharge, and upheaval" (VE, 128), is chaotic with emergent forms. Life moves toward lack – spaces of deficiency, voids – in an excessive movement of expenditure indistinct from loss. "The limit of growth being reached, life, without being in a closed container, at least enters into ebullition: Without exploding, its extreme exuberance pours out in a movement always bordering on explosion" (AS, 30). When the limit of growth is reached, energy turns inward, raising pressure within the system, threatening explosion unless that system can find new, more complex, more intensive ways to organize and thereby displace its energies. In this vision of "the history of life on earth … the dominant event is the development of luxury, the production of increasingly burdensome forms of life" (AS 1, 33): intricate or complex forms, intense forms of life, luxurious forms. Amid "the unconditional splendor of material things" (VE 128), the omnivorous human animal – the cultural, poetic, meaning-making animal – is the animal best situated to produce those forms: civilization itself is a tremendously intricate flowering of excess.

In the essay "Sacrificial Mutilation and the Severed Ear of Vincent Van Gogh," Bataille describes a physiological and psychological "necessity of throwing oneself or something of oneself *out of oneself*" (VE, 67). This would be the means by which human beings experience their complicity with thundering and torrential nature. The physical or psychological projection of a part of the self outside the self results in the "rupture of personal homogeneity" and the "radical *alteration* of the person." Individual life overflows the borders of the self, and in the moment of overflow, we find new ways of being, new outlets of expression, new capacities for investing our world with energy and concern. Such actions have "the power to liberate heterogeneous elements and to break the habitual homogeneity of the individual" (VE 68–70). Simply doing something different or even just *differently* releases pent up energies and re-orients our experience of the world. At another level, organizing our lives and the lives of our communities around large scale expenditures – as in the sacrificial acts and festivals that traditionally accompanied transitional moments in individual life, births, adolescence, marriage and death, as well as transitional moments in natural life, the passages of the earth through the solar year – links human life to larger patterns of expenditure. Through the mimetic gesture of sacrifice, Bataille argues, "man puts himself in the rhythm of the universe" (OC VII, 255). Intentionally or not, "man's activity in fact pursues the useless and infinite fulfillment of the universe" (AS 1, 21). The purpose of Bataille's work is to clarify the mechanisms of this fulfillment and to help us find ways to live our lives in conscious coincidence with it rather than unconscious and potentially catastrophic denial.

Beyond the individual, at the level of society, the notion of expenditure demands the articulation and adoption of a "politics of expenditure" (OC VII, 556), a social organization founded on the recognition of expenditure. In "The Use Value of D.A.F. de Sade," Bataille envisioned social revolution as an "outlet for collective impulses," but he also went on to propose the post-revolutionary division of society into two spheres, one devoted to economic and political organization, the other to an "anti-religious and asocial organization having as its goal orgiastic participation in different forms of destruction, in other words, the collective satisfaction of needs that correspond to the necessity of provoking the violent excitation that results from the expulsion of heterogeneous elements" (VE, 101). The first of these spheres performs a homogenizing, stabilizing function through traditional institutions – the individual, the family, the state, and religion. The second sphere is that of the heterogeneous in all of its forms, glorious as well as possibly catastrophic. These two spheres coexist, giving shape to experience overtly and covertly, as well as consciously and unconsciously. The politics proposed and pursued by Bataille recognizes the dual primacy of both spheres, of the rational and of that which exceeds reason.

Unfortunately, in the modern era, in Bataille's view: "Everything that was generous, orgiastic and excessive has disappeared [...] wealth is now displayed behind closed doors, in accordance with depressing and boring conventions" (VE, 124). Here we might quibble with him but only to express an even greater horror. In the contemporary world, while the excesses of the extremely wealthy are indeed obscured from common view, many of our most astonishing expenditures parade directly in front of us, such as sporting events and other spectacles of entertainment. Others come to us through rumors and reports ranging from the horrors of war to heaps of rubbish accumulating in distant and not so distant corners of the globe. Worse, far from opening passageways beyond servitude, the orgiastic and excessive have been desecrated, demoted from fonts of community to formulaic and convention-bound spectacles of consumption. In uncharacteristic understatement, Bataille remarked that "the necessity of satisfying such a need [for expenditure], under the conditions of present day life, leads an isolated man into disconnected and even stupid behavior" (VE, 73).

Reflecting upon and proposing alternatives constituted much of his life's work. In his final book, *The Tears of Eros*, Bataille wrote: "Unless we consider the various possibilities for consumption which are opposed to war, and for which erotic pleasure – the instant consumption of energy – is the model, we will never discover an outlet founded on reason" (TE, 149). Alongside eroticism, some of those possibilities, for human beings, include eating, intoxication, laughter, ecstatic forms of religious meditation, and the effusions of the aesthetic realms of art, literature and design – all types of experience that cannot be circumscribed by mere utility. But these are not our only options. Even extending the realm of the explicable, through science pursued beyond purely instrumental concerns, should properly be viewed as a mode of excess.

In notes for a new collection of aphorisms written alongside *The Tears of Eros*, Bataille wondered: "Is there – or not – a relationship between the accursed share and gambling" (US 273). The word translated as *gambling* is *jeu*. It also means *play* or *risk*. What possible relationship can there be between the accursed share – the luxury and excess present in all natural and cultural systems – and gambling, play, or risk? After the serious work of the day is done, what should we do with our excess energies?

Notes

1   Written in 1927, *The Solar Anus* was first published as a small booklet with etchings by André Masson in 1931 by the Galerie Simon. "The Notion of Expenditure" first appeared in 1933, in the pages of *La Critique Sociale*, the journal of the Democratic Communist Circle edited by Boris Souvarine, preceded by a note making clear that the essay was in contradiction with "our general orientation of thought" (OC I: 662) and promising a response in a future issue. Editions de Minuit published *The Accursed Share* in 1949, in a short-lived series of books edited by Bataille under the title "The Use of Wealth." Other titles in the all-but-abortive series were to have been written by Jean Piel, Mircea Eliade, Claude Lévi-Strauss, and Max Weber, among others.
2   For a history of the development of these theories, see Oliver Morton (2007).
3   See Stuart Kauffman (2008).
4   For an exploration and extension of the relationship between quantum mechanics and the thought of general economy in Nietzsche, Bataille, and Derrida, see Plotnitsky (1993).

References

Descartes, René. 1985. *Discourse on the Method* (1637) in *The Philosophical Writings of Descartes*, volume 1. Translated by John Cottingham. Cambridge: Cambridge University Press.

Heraclitus. 2001. *Fragments.* Translated by Brooks Haxton. New York: Penguin.

Hesiod. 1953. *Theogony.* Translated by Norman O. Brown. New York: Bobbs-Merrill.

Kauffman, Stuart. 2008. *Reinventing the Sacred: A New View of Science, Reason, and Religion.* New York: Basic Books.

Mauss, Marcel. 1990. *The Gift: The Form and Reason for Exchange in Archaic Societies.* Translated by W.D. Halls. London: Routledge.

Morton, Oliver. 2007. *Eating the Sun: How Plants Power the Planet.* New York: Harper Collins.

Nietzsche, Friedrich. 1954. *Thus Spoke Zarathustra,* in *The Portable Nietzsche.* Translated by Walter Kaufmann. New York: Viking.

Nietzsche, Friedrich. 1967a. *Beyond Good and Evil* in *The Basic Writings of Nietzsche.* Translated by Walter Kaufmann. New York: Random House.

Nietzsche, Friedrich. 1967b. *The Will to Power.* Translated by Walter Kaufmann and R.J. Hollingdale. New York: Random House.

Plotnitsky, Arkady. 1993. *Reconfigurations: Critical Theory and General Economy.* Gainesville: University Press of Florida.

de Sade, D.A.F. 1965, *Justine, Philosophy in the Bedroom, and Other Writings.* Translated by Richard Seaver and Austryn Wainhouse. New York: Grove Press.

6 Heterology

Marcus Coelen

In the early 1930s, the word "heterology" appears in Georges Bataille's writings and with it the promise of a science or a quasi-scientific adventure that would give some form of life to the term. The project of developing an explicit "heterology" can be seen as an endeavor limited to this specific moment in Bataille's life and thought – around the year 1932–33 – and responding to one particular problem – how to introduce the insights, intuitions and methodological moves associated with *Documents* and *The Story of the Eye* and to delimit these from Surrealism. Alternatively, "heterology" can be taken as a name designating the entire spectrum of Bataille's writings and activities, spreading over more than four decades, from scientific materialism to general eroticism, from the most intimate suffering to the public affirmation of life, from archival diligence to pornographic passion, from the exactitude of minute poetic expression to the most sweeping assertion in the political sphere. This somewhat strange term can be set in an open chain or illimitable constellation with others – "base materialism", "general economy", "evil", "erotology", "sacred sociology", "hatred of poetry", "inner experience", even "laughter" and "anxiety", to name just some – each of which mark certain texts or periods in Bataille's career, and all of which share the same characteristic of resisting their appropriation into a clearly defined and stable category, even while continuing to appeal to categorization. These terms place themselves outside the reach of critical, systematic, or historic comprehension while nevertheless inviting it. In this manner, they expose a principle formulated by Bataille in a text called "The labyrinth" in 1936: the *"principle of insufficiency"* which is also a principle of *contestation:* "The sufficiency of each being is endlessly contested by every other" (VE, 172). Bataille, who was convinced that writing, if done in a certain way, is able to cut open a blasé and self-sufficient body of knowledge and conviction, set forth terms and poetic twists that contest as much as they invite contestation in the very moment they are put on paper, giving voice, as it were, to the insufficiency of the being that advances them. Taken in this way, "heterology" is neither the part of a whole – Bataille's "life project" or "work" – nor an essential name for the whole itself. It rather contests elementary and pitilessly unavoidable categories such as "part" and "whole". Faithful to the maddening thought that "my existence" contests the truth of the universe, the term marks more than others the singularity of what is linked to the name of Georges Bataille as insufficient and contested, leaving criticism the task of attuning its language and sensibility to his ontology of insufficiency. "Heterology," perhaps a cry more than a concept, would thus have to be read as fundamentally deficient and defective, in a reading that itself falters by affirming "heterology" as the quest for truth in *"lived experience"* (VE, 113) without the horizon of totality or secure identification.

The remarks here base themselves on the hypothesis expressed in this third way of reading "heterology". While indicating how "heterology" names a fiber detectable in almost all writing by Bataille, they will be limited to indicating and commenting on the more or less explicit occurrence of the term in one text – "The Use Value of D.A.F. Sade" – and in some notes and passages surrounding or resonating it.

Some reflections on the term itself as well as on its linguistic matter will help to approach it. The word *"hétérologie"*, when conceived by Bataille in the early 1930s, was a neologism in French. It has still not made its way into the main dictionaries of that language. The cognate adjective *"hétérologique"*, however, does exist as a technical term in linguistics, where it designates a word that does not describe itself: the word "red" is not red, unlike words that are *"autologique"*, such as "short", which is a rather short word or "awkward", which is an awkward word, and which are therefore in line with themselves. The same technical linguistic meaning exists for the English equivalent "heterologous", while the term is also used in the Anglophone bio-medical vocabulary where it is opposed to "homologous", both being used mainly in the field of immunology; the noun "heterology" is exclusively lexicalized in those two contexts and meanings.

The term *"hétérologie"* – as well as "heterology" – is thus *autologous* to a certain extent. Though it persists as a word, it is not completely recognized as one, or at least it could not be assimilated into the lexicon and accepted by the official safeguards and archives of the language. This is surprising for at least two reasons: firstly, it is frequently used in critical language, and at least one major figure in the field of theory besides Bataille has promoted it to the status of a name for a specific methodology, namely, Michel de Certeau (see Girard, 1991). For this author, "heterology" promised a new epistemology and "science of the other". Secondly, the term follows a clear compositional principle combining two very common parts of words: "*hétéro-*" deriving from the Greek *heteros* meaning "other" and being employed in such terms as "hétérogène" or "hétérosexuel", as well as "-*logie*" designating most frequently a science, a field of knowledge, or a specific theory. Very easily, then, the word could be recognized to signify the "science of otherness", the "knowledge about heterogeneous things", or "language and discourse pertaining to heterogeneity" – but instead, the term itself remains heterogeneous to the language insofar it is homogenized – or pressured to become so by official linguistic politics.

This is not without an ironic logic. For when Bataille introduced his neologism, he both asserted the possible – and for him even necessary – existence of that to which the coinage of the term refers, and yet immediately withdrew from it its validity. The paradox value of the term is clearly stated. Bataille "does not mean that heterology is, in the usual sense of such a formula, the science of the heterogeneous" (VE, 97). In *what* sense then can heterology be a science of the heterogeneous? And how can we account for the relation between the heterogeneous, the scientific and the heterological? These questions appear abstract, but we might be able to both provide them with some concreteness and answer them by referring to the *place* where they were able to occur. Yet again this "place" itself is indicated in an abstract manner: "The heterogeneous is even resolutely placed outside the reach of scientific knowledge, which by definition is only applicable to homogeneous elements" (VE, 97). The place of heterology is outside, as the place of the heterogeneous is: outside the homogeneous of human social existence in the case of the latter, outside science in the case of the former. And Bataille attempts to attain this "outside", neither as the negative of the describable inside nor, as it were, from its "own inside". Positioning philosophy vis-à-vis science, he writes in "The Use Value of D.A.F. Sade":

> The interest of philosophy resides in the fact that, in opposition to science or common sense, it must positively envisage the waste products of intellectual appropriation. Nevertheless, it most often envisages these waste products only in abstract forms of totality (nothingness, infinity, the absolute), to which it itself cannot give a positive content
>
> (VE, 96)

But philosophy, he continues, will necessarily transform the "waste products" into an object of speculation: in what science cannot comprehend, it will see the infinite of the world. Therefore, it cannot be the philosopher who exposes this waste, giving it to thinking without appropriating it and thus making it homogeneous to knowledge and thought, in the form of common sense and a system. Rather:

> Only an intellectual elaboration in a religious form can, in its periods of autonomous development, put forward the waste products of appropriative thought as the definitively heterogeneous (sacred) object of speculation.

(VE, 96)

But then religion also does not address and maintain the heterogeneous *as* heterogeneous. By separating a "superior world" from an "inferior", it also renders the totality homogeneous. Christianity is obviously the model here, more precisely, the *kenosis* of Christ, his incarnation not only as human but as the "lowest" of humans. Bataille writes: "God rapidly and almost entirely loses his terrifying features, his appearance as a decomposing cadaver, in order to become, at the final stage of degradation, the simple (paternal) sign of universal homogeneity" (VE, 96).

The space is thus opened for something new, for "a practical and theoretical *heterology*." That would be neither science nor philosophy nor religion: A new science is born: the "science of what is completely other" as Bataille explains in a footnote immediately following the introduction of the newly coined term. Yet the note continues arguing for the instability of that very name for the scientific endeavor just introduced. Referring to the Greek terms *agios* (sacred, holy; but also accursed, execrable) and *scor* (excrements), he underlines the fundamental ambiguity not only of the objects of this new science, but of itself as well as of its designation:

> The term *agiology* would perhaps be more precise, but one would have to catch the double meaning of *agio* (analogous to the double meaning of *sacer*), soiled as well as holy. But it is above all the term *scatology* (the science of excrement) that retains in the present circumstances (the specialization of the sacred) an incontestable expressive value as the doublet of an abstract term such as *heterology*.

(VE, 102)

Heterology, a science, is threatened precisely by what it is: science, i.e. the elevation of the concrete to the level of abstract understanding and the deduction of laws of occurrence. Strangely, Bataille partakes here in a genuine *philosophical* concern, having perhaps Hegel's rhetorical question "But whoever thinks abstractly?" in mind. (He started to read Hegel at around this time.) Maybe the heterogeneous – "sexual activity ...; defecation; urination; death and the cult of cadavers ...; cannibalism; the sacrifice of animal-gods; omophagia; the laughter of exclusion; sobbing ...; religious ecstasy; the identical attitude toward shit, gods, and cadaver" (VE, 94) – is not so much a specific concreteness to be intuited by a new science as the *figure* of the concrete as such. It is not "shit" in itself that would be posited with the heterological quasi-science, but the concreteness and formlessness of matter before or after taking shape as an object. The shapeless shit of matter, after having been an object of consumption, would be the concrete figure of what it also is: concreteness before turning into the understandable. And the cadaver, the essentially decay*ing*, after having been a living being, would project in front of the eyes of science and common sense, sensual corporeality before it becomes a body.

In this sense, Bataille's endeavor would not only be directed to the appreciation of the waste products of culture, the low elements of productivity; it not only wants to render justice to the fundamentally ambivalent nature of society and human life; it is also the insistence of an intellectual movement "toward the concrete" – to take up the title of a book by the philosopher Jean Wahl (1932) who, although referring to very different philosophical authors (James, Whitehead, Marcel), made productive the same discontent inherent to philosophy which Bataille had grasped starting with *Documents*: discontent due to the betrayal of the concrete as soon as it is thought as something else, i.e. as something thinkable, as well as the dissatisfaction with the traditional means of working through this discontent (sensualism, empiricism). Despite his attempts at delimiting himself from philosophy – "Above all, heterology is opposed to any homogeneous representation of the world, in other words, to any philosophical system" (VE, 97) – Bataille's project might nonetheless be seen as a genuine philosophical endeavor, an attentive listening to Aristotle's exhortation "to save the phenomena".

The heterological is a both weak and excessive response, the necessarily ridiculous answer to a question that would be asked by the homogeneous forces of society – science, religion, economics, politics – about themselves. If "excrement" is the answer to the question as to what food is for – an obviously ridiculous answer – then *excretion* does away with both question and answer, with the objects positioned in them, with the economy of consumption leaving the excrement only as useless remainder or recyclable matter for new consumption. Excretion does not *produce* the excrement, heterological writing does not *propose* a science, both contest economy and thought, and what appears with them, i.e. excremental elements of physiology and heterology, shit, pamphlets, sweat, sperm, scandalous stories, saliva and incoherent, laughable propositions, is not "reinvested" in the useful and the immanent machinery of the world, but concatenated with what is supposed to transcend it, the divine, holy and sacred. What heterology is after belongs to the logic and writing of this concatenation: its letters and phrases are laughs, tears, screams, trance, anxiety, horror, passion, its schematics are attraction, repulsion and convulsion, and it is neither bound by the immanent nor arrested in its direction towards the transcendent. Heterology does not speak *about* what breaks away from the homogeneous, it rather partakes in it.

Therefore, the linguistic characterization of "heterology" given earlier has to be extended: the term does not predominantly refer to the *logos* – to the science or discourse – on the heterogeneous; it indicates the "logic" of the heterogeneous, in the same way as the "physiology" of a living organism does not so much describe it, but rather *is* its logic, the logic of the *physis*, its functioning according to the specificities of the living. Heterology is the logic of the heterogeneous itself, which is not opposed to the homogeneous, but is rather opposition itself or, as Bataille expresses it, "polarity": "The *heterogeneous* (or sacred) is defined as the very domain of polarity. Which means that the strongly polarized elements appear to be *wholly other* in relation to vulgar life" (OC II, 167). The identification of the heterogeneous with the sacred here shows the fundamental ambiguity of heterological terminology. For the sacred is both one extreme of the polarity and the extremism of polarization:

> The notion of the (heterogeneous) foreign body permits one to note the elementary subjective identity between types of excrement (sperm, menstrual blood, urine, fecal matter) and everything that can be seen as sacred, divine, or marvelous: a half-decomposed cadaver fleeing through the night in a luminous shroud can be seen as characteristic of this unity
>
> (VE, 94)

The same can be said about the other extreme of polarization, the base material, faecal matter, etc. It is both the low and the notion embracing polarity in the name of an equally base science.

Excretion and appropriation are important and scandalous in the human; they are "important" and objectively describable in the realm of the (so called higher) animals; they are less important and not even clearly describable in the process of "living nature" where they are completely absorbed into general metabolism. To describe physiology as appropriation and excretion would both be a truism, and the assertion of an unspecific, and thus incorrect, objectivity. In this sense, the "scandalous nature" of the raw facts of consumption and waste defecation in the human is dissolved into the homogeneity of abstract knowledge. "The only way to resist this dilution lies in the practical part of heterology, which leads to an action that resolutely goes against this regression to homogeneous nature" (VE, 98). This "action," however, is a peculiar one, for it is neither an *action* based on deliberation nor an *act* following a decision – it is rather the *activity* of the heterological physis itself, in *spite* of its metabolic law: laughter, orgasm, insignificant spasms of the "organism" insofar as it is inscribed into the economy of appropriation and excretion: laughing at the ridiculousness yet irrefutability of a philosophical argument, having an orgasm at the border of reproduction, losing one's head in the process of thinking. The *Solar Anus* (1927) presents the following images: "An abandoned shoe, a rotten tooth, a snub nose, the cook spitting in the soup of his masters are to love what a battle flag is to nationality" (VE, 6). By spitting into the soup, the cook celebrates digestion in the open. The subject of heterological practice or "action" does not affirm shit as something, but says Yes nevertheless to excretion. This subject thus acquires "the capacity to link overtly, not only his intellect and his virtue, but his *raison d'être* to the violence and incongruity of his excretory organs, as well as to his ability to become excited and entranced by heterogeneous elements, commonly starting in debauchery" (VE, 99).

A thin line is drawn: neither the affirmation of the parts and practices negated by homogeneous societies, systems, and subjugations; nor the affirmation of the "products" of those practices *as such*. The thin line of the *"insignificant"* (VE, 99) is in the vast and indeterminate terrain of what Bataille understood as "subjectivity". The subjectivity is thought and written by him as "lived experience", torn and turned outside into the unrecognizable night and upwards into the blinding sun, basing its life on the "hypothesis of an irrevocable insignificance" (G, 113) as he wrote in his famous letter to Kojève. This insignificance is, however, also that of "the fathomless multitude of insignificant lives" (VE 221). One can ask, then, why debauchery and public transgression are necessary forms of the affirmation of "insignificance". As far as the moment of the "Use Value of D.A.F. Sade" is concerned, the answer is clear: at the end of the heterological practice stands the "revolution", the overthrowing of the system of injustice and exploitation of which the legalization and morality of restricted economy and restrained reason are an integral part. The "revolution" which Bataille envisions here, in the early 1930s, is not the fascist revolution: this is a perverted revolution, leading to "the accomplished uniting of the *heterogeneous* elements with the homogeneous elements, of sovereignty in the strictest sense with the State" (VE, 155). Nor is it the communist revolution, which is too exclusively based on the economic conditions, and not on the "actual psychological structure" (VE 157) of society. It is the revolution of a different proletariat: "This proletariat cannot actually be limited to itself: it is in fact only a point of concentration for every dissociated social element that has been banished to heterogeneity" (VE, 157). The liberating process that responds to the urges of the day "requires worldwide society's fiery and bloody Revolution." The "Use Value of D.A.F. Sade" ends on this affirmation, and the adjectives qualifying the revolution – "fiery", "bloody" – are not accidental. Spilled blood, burning fire, violent frenzy *are* the revolution here, and not its by-products. The "Propositions" from Acéphale make this very clear by underlining that the goal of revolution is "universal existence" and not the dictatorship of an identifiable proletariat. The enemy, the one to be killed, is not so much the capitalist – a laughable and transient figure – but God, or the refusal to recognize the death of God.

> For universal existence is unlimited and thus restless: it does not close life in on itself, but instead opens it and throws it back into the uneasiness of the infinite. Universal existence, eternally unfinished and acephalic, a world like a bleeding wound, endlessly creating and destroying particular finite beings: it is in this sense that true universality is the death of God.
>
> (VE 201)

The adjectives of the "fiery and bloody Revolution" are "waste", but this waste is to be fed back into the organism of thought, or rather, into the acephalic *physis* of writing, in order to re-emerge – as if it were more waste or even vomit – as the affirmation of a general notion of expenditure "endlessly creating and destroying the particular finite beings" called concepts and projects. For the goal of the revolution has to put an end to servitude, and this means for Bataille, a specific, unsecured and risky life: "What escapes servitude – life – risks itself; in other words, it places itself on the level of the chances it meets" (VE, 231). One could say that heterology – passing through a parody of science, a call for blood and fire, a hyperbolic affirmation of mythology, scandalous literature and untenable propositions for equally untenable communities – leads to a quasi-anthropological affirmation of the human as the animal of chance and contingency.

Neither the political – *zoon politikon* – nor reason and language – *zoon logon echon* – nor fundamental lack – *Mängelwesen* – determine this being called human. Yet the human is – in most cases – called by a name, and it is this name that befalls him by chance: as "George" carries a reference to the "worker of the earth" – "*geo-orgos*" in Greek – as well as to the military saint; or a man given a surname calling war and battle into the mind of everyone meeting him. Or both. In the name of being, life is thus put to risk, because it is called by chance. This is what the "Sorcerer's Apprentice" calls "*living* myth" (VE 231), exposing the author *Georges Bataille* to the ridicule of any reader wanting to ground general statements in generality, or even universalism in universality:

> And living myth, which intellectual dust only knows as dead and sees as the touching error of ignorance, the myth-lie represents destiny and becomes being. Not the being that rational philosophy betrays by giving it the attributes of the immutable, but the being expressed by the given name and the surname, and then the double being that loses itself in an endless embrace, and finally the being of the city "that tortures, decapitates, and makes war".
>
> (VE, 231)

From the being called by chance, living this name as myth and lie, through the lovers transcending themselves, and the supposed unity of their entity as two in fusion, to the disseminated being of the conflicted society quoting the acts of violence and at times resorting to them – this sequence seems to describe an itinerary. But it is rather a constellation without direction. Bataille's texts and action of the thirties at least go both ways: from the city-dwellers' activism verging on war, with Contre-Attaque, to the beginning of an *Inner Experience* concerning first of all, though not exclusively, the one named Georges Bataille; from the concern of a subject stretched out in the personal phantasmatology of a singular body between its "Solar Anus" and its "Pineal Eye", concerned with exhorting some comrades to engage in a political adventure hetero-geneous to communism and fascism as well as to bourgeois democracy, to the founding of secret and public institutions addressing as well as being addressed by the violent fractures of society. Those are the pathways of practical heterology. And somewhere on these roads or in the soil they trace, meet the lovers.

At least twice in the course of these itineraries, heterology embraces the "true world of lovers" (VE 229). The "Sorcerer's Apprentice," which was published in 1938 as the opening article in a special issue of the *Nouvelle Revue Française* calling "For a College of Sociology", posits the act of lovers as the only truth, besides the sociology of the sacred and its rites itself, surpassing the life oppressively fractured in the restrained domains of science, art, and politics and thus open to "*total* existence" (VE 232). And a novel written 1934/35 yet published only in 1957, *The Blue of Noon*, gives with the encounter of *Dirty* and *Troppmann* another lovers' world. Its mode, reminiscent of *The Story of the Eye* and resonating with *Madame Edwarda* to come, contrasts with the surprisingly serene tonality of the "Sorceror's Apprentice". Here the movement of transcendence is heterological in the more scatological sense, informed by horror and the direction downward: Dirty keeps vomiting, anxiety projects the narrator beyond himself and his copulations. The "world of the lovers" is set on the stage of all the political, literary, scientific, phantasmatological, and sexual issues addressed in the project of heterology. It has been pointed out that "the best commentary on *The Blue of Noon* can be found in the series of schemata in which Bataille analyses the forms and degrees of heterogeneity analyses" (Louette 2004, 1050). (The schemata referred to here can be found in the posthumous "*Cahier de l'hétérology*", OC II, 178–202.)

While being conspicuously a *roman à clé*, *The Blue of Noon* can be read as Georges Bataille's practical heterology, spelled out in a more detailed manner than anywhere else in this heterogeneous corpus. This "literature", driven by the hatred of poetry, i.e. by the execration of everything edifying and aestheticizing in fictional writing, appears as the ultimate excretion. Yet since nothing is excreted here, except the nothing of its "fiction" – the raw *making* of it; the invention of a matter to be passed – the heterology of the *Blue of Noon* is free to be experienced while waiting for a movement of liberation to take place.

With some other adventures of the 20th century, such as Freud's psychoanalysis and Barthes' *nouvelle critique*, heterology is a quasi or ironically scientific undertaking moved by an idiosyncratic and singular affection by the other of mind and body – drive, mourning, anxiety – escaping into the labyrinth of a partly affirmed, partly checked anarchy of writing and literature. These projects are "autobiographies" in a sense not easily avowed either by their authors, or by their readers insofar as they maintain their will to be followers as well. Georges Bataille's autobiographical heterology did not fail to discourage such an approach: "The simple project of writing implies the will ... to provoke one's fellow-beings to a point that they vomit you up" (OC II, 140–141). A different metamorphosis of metabolism will thus have to be invented by those desiring to continue to read Bataille's heterology.

References

Girard, Luce. 1991. "Epilogue: Michel de Certeau's Heterology and the New World". *Representations* 33, 212–221.

Louette, Jean-François. 2004. "*Notice de Le bleu du ciel*" in Georges Bataille. *Romans et récit*. Paris: Gallimard.

Wahl, Jean. 1932. *Vers le concret*. Paris: Vrin.

7 Sacrifice

Elisabeth Arnould-Bloomfield

Jean-Luc Nancy has noted that sacrifice held an almost obsessive sway over Bataille's work. Bataille, he writes, "sought not only to think sacrifice, but to think *according to* sacrifice. He willed sacrifice itself, in the act; at least he never ceased presenting his thought to himself as a necessary sacrifice of thought" (Nancy 1991a, 20, my emphasis). Such engagement means that sacrifice was never, for Bataille, a mere historical object, a religious artifact or a figure of fiction. From his very first essays, Bataille saw sacrifice as "life's necessary games with death" (O, 62).[1] He believed that its "tragic terror and sacred ecstasy" were linked to the very essence of man's communal being (O, 61). And it is because sacrifice was, for Bataille, the very archetype of his atheological experience that he identified his own thinking with the exigency of its transgression.

It is not a simple affair, however, to study and elucidate a motif, which looms as large in Bataille's work. Sacrifice's ubiquitous presence throughout his texts gives it a lot of figural as well as critical play but it also complicates its theory and muddles its figures. From the sacrificial fantasies of *The Pineal Eye* to the last images of the *Tears of Eros*, sacrifice is present in virtually every single one of Bataille's texts, but it changes constantly. There is a lot of continuity but also much difference between the "Aztec revival" of the thirties and the ecstatic self-immolations of *Inner Experience*, written in the war years. There are also significant variations between these last atheological sacrifices and the archeological studies Bataille publishes after the war. The former explores the problematic pertinence of the sacrificial model for Bataille's non-knowledge, while the latter speculates on the origin and role of the ritual in the birth of religious man. And while both are variations on a similar exposure to the sacred and to finitude, they have a significantly different way of negotiating their relationship with knowledge.

An exhaustive study of the sacrificial motif in Bataille would have to register these differences and carefully map out chronologically changes in sacrifice's roles and forms. I will not, however, for reasons of economy, base my study on such variations. Instead, I shall focus on the fact that, despite obvious differences in discourses and contexts, Bataille's sacrificial writings present a remarkably united front. All of Bataille's many sacrifices – whether they be anthropological reconstructions or his own rapturous inner drama – share the same structure and ambition. They have no clear *use value* but strive instead to reveal the violating force of excess. They also partake of exactly the same ambiguities and paradoxes. For sacrifice is as vexed and inauthentic, for Bataille, as it is illuminating. It is both the tragedy and the comedy of death. And we will attempt, here, to understand the ambiguity of its fascination.

Chapter VII of *The Limit to Usefulness* is one of the most luminous texts of Bataille on sacrifice. Written between 1939 and 1945 as one of the several unfinished versions of *The Accursed Share*, the unpublished essay belongs to the series of drafts Bataille wrote on general economy and the principle of expenditure. Chapter VII, composed well after the initial fictional as well as theoretical forays of the thirties, proposes a precise recapitulation of Bataille's theoretical positions and scientific sources on sacrifice. Bataille here addresses what was most probably his contemporaries' main objection to his previous reflections on sacrifice. Denying that he ever intended to revive sacrifice and "start new cycles of holocaust," he minimizes this early aspect of his writings and emphasizes instead his interest in sacrifice as a universal "enigma" (O, 61).

Bataille is being less than honest when he denies having attempted to revive sacrificial rites. In 1936, he co-founded with André Masson the journal Acéphal whose headless figure became the symbol of the publication and of the secret society of the same name. It is well known that the secret society, which embodied the *College of Sociology*'s dream of a "sacred sociology," planned to carry out a human sacrifice.[2] And in 1939 Bataille's memory of Acéphale and its fantastic project of human sacrifice must have still been fresh. He could also scarcely have forgotten his intention during the pre-war years to recreate a "virulent and devastating sacred, whose epidemic contagion would end up affecting and exalting the entire social body" (Caillois 1974, 58).[3] In the "Sorcerer's Apprentice," one of the texts presented at a 1938 session of the *College of Sociology*, Bataille was clear in his desire to invent a "ritually lived myth" assembling communities around the sacred intimacy of its tragic ebullience (Hollier 1995, 322).[4] This "living myth" was not, in this text, identified solely with sacrifice. And Bataille was already aware of the fictitious nature of "a myth revealing the totality of existence" (Hollier

1995, 342) Yet sacrifice was very much, in this text as in others – *The Pineal Eye* also comes to mind – at the core of the "total existence" Bataille wished for. And most essays of the period were indeed haunted by the fiction of reviving, through "bloody fantasies of sacrifice," man's lost intimacy with the sacred (O, 61).

Bataille's disavowal is not, however, entirely mendacious or unjustified. After 1939, Bataille does abandon the dream of reintroducing ritual violence in modern society.[5] And he turns towards a more sober reflection on sacrifice. His understanding of the sacred – and of sacrifice's role as a fundamental manifestation of man's drive towards totality – has not changed. But Bataille is now more attuned to the historical as well as epistemological contexts of the sacrificial experience and pursues his reflections on two fronts. On the one hand, in *Theory of Religion* and other anthropological studies, he investigates the birth of the sacred and the role of sacrifice in primitive societies. On the other, in the *Atheological Summa*, he pursues the project of a contemporary "limit experience" whose sacrificial rapture requires an abolition of the Hegelian subject and an excess of his absolute knowledge.

What are then Bataille's views on sacrifice? Chapter VII of *The Limit to Usefulness* is again helpful here, because it describes clearly the complex mix of scientific rigor and ontological intuition that is behind Bataille's theories. From his earliest essays in *Documents*, Bataille's reflections are grounded in contemporary sociological theories, particularly those of the Durkheim school. Bataille was well versed in the history as well as the sociology of sacrifice. By the time he wrote *The Limit to Usefulness*, he had already done a decade's worth of theoretical readings. Some of these readings – Robertson-Smith, *Lectures on the Religion of the Semites*, Frazer's *Golden Bough*, Freud's *Totem and Taboo* as well as Hubert and Mauss's important *Essay on the Nature and Function of Sacrifice* – are mentioned in one of the first theoretical essays Bataille devotes to sacrifice: "Sacrificial Mutilation and the Severed Ear of Vincent Van Gogh".[6] Bataille will continue to study these sources and add others (Sylvain Levi, Emile Durkheim) to refine his understanding of the sacred in subsequent texts such as *The Accursed Share, Theory of Religion* and *Eroticism.*[7] And his dialogue with ethnographic science is constant throughout.

Yet, as the text informs us, the signature of Bataille's sacrificial approach is the way it reframes social scientific theories inside a much larger and fundamental enquiry. "One must not linger, Bataille says, over [scientific] answers already received" but concentrate instead on the larger and more profound question of sacrifice's *cause* (O, 61). Ethnographic studies focused on specific cultures are oriented towards an explanation of sacrifice's *effects*, interpreting the ritual as a means to an end – a gift, or a tool for propitiation or expiation. But these interpretations ignore a fundamental aspect of the ritual that is as provocative as it is enigmatic. Sacrifice is universal. It is present for men of all times and places and transcends, as such, the bounds of scientific, contextual enquiry. The universality of ritual sacrifice raises a question far more fundamental than the concern for the use value of individual rites: the ultimate question of a "why"? Why indeed, or "How was it," asks Bataille, "that everywhere, men found themselves, with no prior mutual agreement, in accord on an enigmatic act, they all felt the need or the obligation to put living beings ritually to death" (O, 61)? The answer Bataille gives to that question is at the very core of his general theory of sacrifice. It suggests that man's consciousness is constitutively bound with tragic terror and sacred ecstasy and that communities murder ritually to share in the violent exuberance of being. Sacrifice is, for Bataille, nothing less than a manifestation of the sacred, i.e. "the continuity of being, revealed to those who focus their attention, during the course of a solemn rite, on the death of a discontinuous being" (E, 82 trans. mod.).

Bataille's conception of sacrifice is the result of this uneasy yet productive tension between the historical and ethnographic knowledge of sacrifice and the tragic Nietzschean ontology that reframes it. To understand the intricacies of that thinking – and elucidate, for example, why Bataille keeps to a model he also deconstructs – one must investigate further what Bataille borrows as well as contests from scientific sources. I mentioned earlier that Bataille kept well abreast of recent theoretical developments in the sociology of sacrifice. He was quite familiar with Hubert and Mauss's *Essay on the Nature and Function of Sacrifice*, and recognized the importance of this essay, whose novel definition of sacrifice he partially appropriated. The originality of Hubert and Mauss lies in their attempt to define sacrifice solely in terms of its basic social function and procedure. Contrary to their predecessors, who search for the unity of sacrifice in what Hubert and Mauss felt were "arbitrarily selected principles" – such as communion[8] – the French sociologists propose to identify a kind of *zero degree* of sacrifice: a common structure anterior to its changing forms and economic ends. Sacrifice, they write, can be defined, as "a religious act, which, through the consecration of the victim, modifies the state of the moral person who accomplishes it or that of certain objects with which it is concerned" (Hubert and Mauss 1968, 14).

Hubert and Mauss's minimalist definition may not seem revolutionary or even particularly suited to Bataille's more transgressive ends.

Yet it works quite well with his approach. For Bataille, indeed, the most fundamental aspect of sacrifice is its ability to tear the veil of the profane world and to bring about a communication with the sacred. Hubert and Mauss's definition, by stating that sacrifice's first function is to *make sacred*, allows him to fit his tragic vision into their basic scheme. Bataille's theoretical accord with the theories of the French school is limited, however, as he takes issue with Hubert and Mauss's procedural descriptions of the phases of sacrifice. Their essay on sacrifice identifies three successive phases in the ritual: the first phase of the initiatory rites designed to sanctify the participants, the solemn moment of ritualized murder and the aftermath of the rite marked by the ceremonial and utilitarian disposal of the sacred remains. For Bataille, the second moment of ritual slaying is the apex of the ceremony. It is the only truly significant moment of the rite because its deadly violence allows the contagion of the sacred to flow out into the world. But, for Hubert and Mauss, this phase, as important as it may also be, is eventually superseded by a final moment whose utilitarianism belies the excessive and sacrilegious violence of the previous phase. In this third and last phase of the rite, the sacrifier disposes of the victim's consecrated body in communion or offerings. Gifted to the gods or used as an instrument of appeasement (propitiation) or amends (expiation), the victim's body becomes a means of negotiation with the religious sphere.

Bataille takes issue with the importance Hubert and Mauss grant this final, "useful," phase of sacrifice. He did not, of course, disagree entirely with the suggestion that a portion of the ritual could be used for profane purposes. He knew full well that sacrifice was inherently ambiguous and served various religious purposes beyond that of ritual destruction.[9] Yet Bataille never wavered in his belief that sacrifice's "essential phase" was to be found in the cruel participation of the "sacrifiers" in the victim's violent slaying (VE, 70).[10] This moment of contagious communication with the sacred is, for him, the only veritable goal of a rite whose destructive modality is paramount. And Bataille always believed that sacrifice's true purpose was to bring men to commune with the anxious yet joyous rapture of death.

What is exactly, however, this essential phase of sacrifice? What does its rapture communicate? And what is the purpose and power of its ritual destruction? These questions have different answers according to the various experiences and epochs Bataille considers. It is possible to find the same fundamental postulates, however, in virtually all Bataille's reflections on sacrifice: firstly, that sacrifice is the necessary *alteration* of individuals and objects; and secondly, that sacrifice's destruction is the very mimesis of the universe's excess. These principles are illustrated in Bataille's first essays on sacrifice, "Lost America" and "Self-mutilation and the severed ear of Vincent Van Gogh." If Bataille is drawn, for example, to the bloody apex of the Aztec's rite, it is because the destruction of the victim is readily apparent in the image of the bloody heart offered, pulsating still, to the sun. Likewise, when he proposes – somewhat counter-intuitively – to identify Van Gogh's self-mutilation with sacrifice, it is because he sees the "rupture of personal homogeneity and the projection *outside the self* of a part of oneself," as the very paradigm of sacrificial destruction (VE, 68).

The purpose of sacrificial destruction, Bataille writes in *The Accursed Share*, is to restore to the sacred world that which servile use has degraded, rendered profane:

> Servile use has made *a thing* (*an object*) of that which, in a deep sense, is of the same nature as the *subject*, is in a relation of intimate participation with the subject. It is not necessary that the sacrifice actually destroy the animal or plant of which man had to make a thing for his use. They must, at least, be destroyed as things, that is *insofar as they have become things*. Destruction is the best means of negating a utilitarian relation between man and the animal or plant.
>
> (AS 1, 56)

Sacrificial destruction is a compensatory act, which is intended to regain communication with a world free of labor and the constraints of objectivity. Whether it is the Aztecs restoring prisoners to the magnificence of the sun, or Van Gogh freeing himself from the poverty of self, sacrifice frees. Its consummation liberates the "violent truth of the intimate world," and this explains why men of all epochs and cultures have practiced sacrifice. It also explains why sacrifice seems to preside over the birth of the sacred and the origin of religious man. As Bataille explains in *Theory of Religion, Eroticism* and the essays on *Lascaux and the Birth of Art*, the birth of man is far from being straightforward. It is a dual process marked, first, by the birth of industrious man and, second, by a religious birth bringing with it a "restoration to the truth of the intimate world" (AS 1, 58). If Bataille believes, as most paleo-anthropologists do, that our first true ancestors were *homo sapiens* who gained mastery over the world through their use of language and tools, he also believes that their true birth as sacred and artistic beings starts with man's rebellion against the poverty of his instrumental world. Having reduced the universe to a profane "order of things," "man himself became one of the things of this world, at least for the time in which he labored. It is this degradation which man has always tried to escape. In his strange myths, in his cruel rites, man is *in search of a lost intimacy* from the first" (AS 1, 57).

Destruction is the key to sacrifice as a religious phenomenon because it opens the door between the discontinuous world of work and the intimacy of the sacred realm. But this negativity of sacrifice is also essential in that it *represents* the very excess of this realm. As we noted above, the idea that sacrifice negates utilitarian relationships with the world is almost always linked to the corollary that sacrificial consumption is the *mimesis* of the universe's excess. In the solar rites of the Aztecs or Van Gogh's self-mutilation, for example, Bataille saw a "desire to resemble perfectly to an ideal term generally characterized, in mythology, as a solar god" (VE, 66). And he often understood sacrificial destruction as a desire to join, in consumption, the ever-changing fluidity of being – whose preferred trope is indeed, the sun. It is not always easy to interpret what lies behind Bataille's mimetic paradigm – the idea that excess might be imitated goes against its very insubstantiality and lack. But I believe that Bataille's image of sacrifice as a mirror of being's excess is less designed to comment on the quality of sacrifice's representation than it is to help us measure the exhaustive character of its destruction.[11] Bataille, in other terms, is attempting to convey the fact that sacrifice, to be authentic, must not simply "destroy what it consecrates" and give its participants access to a lost world of violent immanence. It must also communicate that world's radical inaccessibility (a message which impels sacrifice to self-destroy in order to "imitate" the impossibility of the sacred world of excess).

This last point is essential for anyone wishing to understand the economy of sacrifice in Bataille's work. When Bataille reinterprets Hubert and Mauss's sacrificial paradigm and emphasizes the moment of destruction at the expense of any other phases of the ritual, he is saying, indeed, that the destruction of the consecrated offering is paramount and that "this offering cannot be restored to the real order" (AS 1, 58). But he is also saying that this principle of absolute heterogeneity "liberates violence while marking off the domain in which violence reigns absolutely" (AS 1, 58). What Bataille means by this last statement is that there can be violent communication with the sacred world opened by sacrifice but no rational appropriation of it. "The world of intimacy is as antithetical to the real world as immoderation is to moderation, madness to reason, drunkenness to lucidity" (AS 1, 58). Because it is the very negation of the objective world, it does not share its separateness and definition. It is therefore impossible to substantialize as well as to conceptualize. No more durable than the blinding flash, which restores life's fullness at the very instant of sacrificial death, it communicates nothing but "the *invisible* brilliance of life which is not a thing" (TR, 47). Far from revealing death or opening for us the mysteries of the sacred, it blinds us to the very intimacy it illuminates. And Bataille's sacrificial experience is ultimately a question without an answer. As a sacrifice "without reserve or gain," it is also a sacrifice "for nothing" (ffrench 2007, 75).

Bataille's sacrifice, it should now be clear, owes little to the traditional sociological phenomenon we call sacrifice. It is a "sacrifice in the second degree," whose redoubled destruction is aimed not only at the victim but also at sacrifice itself. Because it refuses to give its ritual a result and identifies its only moment of truth with the rapture of death, it questions its own operativity. Indeed, the suggestion that sacrificial death *reveals nothing* leaves sacrificial negativity "unemployed." It destroys the process by which habitual sacrifice instrumentalizes the victim's destruction to gain mastery over death, and it frees the rapturous moment of death from any appropriation by the participants. Such "total immolation," which Bataille has also described as a "sacrifice where everything is a victim" has little to do with the traditional transitive sacrifice (IE, 130). As an "access without access to a moment of disappropriation" it is scarcely more than a simulacral gesture towards an impossible experience of finitude (Nancy, 30). And sacrifice is ultimately, for Bataille "a notion violently separated from itself" (Blanchot 1983, 30).

It is hard to say if Bataille believed in the authentic existence of such a purely excessive ritual. He believed that "the man of sacrifice" "act [ed] in ignorance (unconscious) of sacrifice's full scope" and was therefore "closer than Hegel's Sage" to its expensive spirit (HDS, 19). But Bataille also set himself the task of renewing, in the modern world, the forms and conditions of a sacrificial experience equally rapturous and free. This project gives birth, in the war years, to the *Atheological Summa* and, in particular, to *Inner Experience*, texts dedicated to reviving, in this post-Hegelian era, the difficult dream of a sacrifice without speculation. It also marks, however, a turning point in Bataille's attitude towards sacrifice and seems to inaugurate "the long drifting that led [him] to denounce the theater of sacrifice and consequently to renounce its successful accomplishment" (Nancy 1991a, 21). Bataille appears, indeed, to have become wary of his reliance on sacrifice in the very texts that were to define his atheological experience as an ever-deeper sacrifice of the Subject. At this point his critique of sacrifice makes the transition from a critical attitude towards the rites' functional economy to a full-blown denunciation of sacrifice's spectacular subterfuge.

There is no doubt that Bataille was already aware of sacrifice's "theater" before 1939. Texts such as "Self-Mutilation and the Severed Ear of Vincent Van Gogh" showed clearly that he was already mindful, in 1928, of the essential danger posed by the specular nature of sacrifice. The exemplarity he gave self-mutilation – or the immediate form of self-destruction he calls "sacrifice of the god" – was already an expression of a struggle with the vicarious economy of the ritual. But Bataille did not, then, thematize explicitly this theater, which becomes a *topos* of his later texts. In *Eroticism*, he denounces sacrifice as a "novel" or a "story illustrated in a bloody fashion" whose efficacy depends on a ficti-tious and vicarious identification with the victim's death (E, 86). And in "Hegel, Death and Sacrifice" (1955), he writes:

> In sacrifice, the sacrifier identifies himself with the animal that is struck down dead. And so he dies while seeing himself die, and even, in a certain way, by his own will, one in spirit with the sacrificial weapon. But this is theater.
>
> (HDS, 19 trans. mod.)

The text, it is true, adds, in the next sentence, that this theater is essential to the experience of death as "no other method [exists] which could reveal to the living the invasion of death" (HDS, 19). Yet, inevitable or not, this element of theatrical drama casts a problematic shadow over Bataille's version of a sacrifice without gain or reserve. In Bataille's zero-sum sacrifice, nothing is to be gained from the essen-tially rapturous moment of identification with the victim's death. But if, as Bataille also believes, this rapturous ordeal remains vicariously bound to a sacrificial subject, it becomes as appropriative as any cath-arsis and as economical as any dialectics. As long as the sacrificial subject can gaze upon, and identify with, the staged death-throes of the victim, she is appropriating her own "negativity." And since there is, obviously, no sacrifice without a scenic dimension – since self-sacrifice itself is also spectacular or…completely abstract – sacrifice reveals itself to be, for Bataille, somewhat of a "red herring" (OC XI, 101).[12] Instead of exposing us to the non-appropriable excess of finitude, it simulates the very type of totalizing knowledge Bataille wanted to displace.

One might wonder, at this point, if Bataille ever reached any conclusive condemnation of sacrifice or if his approach remained ambivalent throughout. It may seem strange indeed that he could both carry out a vigorous critique of sacrifice's economy and remain inconclusive in his renunciation of its drama. Such critical indecisiveness is precisely what

Jean-Luc Nancy – one of the most intelligent, and critical, readers of Bataille's sacrificial scheme – finds wanting in Bataille's otherwise revolutionary thinking of finitude.[13] In "The Unsacrificeable," for example, Nancy reiterates Bataille's own denunciation of sacrifice as a speculative comedy by which the subject appropriates, "by means of the transgression of the finite [...] the infinite truth of the finite" (Nancy 1991a, 25). But unlike Bataille, Nancy leaves no room for any prodigal form of sacrifice claiming to reverse and replace sacrifice's "trans-appropriative" death by a rapturous one. There can be, for Nancy, no sacrifice free of speculation. And Bataille's rapturous rewriting of sacrifice is illusory, firstly because sacrifice's comedy is structural, not incidental, secondly because, as soon as it is staged through the sacrificial process, death's rapturous "non-knowledge" becomes a figure of truth.

This last caveat is, I believe, one of the most important points of Nancy's critique. It is certainly the most decisive of his attempt to invalidate Bataille's atheological version of sacrifice. But it is also, I believe, the critical core of Bataille's *Inner Experience* and the very point Bataille seems to address in the last parodic moment of the volume. I will not be able to show in sufficient details why I believe Bataille anticipates Nancy's objection and renounces sacrifice as a literal model for his experience of non-knowledge. But I want to reiterate the fact that, after 1939, Bataille separated implicitly his reflections on sacrifice as a sociological object and his textual treatment of sacrifice as an inner experience. Nancy's readings pay scant attention to the latter texts, which may be found in the *Atheological Summa* and *The Impossible*. But many critics have noted, as I do, that it is precisely in those texts that Bataille problematized his former critical idyll with sacrifice. Whether they describe his *Inner Experience* as a supremely self-aware parody of Hegel's own sacrificial Absolute (ffrench); or whether they note that, in the same text, Bataille's sacrifice is undone by writing and replaced by poetry (ffrench, 2007; Arnould, 1996, 2009; Amano, 2004), these critics show how Bataille's *Atheological Summa* writes sacrifice into its very playful demise. The end of the *Inner Experience* is, in this respect, exemplary. For it is at the very threshold of the text that Bataille addresses (a last time, but ironically and conclusively) the last strenuous objection Nancy raised against sacrifice.

Nancy's argument in "The Unsacrificeable," we recall, was that the death to which sacrifice exposes us is always defined by the violence that brings it about. Rapturous or not, it appears, through the breach of the victim's body, as an "outside" of finitude, an "obscure God" as haunting as it is infinite. This presents the great inconvenience, says

Nancy, of locating a finitude, the "in between" of which should remain un-locatable and impenetrable.

> One does not enter the *between* [...], not because it would be an abyss, an altar or an impenetrable heart, but because it would be nothing other than the limit of finitude and lest we confuse it with, say, Hegelian "finiteness," this limit is a limit that does not soar above nothingness.
>
> (Nancy 1991a, 37)

Now, Bataille did, I believe, intend a similar critique of sacrifice's theological "Outside" when, at the end of his *Inner Experience*, he throws a handful of poems into the sacrificial night.[14] The gesture is complex and is meant to remain somewhat ambiguous. But it is, without a doubt, a disclaimer of the sacrificial regime of an *Inner Experience,* which never ceases, to the very end, to immolate its subject, its writing, its very experience. Bataillian inner experience is indeed conceived as a perpetual sacrifice – incessantly redoubled. As such, it remains, as Nancy would say, caught inside a dialectical logic where sacrifice is forever immolated to itself, to the infinitely held up possibility of its non-knowledge. What Bataille has described as the "torment" of the perpetual contestation of his experience is nothing but the struggle against its own inability to free itself from the pull of sacrificial "trans-appropriation." But the last gesture of the book interrupts this infinitization of the sacrificial dialectics. By letting us know that the final self-immolation of the experience's subject does not reveal sacrifice's nocturnal "Outside" but a handful of poetical tropes, Bataille puts an ironical end to sacrifice's "trans-appropriation." He shows us that finitude cannot be revealed through the sacrifice of the subject. He shows us as well that the truth of the sacrificial night is always already a literary one and that sacrifice, itself, is not much more than a "flower," a figure.

There would be much to say about this last statement and the complicated relationship Bataille establishes between sacrifice and literature. I would like to reiterate, however, that it is in the complication of that relationship that Bataille liberates his own experience of finitude from the illusion of a "sacrificeable" death. Bataille never truly renounced sacrifice because it offered him an irreplaceable figure of rapture. Neither did he cease to be tormented by the ambiguities of its cruel theater. But in his atheological texts, Bataille did stage some of his most parodic sacrificial dramas. These may still have been too speculative for Nancy's inoperative finitude, but they certainly did not take seriously their own bloody staging.

Notes

1 Unless specified otherwise, translations of Bataille's quotations from his *Complete Works* in French are mine. Where possible, I have used the English translation available.

2 On this topic, see Surya (2010).

3 Quoted and translated by ffrench (2007, 18). Caillois' original quotation states that the contagious violence of the sacred was to "exalt whoever had sown its seed".

4 "The Sorcerer's Apprentice" is the title of a talk presented in 1938 at the *College of Sociology*, in response to Kojève's critique of Bataille's immediate and violent theory of the sacred.

5 On the subject see Patrick ffrench's enlightening chapter "Affectivity without a subject" in *After Bataille, Sacrifice, Exposure, Community* (ffrench 2007, pp. 10–59).

6 With "Lost America," published in 1928, this essay, included in 1929 in *Documents*, is one of the first texts to use historical as well as sociological sources to support the author's intuitions on sacrifice.

7 Bataille refers to Sylvain Levy, *La Doctrine du Sacrifice dans les Brahmanas* (1898) in *Theory of Religion*.

8 Hubert and Mauss's essay is written in partial response to Robertson-Smith's *Lectures on the Religion of the Semites* (1889), which places communion between God and worshipper at the center of the sacrificial system.

9 See, for example, Bataille's reflections on "festivals" in the *Theory of Religion*, 52–57.

10 "Sacrifer" is a term Bataille borrows from Hubert and Mauss who discriminate between victim, sacrificer (the one who wields the knife) and sacrifer (participants and beneficiaries of the rituals).

11 The question of sacrifice as mimesis is complex and would have to include an analysis of how Bataille links religious sacrifice to the very structure of being. For him, being is the fluid passage between unstable objects. Such being has no unity, and is made of currents and circuits from series of beings to others. To access this instability (to communicate) means to strive to transcend the separation between beings. It means to "imitate" through the violence of the sacrificial passage, the ungraspable fluidity of being. For descriptions of being's labyrinthine or communicative structure see "The Labyrinth" in *Inner Experience* or *Sacrifices*, 64–74.

12 Bataille uses the expression "pavé de l'ours" in an article entitled "From the Stone Age to Jacques Prévert," published in *Critique* in 1946. I have chosen Patrick ffrench's translation of the expression (ffrench 2007, p. 91) over Richard Livingston, the translator of Nancy's "The Unsacrificeable," whose translation "definitely a shocker" misses the meaning as well as critical impact of the expression ("The Unsacrificeable," p. 30).

13 Jean-Luc Nancy and Maurice Blanchot have debated Bataille's contestation of sacrifice and its relationship to community and literature in their twin books: Nancy's (1991b) *Inoperative Community* and Blanchot's (1983) *Inavowable Community*.

14 See the section entitled "Manibus date lilia plenis" (EI, 157–167).

References

Amano, Koichiro. 2004. *Georges Bataille, la perte, le don, l'écriture*. Dijon: Presses Universitaires de Dijon.

Arnould, Elisabeth 1996. "The impossible sacrifice of poetry, Bataille and the Nancian critique of sacrifice." *Diacritics* 26, 2: 86–96.

Arnould, Elisabeth. 2009. *Georges Bataille, la terreur et les lettres*. Villeneuve-d'Asq: Presses Universitaires du Septentrion.

Blanchot, Maurice. 1983. *La communauté inavouable*. Paris: Minuit.

Caillois, Roger. 1974. *Approche de l'imaginaire*. Paris: Gallimard.

ffrench, Patrick. 2007. *After Bataille, Sacrifice, Exposure, Community*. London: Legenda.

Hollier, Denis, ed. 1995. *Collège de sociologie*. Paris: Gallimard.

Hubert, Henri and Mauss, Marcel. 1968. "Essai sur la nature et la fonction du sacrifice." *Oeuvres*, I. Paris: Les Editions de Minuit.

Nancy, Jean-Luc. 1991a. "The Unsacrificeable." *Yale French Studies* 79: 20–38.

Nancy, Jean-Luc. 1991b. *The Inoperative Community*. Translated by Peter Connor et al. Minneapolis: University of Minnesota Press.

Surya, Michel. 2010. *Georges Bataille : an Intellectual Biography*. Translated by Krzysztof Fijalkowski. New York: Verso.

8   Inner Experience

Gerhard Poppenberg

The concept of "inner experience" derives from the religious tradition. It is associated with the spiritual dimension of religion and develops its particular character above all in Christian mysticism. Here it signifies an access to the reality of God and the sacred in an emotional and ecstatic mystical experience, and not through rational and discursive knowledge, as in theology. Since God and the sacred are the absolute other in relation to the profane reality of the human, the experience of this encounter takes place as ecstasy. The Greek word ἔκστασις signifies being-outside-the-self, rapture. The corresponding verb ἐξίστασθαι literally means "to step outside of oneself, to stand outside oneself". The paradox of mystical experience is that it is an inner experience which at once implies being-outside-oneself. In the Christian tradition this experience has been evoked ever again in erotic metaphors. The Old Testament Song of Songs, describing a pastoral love-story in ardent erotic imagery, was taken by Christian exegesis as an allegorical representation for the encounter of the individual soul with God. The human soul is the bride, anticipating marriage with the divine bride-groom, Christ. Bride-mysticism is an essential part of the tradition of inner experience. Georges Bataille draws on this tradition in developing the concept of inner experience, although certainly without binding himself to any specific religious doctrine. He attempts to save the experience of the sacred, beyond institutionalized religion:

> Religion in the sense I mean it is not just *a* religion, like Christianity. It is religion in general and no one religion in particular. My concern is not with any given rites, dogmas or communities, but only with the problem that every religion sets itself to answer

> (E, 32)

Erotic ecstasy is also an access to inner experience for Bataille, one with a privilege equal to that of mystical experience. *Eroticism* begins with a chapter on "Eroticism in inner experience". And the erotic novels and stories should also be understood as explorations and representations of inner experience. The novella *Madame Edwarda* is closely related to *Inner Experience*. In some notes for a preface, reproduced in the notes to the *Oeuvres Complètes*, Bataille writes: "I wrote this little book in September-October of 1941, just before 'The Torture', which makes up the second part of *Inner Experience*. For me, the two texts are closely related, and one cannot understand the one without the other [...]. I could not have written 'The Torture' if I had not first provided its lewd key" (OC III, 492). Peter Connor, whose book on Bataille is among the best one can read on the subject, describes *Inner Experience* as an "eroticization of thought itself" (Connor 2000, 36).

Given the religious connotations of the concept of inner experience, Bataille had to engage with the forms in which it had been developed within religious tradition in order to become familiar with its essential elements and to continue its practice beyond the limits of religion. "By inner experience, I understand what one usually calls mystical experience: states of ecstasy, of ravishment, at least of meditated emotion. But I am thinking less of confessional experience, to which one has had to hold oneself hitherto, than of a bare experience, free of ties, even of an origin, to any confession whatsoever" (IE, 9).

Inner Experience was published in 1941. It is the first of three works to which Bataille gave the collective title, *The Atheological Summa*. The reference to the *Summa theologica* of Saint Thomas Aquinas makes Bataille's question explicit. It concerns an experience of the sacred without any religious commitment and without any relation to God. What becomes of mysticism and inner experience after the "death of God", dramatized by Nietzsche in *The Gay Science*? Can there be a mysticism without God, a "profane illumination", in the words of Walter Benjamin? Michel Leiris referred to his friend Bataille as a "mystic of debauchery" (CL, 5).

The idea of a mysticism without God first appears towards the end of the 19th century and recurs often in the 20th century. Nietzsche in *Thus Spoke Zarathustra* is one of the initiators; the motto to *Inner Experience* is taken from the "Night-Wanderer Song": "Night is also a sun". In his foreword, Bataille writes that he would like his book to share the spirit of *The Gay Science*, which brings together "depth and cheerfulness", and which "plays naively" with all that is sacred, but in such a way as to allow "the great seriousness" to begin (Nietzsche, cited by Bataille, IE, 3). The third part of the *Atheological Summa* is centered on reflections on Nietzsche (cf. Part 1, chapter 4 of the present book).

Atheist mysticism and profane illumination seek to preserve the luminous core of religious experience under the conditions proper to enlightened modernity. Paul Valéry's Monsieur Teste is said by his wife to be a "mystic without God" (Valéry 1947, 35). The Abbé, to whom she confides this comparison, dismisses it as nonsense. What is possible for humans, he tells her, has to be directed towards a genuine reality, and have its telos in this reality. An atheist mystic is attempting something that is not in his reach. He wants the impossible, and he wants it in the domain of the "totality of what is possible to him" *(l'ensemble de ce qu'il peut)*. Bataille takes the objection of the Abbé seriously; his profane mysticism is centered on the concept of the impossible.

The implications of atheological inner experience can be developed by reference to Bataille's conception of laughter. *Guilty*, the second volume of the *Atheological Summa*, contains a chapter entitled "The divinity of laughter". This correspondence between laughter and the divine has a theological authority. According to the Church father, John Chrysostom, Christ never laughed; in consequence, laughter was condemned in Christianity. Bataille's chapter title "Laughter and trembling" alludes to Kierkegaard's *Fear and Trembling* (which itself alludes to chapter 2 of the *Letter to the Philippians*); it indicates that, for Bataille, the theme of laughter signifies a reversal of religious doctrine. Laughter is the essence of man: "to be what I was: laughter itself" (G, 89).

Laughter is the experience of the loss of the self: "Uncontrollable laughter leaves behind the sphere that is accessible to discourse, it is a leap that cannot be defined in terms of its initial conditions – [...] Laughter is a leap from possible to impossible and from impossible to possible" (G, 101 trans. mod.). The leap consists in the abandonment of discursive and conscious thought, and access to another reality, which Bataille conceptualizes as "the impossible". The possible and the real can be related back to their causes, and thus explained through them. If an effect and a reality are not brought about by a cause, if they cannot be explained by a cause, then they are, in a strict sense, "impossible".

Laughter brings about an immanent ecstasy, which is at the same time an opening to an exterior. "In laughter, ecstasy is freed, is immanent. The laughter of ecstasy doesn't *laugh*, instead it opens me up infinitely. Its transparency is traversed by laughter's arrow, released by a mortal absence" (G, 103 trans. mod.). The metaphor of the arrow also comes from religious tradition. The transparency of the illumination in ecstasy is penetrated by the arrow of laughter, just as the heart of Saint Teresa of Avila is struck by the arrow of God's love. The arrow of laughter for Bataille, however, issues from a "mortal absence". The death of God makes human death into an absolute absence. If laughter is the essence of humanity, it is a laughter about this absence – and it is not an hysterical, but a sovereign laughter.

Among the authors cited in *Inner Experience*, a great number stem from the spiritual and mystical tradition – Dionysos the Areopagite (5th century), Angela of Foligno (1248–1309), Ignatius of Loyola (1491–1556), Teresa of Avila (1515–1582), and above all, Saint John of the Cross (1542–1591). For Bataille, Saint John of the Cross is the most important of the spiritual teachers because, within the domain of Christianity, he is the one who radically poses the question of inner experience, instead of simply reducing ecstasy back to "satisfaction, happiness, platitude". "Saint John of the Cross rejects the seductive image and the rapture, but finds repose in the theopathic state. I have followed his method of reduction right to the end" (EI 57, trans. mod.). Pierre Klossowski, therefore, argues that "Bataille, despite his atheist attitude, remains in solidarity with the whole Christian cultural structure" (Klossowski 2007, 68).[1]

In inner experience as it is conceived in the mystical tradition, the soul becomes the space for the encounter between God and the human. The human being was made in the image of God, and so it is possible for us to find this image in our own interior. Inner experience, then, is not so much a cultivation of the self, as a means to go beyond the self, a form of transcendence. The self has to be dissolved and annihilated in order to unite with the absolute other that is God. This transformation of the self into the substance of the divinity is what is meant by "inner experience". It is something different from the knowledge of scholastic theology, and exceeds the relation to God supposed by theology. It creates another form of knowledge: Bataille distinguishes between "the facts of a common and rigorous emotional understanding and those of a discursive understanding" (EI, 5). Their union at a "precise point" gives rise to a new form of ontology.

Saint Augustine systematically elaborated the theological understanding of man as an image of God in his treatise on the Trinity. Since God is a trinity, the human soul also consists of three moments; these are the faculties of the soul, which are matched to the trinitarian persons. The memory corresponds to the father, the understanding to the son, and the will to the holy spirit (*De Trinitate* X, XI). The dynamic center of inner experience is the conversion. It is a caesura, dividing the individual life into a before and an after. As Christ redeemed sinful man through his sacrificial death, so each individual has to make the transformation from the sinful to the blessed life. This metamorphosis is a *psychomachia*, an inner struggle against the malevolent powers of evil. Augustine's account of his conversion in the *Confessions* (VIII) became the defining model for the Christian era.

Saint John of the Cross formalized this complex of inner experience. The Catholic Church named him as a Doctor of the Church in questions of spirituality; his writings have been incorporated into the dogma of the Church. Therefore Bataille could take him as the point of departure for his re-writing of the tradition. In Saint John of the Cross, the *psycho-machia* is a confrontation of the soul with its own negativity. This conception responds to a formal imperative. If the soul is to have an experience of the supernatural, then it must put off everything that is natural. Since the divide separating man and God is infinitely great, there is no mediating instance on the human side which could make the transition possible. All that is human has to be negated in pre-paration for the union with God, as the absolutely other of man. This negativity in the human corresponds to the negativity on the side of God, who negates his own divinity, in becoming a mortal man, and dying on the cross. This double negativity now becomes the medium for the conversion, and the mystical union of the soul and God.

The transformation of the soul takes place in the intellectual faculties. These faculties belong to the non-divine part of man, and therefore must be destroyed (St John of the Cross 1934, *Ascent of Mount Carmel*, II.v.7). This destruction is not to be thought of as a loss, since it is the pivotal moment of the conversion. The three intellectual faculties correspond to the three cardinal virtues: the intellect to faith; memory to hope; and the will to love. These virtues are conceived in terms of their contrast to the intellectual faculties. The light of reason becomes darkness through faith because faith enters into play precisely where there is and can be no knowledge. Nonetheless, the certainty of faith transcends the knowledge of reason; the non-knowledge of faith is a higher form of certainty (*Ascent*, II.vi.2). In a similar way, memory is reduced to forgetting by hope. God cannot be apprehended through anything earthly, and so the contents of memory have to be erased, in order that in its place, hope, which is oriented towards the future, can prevail (*Ascent*, III.vii.2). Finally, the will is transformed into a passive letting-be by love (*The Dark Night of the Soul*, II.xviii.3). It is this passivity, and not the will (which has been destroyed), which brings about the conversion.

The power of the negative comes from its correspondence to the passion of Christ. The transformation of the intellectual faculties takes place through negation. The experience of this annihilation is "horrible and awful to the spirit"; it is "the dark night of the soul". But such a privation is required in order "that the spiritual form of the spirit may be introduced into it and united with it, which is the union of love" (*Dark Night*, II.iv.3). The non-knowledge of the intellect becomes faith, the forgetting of the memory becomes hope, the passivity of the will becomes love. Thus the soul, through the negation of the three intellectual faculties, and their metamorphosis into the three cardinal virtues, enters into relation to the three persons of the Trinity.

The negation of the intellectual faculties is a spiritual death, an imitation of the sacrificial death of Christ. It goes as far as the *eli lama sabachtani*, the despairing words spoken by Christ on the cross (Mark 15, 34; Matthew 27, 46). The God who is abandoned by God and descends into his own negativity is the model for the human spiritual death and sacrifice. "What the sorrowful soul feels most in this condition is its clear perception, as it thinks, that God has abandoned it, and, in his abhorrence of it, has flung it into darkness; it is a grave and piteous grief for it to believe that God has forsaken it" (*Dark Night*, II.vi.2). The sacrifice consists in the abandonment of the self; in this way, the believer becomes another. The unification with God *via* the mediation of a negation signifies here losing oneself rather than finding oneself.

The moment at which God is absent from himself is also the moment of his highest love, and so the highest form of divinity. The deity comes to itself in descending into the depths of that which, in God, is not God himself. Thus, the death of God is a moment of God himself. This is the path that is taken in the passion of Christ; and it is the same path that is taken in inner experience. The cultivation of inner experience is the wild heart of Christianity. The sacrifice of Christ is the most extreme giving or expenditure of oneself: the God that dies as a man gives up his divinity. And this sacrifice invites a similar gift of the self on the part of humanity.

The religious conception of transcendence as a transition to a higher world, reserved for what is holy and divine, is transformed by Bataille into a model of immanent transgression. Inner experience takes place between humans; thus "the sacred" becomes an inner-worldly event. The title of the 4th section of *Inner Experience* – "The new mystical theology" – should be understood in this sense. The new theology "only has the unknown (*l'inconnu*) for its object" (EI, 104). Bataille finds the same question at work in Maurice Blanchot's *Thomas the Obscure*. And it is from Blanchot that he derives the conditions for an atheological spirituality: "to have its principle and its end in the absence of salvation, in the renunciation of all hope; to affirm of inner experience that it is the authority (but that all authority expiates itself); to be contestation of itself, to be non-knowledge" (EI, 104).

In Christianity, God is the instance that gives unity and wholeness to the world, and meaning and truth to human life. Bataille's atheological inner experience begins with an insight into the non-totality of world and life (EI, 4). This insight is at the origin of the concept of non-knowledge. "To no longer want to be everything is to question everything. Anyone who, slyly, wants to avoid suffering identifies himself with the entirety of the universe, judges each thing as if he were it, in the same way that he imagines, at bottom, that he will never die. We receive these hazy illusions with life, like a narcotic. But what happens when, disintoxicated, we learn what we are" (EI, 4). The desire for wholeness implies not to have to die; it is put in question by the experience of finitude. This desire, the elementary narcotic of life, has been sustained by religion, the "opium of the people", as Marx says. To awaken out of the intoxication of this illusory identification of the self and the whole demands that everything has to be put into question. Bataille's book is about the pains of this awakening – the hangover of the life that begins after religion. If the "desire to be everything" can only be satisfied by an illusion, then to recognize it as such is an act of Enlightenment. And "to put everything in question" becomes the foundation for a genuinely human mode of being.

When the identification with the totality and one's own immortality are seen as illusions, it creates a "void in which one cannot breathe" (IE, 4). This void gives rise to a "singular experience", one composed of anguish and ecstasy. The traditional mystical experience is a revelation of divine truth. The new inner experience begins with the emptiness of the non-totality – and it is itself void and empty. Non-knowledge, then, a key category in Bataille, above all in the *Atheological Summa*, has its meaning as a counterpart to the revelation of religious truth. It must be underlined, however, that such an experience is not a religious revelation: "nothing is revealed, except the unknown". And unlike religious inner experience, it does not lead to the *tranquilitas animi*, to the peace of soul and inner joy: "it never provides anything calming" (IE, 4). Inner experience puts every last certainty in question; therefore it does not exist in view of any pre-given goal: "I wanted experience to lead me where it was leading, not to some end given in advance. And I say at once that it does not lead to a harbor (but to a place of bewilderment, of non-sense)" (EI, 9). Inner experience is a movement without direction and without goal or meaning. The distinction between emotional and discursive knowledge is based on this recognition. Inner experience is not the mediation of any kind of positive cognitive content; it is an event and a movement, nothing more. It communicates, in the literal sense, an "emotional knowledge" (*une connaissance émotionelle*). Such a "knowledge", unlike discursive knowledge, does not come to rest in a conceptual term, which would be its "terminus"; it is knowledge in motion, and knowledge as motion; and for the human subject, it is experienced as emotion, as a movement of the feelings. There is no principle that guides and authorizes it, since it is centered on non-knowledge and the unknown. Nonetheless, if it is to provide a new ontological determination of the human, it cannot be simply arbitrary; it must, then, be justified and authorized.

Bataille finds the resolution to this paradox of a questioning of all authority, which nonetheless has to be authorized, in a conversation with his friend Maurice Blanchot, from whom he borrows the formula: "experience is itself authority: but authority has to be expiated" (EI, 14). Two moments should be noted here. Firstly, the principle of self-authorization is announced by another; it is derived from a conversation, an act of communication and friendship. The origin of the formula is not merely anecdotal; self-authorization requires this articulation with another. And secondly, the authority demands its "expiation". The meaning of the term in this context, and the mode of its accomplishment, is then elaborated under the category of "torture" (*le supplice*), which is the title of the second part of *Inner Experience.* This chapter was written, Bataille claims, "with necessity, in accordance with my life" (IE, 3).

The principle of non-knowledge ends in a "state of nudity". While it leaves particular knowledge and even particular areas of knowledge intact, non-knowledge takes away their final ground. The truth of the human being then appears as a "supplication without response" (IE, 19). It is the non-essential essence of non-knowledge that it never provides a solution or a response. To know signifies precisely to have an answer to a question. Absolute knowledge gives the answer to the absolute question, to the world considered as "an enigma to be resolved" (IE, 4). The search for this answer has to remain unsatisfied. This is what is meant by non-knowledge. The will to lose oneself replaces the will to "be everything". "To lose oneself in this case would be to lose oneself and *in no way save oneself*" (EI, 29). The insight into incompleteness, Bataille writes, is "the highest ambition, it is to want to be a man"; to attain this point is even to "rise above man", to be more than human, given that until the present, humanity has always understood itself in terms of its religious vocation (EI, 32).

In order for this transformation to take place, just as in Christian salvation, the old man has to die and be reborn as the new man. But this is now an entirely human and earthly process; "condemned to become man (or more), I must now die (to myself), give birth to myself" (EI, 39). Here then we have Bataille's version of the Christian conversion narrative, founded on the insight into contingency and finitude.

These theoretical developments are intertwined with the account of a personal experience. Bataille recalls walking through Paris, 15 years earlier, with an open umbrella, his head full of wild ideas, when suddenly the idea of the impossible dawns on him. "A space constellated with laughter opened its dark abyss before me." His laughter is ecstatic: "I laughed as perhaps no one had ever laughed, the final depth of each thing opened, laid bare, as if I were dead" (EI, 40). The umbrella becomes a "black shroud". This is the traditional illumination-experience that reveals the ultimate reason of the world. From Saint Paul to Augustine, to Teresa of Avila and Jakob Boehme, it has been described ever again. In Bataille, the illumination originates with laughter, and accomplishes itself as laughter, which is also an experience of death.

At this point, he is "convulsively illuminated". The illumination is the recognition that "man is only man". That is liberating, but also unbearable, and causes anguish. The aim of Bataille's book, he writes, is to "turn anguish into delight" (EI, 40). This does not mean simply to pass from anguish to joy, but rather to reveal the joy that originates from anxiety, and in anxiety. Anxiety remains the dark background on which joy lights up. It is the agent of the conversion. Hence it has to be experienced in its full terror: the experience ends in a pleading without any hope of being heard: "supplication, but without gesture and certainly without hope" (EI, 41). In *The Concept of Anxiety*, Kierkegaard described this emotion as the original experience of the modern age. Subsequently, Heidegger, in *Being and Time* and "What is Metaphysics", analyzed the structure of anxiety (*Angst*), confirming its status as the fundamental affective disposition of modern humanity. The joy in anxiety, the joy that does not dissolve anxiety, is the joy at having finally attained humanity.

The plea becomes a prayer, in which he calls upon the divine father, who, in a night of despair, sacrificed his son. The relation to God is not a union with the divine plenitude, but an identification with the abandoned and despairing God, the God who experiences "exhausting solitude" in the *eli lama sabachtani* (EI, 41). The answer to the plea is given in the negative revelation that there is no answer. The "revelation" consists in the acceptance and the affirmation of this silence.

The self that assumes its finitude no longer interprets inner experience in terms of its relation to God, but in terms of its humanity, and hence of its relation to other humans. "But in me everything begins again, nothing is ever risked. I destroy myself in the infinite possibility of others like myself: it annihilates the meaning of this self. If I attain, an instant, the extremity of the possible, a little later, I will flee, I will be elsewhere" (EI, 41). The self (*le moi*) is always another, always elsewhere. This is the torment of "being forsaken, drop by drop, in the multitude of the misfortunes of man". But the despair of the dark night – "my different nights of terror" – is also accompanied by an "unspeakable joy" (EI, 42). The humanity of the human, in the horizon of others, is its immanent transcendence. It is a field of "infinite possibility", but it forms no totality, because humanity is made up of a "multitude of misfortunes", and because its history is also finite.

The figure for this infinite non-whole is again taken from the mystical tradition. Teresa of Avila describes the spiritual wedding of the mystical union with God in the metaphor of raindrops, which fall into a river, and dissolve into its water: the river then flows out to the sea, and merges with it. Bataille reverses this figure, which is common in the spiritual tradition. The individual dissolves "drop by drop" into the multitude of human misfortunes. This dissolution ends in death: "Joy of the dying, wave among waves" (EI, 56). Death is not to be understood as dissolution into a totality – the dissolution is anonymous, and its medium is not a determinate something: drops in the sea, waves in waves, individuals in humanity.

A central part of the mystical tradition is the meditation upon the image of Christ dying on the cross. In the *Spiritual Exercises* of Ignatius of Loyola and the reflections of John of the Cross, meditation on the cross is the means by which the self is dissolved in inner experience. In *Inner Experience* the same function is served by the series of photographs – "disturbing pictures" (*images bouleversantes*) – of the torture of the Chinese regicide, which Bataille long kept on his person: "he communicated his pain to me or rather the excess of his pain, and it was precisely this that I was seeking, not to enjoy it, but to ruin that in me which is opposed to ruin" (EI, 122; TE, 205–207).

This tortured Chinese man is the figure of the *Ecce Homo* in the secular world, the figure of a suffering that cannot be redeemed, and of complete dissolution: his body is being cut up and the flesh torn open. This image of "the torture" as a fatal ecstasy and of death as ecstasy becomes the epitome of mortality: irredeemably delivered over to death, without hope or resistance.

Nonetheless, the non-knowledge of inner experience is not simply void and empty; it has its own content, which becomes accessible in "vague inner movements". These are not bound to any specific objects or intentions (cf. EI, 21); they can be triggered by the "purity of the sky", or by the odor of a room, but the sensations are arbitrary, unmotivated. The odor of a room evokes something, the auratic quality of a blue sky allows something to appear, but the manifestation that takes place does not have a specific cause that could be located in some way in the room or the sky. In the chapter "Ecstasy", in the final section of the book ("Post-Scriptum to the Torture, or the New Mystical Theology"), Bataille describes and analyses two basic modes of this experience. The first is triggered on a certain evening, at twilight: "Without giving these words more than an evocative value, I thought that the 'sweetness of the sky' communicated itself to me and I could feel precisely the state within that responded to it. I felt it to be present inside my head like a vaporous streaming, subtly graspable, but participating in the sweetness of the outside, putting me in possession of it, making me take pleasure in it" (EI, 114). He compares the state of "happiness" that overcomes him with "mystic states". The quotation marks around "the sweetness of the sky" are there because *dulcedo* (sweetness) is an essential metaphor of the spiritual tradition of inner experience (Chatillon, 1954). In this term, the element of physical sensation and spiritual experience are intertwined. Such an experience is an "inner presence which we cannot apprehend without a leap of our entire being", carrying the self beyond itself (EI, 115). "The movements flow into an external existence: they lose themselves there, they 'communicate', it seems, with the outside, without the outside taking a determined form and being perceived as such" (EI, 118). This ecstasy is momentary and particular, since the "outside" with which it communicates still has the character of an object: things, world, sky. The experience is finally that between a subject and an object: I experience "the sweetness of things". As long as the experience takes place in the interaction of the self with the external world – even if it is no more than the experience of an indefinite "there" – it finally returns to a definite kind of being that is known and recognized in discourse, and the inner experience comes to an end.

The direction of Bataille's reflection then is towards a mode of experience that departs from recognizable and nameable experience and enters into the sphere of non-knowledge. Non-knowledge is an experience of the night, in which the perception of things and world is no longer possible, in which sight, the basic mode of knowing, is extinguished. "From then on the night, non-knowledge, will each time be the path of ecstasy along which I will lose myself" (EI, 125). In the darkness of the night, however, the desire to see still subsists: "What then finds itself in a profound obscurity is a fierce desire to see when, before this desire, everything slips away" (ibid.). The night, the medium in which every relation to things, every relation to the world dissolves, now becomes itself an object – one whose property is to make every kind of object-relation impossible.

A citation from Blanchot's *Thomas the Obscure* illustrates the point: "He saw nothing and, far from being distressed, he made this absence of vision the culmination of his sight [...] Not only did this eye that saw nothing apprehend something, it apprehended the cause of its own vision. It saw as object that which prevented it from seeing" (cited by Bataille, EI 103). As Blanchot underlines in his essay on Bataille, the dark of night is not simply an absence of light: it is a "surplus of nothingness", "a pure affirmation" (Blanchot 1993, 307, 310). The "night of non-knowledge" is now encountered face to face, and no longer as an object to be defined: "Suddenly I know it, discover it without a cry, it is not an object; it is HER that I was awaiting" (EI, 125 trans. mod.). The experience of the night as the absolute other is evoked in terms taken from the tradition of bride-mysticism: "In HER everything is effaced, but, exorbitant, I traverse an empty depth and the empty depth traverses me. In HER, I communicate with the 'unknown' opposed to the *ipse* that I am; I become *ipse*, unknown to myself, two terms merge into the same laceration, scarcely differing from a void" (EI, 126 trans. mod.).

Such affective movements are disturbed or completely blocked by consciousness and by discursive thought, proceeding in accordance with the "law of language". They are only to be attained – "with a little luck" – through a struggle against language. But since the human mode of being is profoundly constituted by language, this actually means a struggle against oneself. The struggle of the soul (the *psychomachia*) in the spiritual tradition against the obstacles put up by the enemy becomes a struggle with language, an internal struggle with and against oneself as a creature of language.

The linguistic agon appears in formulations composed of mutually exclusive meanings, whose juxtaposition is formally ironic. "Silence" is an example of such a "sliding word". Its signification is the destruction of what it is, as word and phonic form: "among all words it is the most perverse, or the most poetic: it is itself proof of its own death" (EI, 23). Silence is the paradigmatic ironic word, setting sound and meaning against each other in open contradiction. This dimension of Bataille's thought is unfolded a generation later with deconstruction.

Bataille draws one last consequence from this thought. In past attempts to write a book, he broke off the project, before it was finished, having forgotten what it was that had so fascinated him. "I escape myself and my book escapes me" (EI, 62). But in this experience, he now recognizes the movement of inner experience itself: "And if this book resembles me? If the conclusion eludes the beginning: is unaware of it or indifferent to it? Strange rhetoric! Strange means of invading the impossible" (ibid.). Anacoluthon is the figure of language and thought which responds to the impossible. It expresses the inherent impossibility to bring a thought to term, because it ends in non-knowledge. The anacoluthon is the syntactical figure of the "supplication without response".

Hence Maurice Blanchot makes the stipulation, which also holds for the present study, that Bataille's book will not let itself be contained in the critical commentary. "Since Georges Bataille's book is an authentic translation it cannot be described. The book is the tragedy that it expresses. Certainly, if one has discerned its meaning, one can reduce it to a weighty scholarly exposition. But its truth is in the burning of the mind, in the play of the lightning, in the silence full of vertigo and exchanges that it communicates to us" (Blanchot 2001, 41).

Translated by Mark Hewson.

Note

1   Buvik (2010) presents the 1944 discussion between Bataille, Klossowski, Marcel Moré and the theologian Jean Daniélou, which took place in the house of Moré (cf. OC VI 315–359).

References

Blanchot, Maurice 1993. *The Infinite Conversation*. Translated by Susan Hanson. Minneapolis: University of Minnesota Press.

Blanchot, Maurice. 2001. *Faux Pas*. Stanford: Stanford University Press.

Buvik, Pierre. 2010. *L'Identité des contraires. Sur Georges Bataille et le christianisme*. Paris: Éditions du Sandres.

Chatillon, Georges. 1954. "Dulcedo, dulcedo Dei" in *Dictionnaire de spiritualité*, Paris: Beauchesne, 1777–1795.

Connor, Peter Tracey. 2000. *Georges Bataille and the Mysticism of Sin*. Baltimore: Johns Hopkins University Press.

Feyel, Juliette. 2013. *Georges Bataille: une quête érotique du sacré*. Paris: Champion.

Hussey, Andrew. 2000. *The Inner Scar. The Mysticism of Georges Bataille*. Amsterdam (Atlanta): Rodopi.

John of the Cross, Saint. 1934–1935. *The Complete Works of Saint John of the Cross, Doctor of the Church*. 3 vols. Trans. Alison Peirs from the critical edition of P. Silverio de Santa Teresa. London: Burns Oates and Washbourne.

Klossowski, Pierre. 2007. *Such a Deathly Desire*. Translated by Russell Ford. Albany: SUNY Press.

Valéry, Paul. 1947. *Monsieur Teste*. Translated by Jackson Matthews. New York: Knopf.

9 Sovereignty

Claire Nioche

The concept of sovereignty is at the centre of Bataille's ethical project. The most developed exposition of the concept is to be found in *The Accursed Share*, and more precisely, in the third part of this work, entitled *Sovereignty*. In this volume, which was never published in Bataille's lifetime, a certain unity of his philosophical investigation of phenomena becomes perceptible. *Sovereignty* is one of his most ambitious projects. In many respects, it resonates with *Inner Experience* and with the texts on Nietzsche and on non-knowledge. Bataille's analyses of sovereignty are unfolded at several levels, the anthropological and historical, the philosophical, the literary. Yet there is no *logical* way to display the figure of sovereignty.

1 Defined by the principle that "nothing sovereign must ever submit to the useful" (AS 2, 226), sovereignty is an existential disposition towards life and death, towards the sacred and the marvellous, subverting temporality and the relation to knowledge.
2 Defined from the perspective of the "general economy" as a pure expenditure (waste, sacrifice, or destruction), sovereignty refers to the feudal paradigm. Revolution is its utmost contestation. Communism is its most active contradiction. Here the notion of sovereignty enters into the realm of social relations. Yet sovereignty is generally the condition of each human.
3 Defined in terms of inner experience, sovereignty allows man to conceive of life in terms of play, not only in terms of work (synonymous with servility). In this context Bataille introduces the figure of the "man of sovereign art".

We will here present a set of theoretical presuppositions that constitute the heart of Bataille's meditation on sovereignty and that also help to clarify what is at stake in *inner experience*: "essentially, sovereignty is revealed internally; only an interior communication really manifests its presence" (AS 2, 245). We will see how sovereignty submerges the possibility of dialectics and discourse – not simply by means of an interruption, but through an opening, an irruption suddenly uncovering the limit of discourse and the beyond of absolute knowledge.

Sovereignty as an Ethical Horizon

In the *incipit* of the volume on *Sovereignty*, Bataille warns the reader that sovereignty is not so much a question of international relations but rather a question of ethical principles: sovereignty pertains to the inner relation of man to the objects of his desire. The ethics of sovereignty casts aside any value of *utility*. Any enjoyment of possibilities that is not justified by utility is *sovereign*. Thus, the sovereign life begins once the necessities assured, and the possibility of life opens up without limit. Disregarding a purely functionalist conception of life, Bataille asserts that the desire for the sacred and the miraculous is as essential to man as satisfying his needs.

"Life beyond utility is the domain of sovereignty" (AS 2, 198). At the same time, sovereignty is attained through the awareness of the catastrophe of death. This is the Hegelian moment in Bataille's meditation, and arguably a zone throughout which sovereignty remains within a classical philosophy of the subject. Here we can follow Derrida's reading of Bataille in *Writing and Difference*, in the chapter "From Restricted to General Economy" (Derrida, 2005, 317–350). For both Hegel and Bataille, sovereignty is closely related to a conception of death. *The man of sovereign art* is the man who has strength to endure the anguish of death and to face the perpetual work of death. Bataille writes: "The strangest thing is that he [the man of sovereign art] measures up to that measureless catastrophe under the threat of which we are living. This is because he always lives rather as if he were the *last man*" (AS 2, 429).

As Derrida notices, the term "sovereignty" translates the lordship (*Herrschaft*) of the *Phenomenology*, and the operation of lordship precisely consists in "showing that it is not fettered to determinate existence, that it is not bound at all by the particularity everywhere characteristic of existence as such, and is not tied up with life" (Hegel, quoted by Derrida, 2005, 321). Let us recall that in the dialectic of the master and the slave, the master is the one who puts at stake the entirety of one's own life, whereas the servant is the man who wants to conserve his life by all means, to be conserved (*servus*). Bataille takes up this Hegelian idea that by raising oneself above life, by looking at death directly, one accedes to lordship (in Hegelian terms: the for-itself [*für sich*]). The sovereign man is the one who has the strength to endure the anguish of death and to maintain the work of death.

Yet, in the Hegelian paradigm, lordship ultimately *has* a meaning in the systemic construction of knowledge: the putting at stake of life is *per se* a stage in the presentation of essence and truth, a necessary moment in the history of self-consciousness and phenomenality. The master must experience his truth, which means that he must stay alive in order to enjoy what he has won by risking his life: "To rush head-long into death pure and simple is thus to risk the absolute loss of meaning, in the extent to which meaning necessarily traverses the truth of the master and of self-consciousness" (Derrida, 2005, 321). Hence, through a ruse of life that is nothing but a ruse of reason, life has preserved itself – in one way or another. Undoubtedly, like Hegelian lordship, Bataille's sovereignty makes itself independent through the gesture of putting life at stake; it is attached to nothing and conserves nothing. But unlike Hegelian lordship, sovereignty does not want to maintain itself, or collect the profits from its own risk. Bataille defines death as a "negative miracle". He writes:

> The most remarkable thing is that this negative miraculous, mani-
> fested in death [...] is the moment when we are relieved of antici-
> pation, man's customary misery, of the anticipation that enslaves,
> that subordinates the present moment to some anticipated result.
> Precisely in the miracle, we are thrust from our anticipation of the
> future into the presence of the moment, of the moment illuminated
> by a miraculous light, the light of the sovereignty of life delivered
> from its servitude.
>
> (AS 2, 207)

Derrida shows that the Hegelian economy of life still *restricts* itself to conservation, to circulation and self-reproduction as, ultimately, the reproduction of meaning:

> Henceforth, everything covered by the name lordship collapses
> into comedy. The independence of self-consciousness becomes
> laughable at the moment when it liberates itself by enslaving itself,
> when it starts to work, that is, when it enters into dialectics.
>
> (Derrida, 2005, 322)

Through the denunciation of the comical aspect of lordship, Bataille indicates a different horizon of thought.

In the "system" poetry, laughter, ecstasy are nothing. Hegel hastily rids himself of them: he knows no other end than knowledge. To my eyes, his immense fatigue is linked in my mind to his horror of the blind spot. The completion of the circle was for Hegel the completion of man. Completed man was for him necessarily "work": he could be that man, himself, Hegel, being "knowledge". For knowledge "works", which poetry, laughter, and ecstasy do not. But poetry, laughter, ecstasy are not completed man – do not give "satisfaction"

(EI, 113)

For Bataille, any idea of completion, of a completed man, is worthless. His theorization of the burst of laughter is the very example of disruptive explosion of sovereignty (as poetic or erotic effusion, anger, ecstasy...): it withdraws the sovereign instant from the horizon of meaning and knowledge. It pulls sovereignty out of dialectical logics. Derrida writes: "Laughter alone exceeds dialectics and the dialectician: it bursts out only on the basis of an absolute renunciation of meaning, an absolute risking of death, what Hegel calls abstract negativity" (Derrida, 2005, 322). The burst of laughter is the almost-nothing into which meaning sinks, absolutely.

As we said, the non-logic of sovereignty requires another relationship to time and temporality. For Bataille, the employment of the present time for the sake of the future (i.e. considering the *result*) is irrecoverably *servile*. Sovereign is the moment when nothing counts but the moment itself. It can't be calculated, it can't be anticipated. "What is sovereign in fact is to enjoy the present time without having anything else in view but this present time" (AS 2, 199).

Sovereignty, then, can only be a *consciousness* of the moment (but not a consciousness in the Hegelian sense, as a moment in the epic of absolute knowledge). The "experience of the instant" is the temporal mode of the sovereign operation: it is effusive, furtive, and akin to a miracle. The sovereign moment is "the miraculous sensation" of having the world at one's disposal. To freely take advantage of the world and of the world's resources, partakes in some way of the miraculous. "Beyond need, the object of desire is, humanly, the miracle; it is sovereign life, beyond the necessary that suffering defines" (AS 2, 199).

How does a miraculous moment of sovereignty manifest itself? It appears among us in the form of beauty, of wealth – but also in the form of violence, of funeral and sacred sadness: the sovereign partakes at once of the divine, of the sacred, of the ludicrous or the erotic, of the repugnant or the funereal. "It is really the object of laughter, or the object of the tears, that suppresses thought, that takes all knowledge away from us" (AS 2, 203). Sovereignty lies in this immediacy where the process of thought and calculation is suspended. Thus the sovereign moment is for Bataille at the same time, so to speak, an instance of "unknowing".

Knowledge is always, to some extent, instrumental and thus subordinated to useful ends. Even science, although it can be said to be *disinterested*, is always subject to the primacy of the future over the present, and is given to us in a discourse, by unfolding in time. "To know is always to strive, to work; it is always a servile operation, indefinitely resumed, indefinitely repeated. Knowledge is never sovereign: to be *sovereign* it would have to occur in a moment. But the moment remains outside, short of or beyond, all knowledge" (AS 2, 202). On the contrary, sovereignty is the rare state of unknowingness, accessible only in moments: "We know nothing absolutely, of the moment. In short, we know nothing about what ultimately concerns us, what is *supremely* [souverainement] *important to us*" (AS 2, 202–203). In other words, thoughts auto-dissolve into nothing and become sovereign at the instant they cease to be thoughts as such. Overwhelming and ecstatic *effusions* disrupt the chains of thought. Laughter, tears, intoxication, play, festivity, sexual ecstasy, sacred terror are the privileged moments that allow human beings to live in the present. This implies to cede any position of power, of knowledge, of calculation. "Consciousness of the moment is not truly such, is not sovereign, except in unknowing. Only by cancelling, or at least neutralizing, every operation of knowledge within ourselves are we in the moment, without fleeing it. This is possible in the grip of strong emotions that shut off, interrupt or override the flow of thought" (AS 2, 203).

The Archaic Paradigm of Sovereignty

The Splendour and Misery of Archaic Sovereignty

The second part of Bataille's book, after the considerations on method, is constituted by a meditation on specific modes of sovereignty. The notion of sovereignty is historically rooted in archaic sovereignty, embodied in the notion of royalty.

In the past, sovereignty belonged to those who, bearing the names of chieftain, pharaoh, king, king of kings, played a leading role in the formation of that being with which we identify ourselves, the human being of today. But it also belonged to various divinities, of which the supreme god was one of the forms, as well as to the priests who served and incarnated them, and who were sometimes indistinguishable from the kings; it belonged, finally, to a whole feudal and priestly hierarchy that was different only in degree from those who occupied its pinnacle.

(AS 2, 197)

Generally, Bataille remarks, we consider the institutions of the past, if not as curiosities, then as realities definitely alien to what we are. Bataille's ambition is to take these institutions seriously and to reflect on the transition from societies based on the requirements that sovereignty satisfied to societies of the modern type. Sovereignty can be said to be an *institution* in the sense that it is not foreign to the people: the state of mind of the sovereign, of the subject, is subjectively communicated to those for whom he is the sovereign. "The royal splendor does not radiate in solitude. The multitude's recognition, without which the king is nothing, implies a recognition of the greatest men, of those who might aspire on their own account to the recognition of others" (AS 2, 248). Therein lies the profound ambivalence of sovereignty *as a political form*: it generates by itself the possibility of servility insofar as it is distributed and divided into ranks:

Whether priestly or royal, the dignities always compose a hierarchy in which the various functions form ranks that, ascending from one to the other, in some way support that supreme dignity which, surpassing them all, alone possesses the fullness of being. But we have to say, on the other hand, that in this way being is always manifested to us in the degradation of ranks, usually tied to functions. Inevitably, the function is degrading. Anyone who takes it on labors, and is therefore servile. (…) In that comedy of splendor, mankind strove miserably to escape from misery.

(AS 2, 248)

A second paradox follows: on the one hand, revolution is a legitimate though violent reaction to an obscenely wasteful feudalism. It opens the way to the idea and the existence of an egalitarian consumption. But on the other hand, the Soviet system, through the dictatorship of the proletariat, lets the objectivity of power take its place. With the choice of the logic of the objectivity of power, sovereignty is renounced, sovereignty is *denied*. In the socialist world created by Stalin, the free disposal of the excess that characterized the "surplus" in Marx's definition is no longer available, either for non-productive personal expenditures or for accumulation: the product of labour exceeding the personal needs of the worker is immediately re-distributed in accordance with the collective need.

These paradoxes are of decisive importance to Bataille's meditation. The historical forms of sovereignty are analysed in terms of the crucial distinction between profane (productive) and sacred life. It was the major preoccupation of archaic mankind, Bataille claims, to define alongside the profane world, a sacred world; alongside the man constrained to serve, a sovereign man; alongside profane time, a sacred time:

> Archaic man was mainly taken up with what is sovereign, marvellous, with what goes beyond the useful. (...) Modern man disregards or undervalues, he tends to disparage or deny, that which archaic man regarded as sovereign. Archaic man endlessly posed the question of sovereignty; for him it was the primary question, *the one that counted as sovereign in his eyes.* (...) For, in a way, he *knew* that sovereignty cannot be the anticipated result of a calculated effort.
>
> (AS 2, 226)

Within this structural distinction between profane and sacred, the labour of profane existence, Bataille argues, can be understood as ultimately a denial of mortality: the profane individual, forever living for the future rather than in the present, is doomed to a living death. Sacred life is, on the contrary, a repudiation of the profane world's values of utility and productivity. Precisely: traditional sovereignty was defined by the *consumption* and expenditure of wealth, rather than its *production*, which in Bataille's view is always servile and alienated.

But still, the ambivalence of the archaic form of sovereignty is intrinsic: "Royalty was, in one and the same movement, splendor and a miring down. A considerable emphasis was placed on magnificence, but it was never able to lift itself out of the mud" (AS 2, 248–249). This basic disdain for the world of sovereignty, now a thing of the past, is justified by the crudeness of its foundations. And of course, Bataille writes, it would be an aberration to regret the religious and royal edifice of the past. That edifice was only an "enormous failure", and there is no way to imagine for a moment the possibility of a going back. "If we wish in turn to have an acquaintance with sovereignty, we must have other methods" (AS 2, 229). Nonetheless, archaic sovereignty gives us a glimpse of the sudden openings beyond utility that Bataille seeks:

> Laughter, tears, poetry, tragedy and comedy – and more generally, every art form involving tragic, comic or poetic aspects – play,

anger, intoxication, ecstasy, dance, music, combat, the funereal horror, the magic of childhood, the sacred – of which sacrifice is the most intense aspect – the divine and the diabolical, eroticism (individual or not, spiritual or sensual, corrupt, cerebral or violent, or delicate), beauty, crime, cruelty, fear, disgust, together represent the forms of effusion which classical sovereignty, recognized sovereignty, undoubtedly does not conjoin in a complete unity, but which virtual sovereignty would, if we were to secretly attain it. I have not exhausted, I know, those sudden openings beyond the world of useful works, which – even if the supreme value of these openings is denied, as it is in our time, when the political game takes the place of sovereign displays – continue to be given to us.

(AS 2, 2230–231)

Revolution as the Subversion of Sovereign Power

Bataille asserts that the great revolutions (whether bourgeois or proletarian) had as their purpose the abolition of the feudal order, of which sovereignty is the ultimate meaning. "I wish to stress, against both classical and present-day Marxism, the connection of all the great modern revolutions, from the English and the French onward, with a feudal order that is breaking down. There have never been any great revolutions that have struck down an established bourgeois domination. All those that overthrew a regime started with a revolt motivated by the sovereignty that is implied in feudal society" (AS 2, 279). Revolutions, he insists, have occurred in societies of the feudal type, in which the use of wealth was not yet reserved for the accumulation of productive forces (which is the bourgeois paradigm).

The unexpected conclusion of this analysis is that bourgeoisie and the proletariat are *in an equivalent position* with respect to feudality. "All the great revolutions of the modern world, which are linked to the struggle against feudality, have tended to oppose these sumptuary expenditures, regarded as aberrant. They were the doing of masses united by their incomprehension of the preoccupation with and habits of prodigality, which the landed proprietors as a whole represented. When the bourgeoisie established quite different systems, based on the accumulation of a large part of the resources with a view to industrialization, the popular masses never joined together to overthrow the established order. These masses have never united *except in a radical hostility to the principle of sovereignty*" (AS 2, 288). Proletariat and bourgeoisie share the same reprobation of the concern with ostentation, which is the absolute prerogative of sovereignty. According to Bataille, only the June days, the Commune and Spartacus can be considered exceptions since they are the only violent convulsions of the working masses struggling against the bourgeoisie. Wasteful expenditure *versus* accumulation: in the feudal world, there was a preference for a sovereign use, for an unproductive use, of wealth (erection of churches, castles, palaces). The preference of the bourgeois world is reserved, on the contrary, for accumulation (and the multiplication of the means of production: the installation of workshops, factories or mines).

Since both are on the side of the logic of accumulation, the bourgeoisie and the proletariat share a world in which sovereignty is denied. On the part of the bourgeois, accumulation is of course the result of a choice; the bourgeois are free to invest their resources in productive enterprises (and then free to indulge in extravagant spending). The workers, if they accumulate, do nothing but emphasize the *necessity* that accumulation satisfies; but at the same time, they dismiss the possibility of giving the present moment precedence over the future. This is exactly where the ambiguity of the communist project lies, according to Bataille. The situation of communism raises, from the point of view of sovereignty, a new problem – particularly if we consider communism as an objection to those things that men previously held to be sacred. "Thus, communism is the basic problem that is posed to each of us, whether we welcome it or reject it: communism asks us a life-and-death question" (AS 2, 366).

Yet, according to Bataille, nothing can alter the fact that communism, having earned the credit for raising and keeping open the problem of "egalitarian consumption", has not solved it. Even worse, egalitarian consumption is in fact related to a new paradigm of accumulation. Hence, the society that is most antithetical to Bataille's notion of sovereignty is Stalinism, which gave communism an unexpected form. The aggressive economic planning which took place in Russia (an agrarian, industrially backward country, with a juridical structure more or less feudal) in the 1930s might be called the "primitive accumulation" of socialism in one country – in other words, the process was not structurally different from that described by Marx in England, by which one social class accumulated in its hands the means of production, while other classes were being deprived of their land and means of livelihood and reduced to the status of wage-earners. Impelled by the necessity to industrialize a feudal society, Stalin's economics turned out to be another kind of accumulation. From the point of view of the "general economy", this imperative of production and accumulation is in total contradiction to the idea of sovereignty. The result was a society in which the individual's access to pure and extravagant consumption was totally subordinated to the goal of increasing national productivity. Stalinism developed another alienation, by creating a society unable to live in the present moment. In that sense, Stalinism mirrored the economics of the bourgeois worldview.

Sovereignty as a Subjectivity

In order "to consider the problems of sovereignty in the present world" (AS 2, 261), Bataille needed to consider broadly the question of communism. "Present-day humanity has the communist horizon before it. (…) Today, sovereignty is no longer alive except in the perspectives of communism. It is only insofar as the convulsions of communism lend life to it that sovereignty takes on a vital meaning in our eyes. Hence I will not seek the meaning of sovereignty directly, but rather that of communism, which is its most active contradiction" (AS 2, 261).

Neither feudal sovereignty nor communism are able to exemplify the meaning of sovereignty Bataille is looking for. But both are of decisive importance, even if history cannot solve the problem of sovereignty. "I cannot forget that only communism has raised the general question" (AS 2, 365). However, "in a practical sense, the use of resources for non-productive ends cannot be given as the goal of history. I even maintain the contrary: that if history has some goal, sovereignty cannot be that goal, and further, that sovereignty could not have anything to do with that goal, except insofar as it would differ therefrom" (AS 2, 281).

Sovereignty, as the fundamental principle of Bataille's ethics has to be found elsewhere, then. Nietzsche becomes a key reference in this situation: where communism is a system of sovereignty denied, Nietzsche provides a vision of *sovereignty affirmed*. Bataille identifies with Nietzsche: "I am the only one who thinks of himself, not as a commentator of Nietzsche but as being the same as he. Not that my thought is always faithful to his: it often diverges from it […] But that thought is placed under the same conditions as was his. There was nothing sovereign that the historical world offered him that Nietzsche could recognize" (AS 2, 367). What makes Nietzsche a "man of sovereign art" is his refusal of the reign of things, his resistance to the idea that science was mankind's end. Fundamentally, sovereignty is the enjoyment of the miraculous abandonment to objects of desire.

Nietzsche is the "man of sovereign art" *par excellence*: sovereign thought envisages a complete separation from the world of things (i.e. objective activity) and from subjectivity. But "the inner experience that guides me" (AS 2, 241) to an insight of sovereignty, this experience of moments beyond the realm of utility, is hardly communicable. Discourse is forever impotent to give access to the moment of sovereignty, which can only be experienced through eroticism, transgression, intoxication, cruelty, sacrifice... It submerges the possibility of dialectics and discourse, not simply by means of an interruption, but through an opening suddenly uncovering the limit of discourse and the beyond of knowledge. Inner experience is this interior journey in a presence in no way distinct from absence, where "the mind moves in a strange world where anguish and ecstasy coexist" (IE, 4).

The enigma is that we are definitely disarmed: we will never *know* how to make a sovereign moment take place. There can't be any deliberate effort or work *toward* a sovereignty (for sovereignty has no identity, is not self nor toward itself). In order not to govern and in order not to be subjugated to the order of things, the sovereign moment subordinates nothing and is subordinated to nothing or no one. It expends itself without reserve, is indifferent to any possible results, even loses consciousness and memory of itself. "Real" sovereignty frees human existence from the bonds of necessity. But at the same time, "the main thing is always the same: sovereignty is NOTHING" (AS 2, 430).

Reference

Derrida, Jacques. 2005. *Writing and Difference*. Translated by A. Bass. London: Routledge.

10 Eroticism

Nadine Hartmann

> What is peculiar to modern societies, in fact, is not that they consigned
> sex to a shadow existence, but that they dedicated themselves to speaking
> of it *ad infinitum*, while exploiting it as *the* secret.
>
> (Foucault 1978, 35)

> Nothing interests us more than forcing out the secrets of eroticism.
>
> (AC 2, 17)

While eroticism stands at the center of Georges Bataille's earliest
literary writings it does not explicitly enter his theoretical reflections
until the 1940s, only to then take center stage.[1] Bataille even planned
to edit a journal, in collaboration with art historian Patrick Waldberg,
tentatively named *Genèse*, whose programmatic subtitle was supposed
to be "Sexology, Psychoanalysis, Philosophy of Sexuality" (cf. Kendall
2007, 207). This journal would have continued Bataille's attempts to
theorize eroticism in "Alleluia: The Catechism of Dianus", written in
1944 and released as an appendix to *Guilty* in 1961.Written in the
quasi-mystical style characteristic of the greater *Summa Atheologica*
project, the text presents an ode to love, specifically, an ode to Bataille's
second wife-to-be, Diana Kotchoubey (cf. Surya 2002, 353). Bataille
elaborates on his key ideas on eroticism in a more systematic manner in
"The History of Eroticism" and *Eroticism*: these texts treat of the
conjuncture of extreme pleasure and pain, Christian mysticism, the relation of the abject and death. "The History of Eroticism" was intended to
be – and would posthumously become – volume two of Bataille's study
of general economy, *The Accursed Share*. Bataille began working on it
in 1950, accumulating texts he had written for the journal *Critique* in
the years prior and slowly giving definition to what could be called a
"phenomenology of eroticism" (Kendall 2007, 190). Along with

Eroticism, it gives the most concise account of Bataille's understanding of eroticism.

Bataille's aim was to establish a notion of eroticism as a paradigm of the sacred, even as *the* most sacred of all experience. The sacred unfolds itself in all its ambivalence in erotic experience with those aspects that are considered low and animalistic. Reflection on this ambivalence set the grounds for elaborating a specifically human "self-consciousness" that has "nothing as its object" (AC 1, 190). The experience of pleasure in eroticism is tightly bound with seemingly contradictory states of fear and pain. I am going to elaborate on how these antagonistic settings play a cardinal role in Bataille's theory of eroticism and how they are approached by way of transgression and prohibition. I will also address the question concerning the kind of relation Bataille's writing generates between knowledge and pleasure. This question is increasingly addressed in the reflections on methodology in Bataille's writings on eroticism, and it constitutes a principal concern later on for Michel Foucault, particularly in his last writings on the history of sexuality.

Transgression and prohibition

In the predominant figurative meaning that determines today's use of the word, "transgression" denotes primarily the violation of the divine commandment, the intolerable infringement of religious dogma, or, simply, sacrilege. It is already in this context that the ambivalence of the notion emerges from a definition *ex negativo* to become a potentially liberating act in the Pauline interlacement of limit/prohibition/law and transgression: "Moreover the law entered, that the offence might abound. But when sin abounded, grace did much more abound" (Romans 5:20 KJB). In the course of secularization, transgression came to be associated with both the straightforward violation of the law and of the conventions of decency and tastefulness.

For Bataille, transgression constitutes the exceptional moment of a breaking-through the sphere of the profane into the sphere of the sacred. His thought is organized around fundamental dualisms of which "the sacred" and "the profane" are arguably the most essential. The practices and occurrences of the everyday dictated by utility and capital accumulation belong to the sphere of the profane. The sphere of the sacred is characterized by exceptional states of excess and wastefulness in which alone the subject has the chance to experience its own sovereignty. In structural terms, the particular feature of this arrangement consists in the fact that transgression remains contingent on the limit; hence also the challenge to think transgression as movement rather than as a fixed state. The Latin *gressus*, step, hints at the notion of movement that lies at the core of the word. Transgressing is exceeding, crossing a limit that, as Michel Foucault noted, does not come to life until approached in such a way. Foucault meditated on the dialectical interdependence of limit and transgression in his 1963 homage to Georges Bataille, "A Preface to Transgression":

> The limit and transgression depend on each other for whatever density of being they possess: a limit could not exist if it were absolutely uncrossable and, reciprocally, transgression would be pointless if it merely crossed a limit composed of illusions and shadows.
>
> (1977, 34)

It is important to note that in Bataille's understanding, transgression is only momentarily reached in experiences of the sacred in brief instants of continuity, as they occur in practices of ecstasy, one of which is eroticism. The transformation of the first men who negated their own animality by building tools with which they could alter their environment is repeated in the transition from paganism to Christianity, repudiating the former with similar horror (cf. AS 2, 61–63). While in paganism the pure and the impure aspects of the sacred were integrated, Christianity purifies the sacred as such and contrasts it with the profane and impure, forbidden world (cf. AS 2, 132–133). It is at this point, according to Bataille, that transgression needs to be re-mobilized in order to negate these prohibitions in turn, and retrieve the enriched, originally ambivalent nature of the sacred. The historical development takes place as follows:

> The spirit of this early world is impossible to grasp at first; it is the natural world mingled with the divine; yet it can be readily imagined by anyone whose thought is in step with the processes; it is the human world, shaped by a denial of animality or nature, denying itself, and reaching beyond itself in this second denial, though not returning to what it had rejected in the first place.
>
> (E, 85)

The experience of the sacred must not be eliminated in the secular age – since in "an entirely profane world nothing would be left but animal mechanism" (E, 128). The void that is left by the "death of God" needs to be acknowledged, consequently, not as a form of disenchantment, but, as Foucault underscores, as sovereign inner experience: "The death of God does not restore us to a limited and positivistic world, but to a world exposed by the experience of its limits, made and unmade by that excess which transgresses it" (Foucault 1977, 32). As a negation of negation, transgression does not suppress the law but suspends it temporarily – not in a Hegelian suspension or sublation but in a way that exposes a space for the experience of the sacred.

Staying true to the demands of the greater *Accursed Share* project, in "The History of Eroticism", Bataille follows a historical and anthropological line of argument, in which the constitutive role of prohibitions informing society is central. Bataille here draws on Claude Lévi-Strauss' theory of the taboo. The structural truth of prohibition becomes recognizable in the examples given of forbidden objects: prohibition seeks to neutralize and domesticate destructive and violent elements of human life in order to ensure the stability and homogeneity of a society. These prohibitions primarily concern sexual activity and the commerce with the dead. The historical development that separates mankind from animals is advanced by three main developments: (1) prohibitions, (2) the experience of work, and (3) awareness of death, and, along with this, the repulsion for elements related to death and the dead body. Our animalistic origin has to be repressed in human society since it is at once the shameful reminder of our baseness and our finitude: "Mankind as a whole resembles those *parvenus* who are ashamed of their humble origin" (AS 2, 62).

The humble origins of mankind are mirrored in our ontogenetic origins. They emerge in certain repulsive objects associated with the process of birth as well as that of death – that is, with points in time at which we are not yet or no longer a subject. In the chapters headed "The Natural Objects of Prohibitions", we find the foundation for what Julia Kristeva would come to call the *abject* (cf. Kristeva 1982) – a concept closely related to Bataille's idea of the heterological. Bataille speaks of an "object of horror […], a fetid, sticky object without boundaries, which teems with life and yet is a sign of death" (AS, 295); in this object we can recognize the abject, which crosses transfixed boundaries, is neither subject nor object, but can manifest itself in bodily fluids and principally in the corpse. The corpse is at the same time the human subject and the object rendered human – the most unsettling impact of its appearance is precisely in this peculiar instability. These heterological elements are destabilizing, both to the subject and to the homologically formed society and must therefore be kept at bay by taboos and prohibitions. The role these base and abject

elements play in the realm of eroticism becomes an increasingly dominant concern in Bataille's theory. The parts that are rejected from the
body politic have their equivalents in the human body. At the moment
of *Documents*, Bataille's corporeal example for the materialistic base of
the idealized head was the big toe; it is now the "hairy parts under-
neath your dress" (G, 147) that constitute a repressed but – or rather:
therefore – significant part of human truth.

> You must know in the first place that everything with a manifest
> face also has a secret one. Your face is noble. The truth in its eyes
> comprehends the world. But the hairy parts underneath your dress
> have as much truth as your mouth. These parts secretly open on
> filth. Without them, and without the shame associated with using
> them the truth that is known by your eyes would be mean.
>
> (G, 131)

Eroticism implies a return to the animalistic origins of man, yet it can
only be an ecstatic experience insofar as it incorporates the
consciousness of prohibition.

In the first section of his 1957 *Eroticism*, Bataille repeats and minimally modifies his earlier theses, mainly by adding two more sets of
antonyms to the theory. "Continuity" and "discontinuity" are the central
terms in this study. These new categories can readily be integrated into
the Bataillean universe of dichotomies: accumulation-expenditure,
homogeneous-heterological, profane-sacred.[2] Man is characterized as a
discontinuous being, defined by his separation from every other being –
a constitutive separation that cannot be entirely overcome. Continuity
is to be imagined as a "state of perfect immanence" (TR, 19), which is
natural only for animals as they are "in the world like water in water",
as Bataille's dictum from the *Theory of Religion* has it (TR, 23). While
for humans the desired continuity can only be reached in death, it can
be temporarily approached in the moment of transgression. In erotic
experience, one can lose the "feeling of self" which distinguishes the
discontinuous being (E, 99). Eroticism demands that one give oneself
away and abolish the imaginary wholeness of the being, a process
which demands a great deal of violence (cf. E, 17–18). The idea of a
continuity to be approached in eroticism should not be mistaken for
the phantasmatic ideal of a fusion between two individuals. It is rather
an affirmation of the violence of the act described as "the frenzied
desire to lacerate and to be lacerated" (G, 141). In this violence, the
foreignness inherent to one discontinuous being constitutes the point of
communication with the other's foreignness.

Pleasure and desire

The prohibitions that set man apart from animals are reflected in the distinction in terminology, which accentuates the specificity of eroticism: while "sexuality" denotes the physical activity that ideally results in reproduction, "eroticism" is the practice of expenditure and futile enjoyment.[3] Since eroticism is an experience that does not serve any purpose outside itself, it needs to be considered in the sphere of general economy, the term introduced in *The Accursed Share* to designate economic activities governed by the principle of wasteful expenditure:

> The truth is that we have no real happiness except by spending to no purpose, and we always want to be sure of the uselessness of our expenditure, to feel as far away as possible from a serious world, where the increase of resources is the rule.
>
> (AS 2, 178)

The "increase of resources" would in this case not only include reproduction but also the search for unambiguous pleasure, defined as avoidance of pain. This is why Bataille's eroticism should not be conflated with the Freudian *eros*, just as Bataille's pleasure is not continuous with the *pleasure-principle*, the latter being ultimately a restrictive principle, protecting us from experiencing *too much* pleasure. Bataille had recognized this protective function and dismissed the pleasure-principle as merely utilitarian already in his seminal 1933 essay "The Notion of Expenditure", the first statement of the theses of *The Accursed Share*:

> The goal of [supposedly material utility] is, theoretically, pleasure – but only in a moderate form, since violent pleasure is seen as *pathological*. On the one hand, this material utility is limited to acquisition (in practice, to production) and the conservation of goods; on the other, it is limited to reproduction and to the conservation of human life (to which is added the struggle against pain, whose importance itself suffices to indicate the negative character of the pleasure principle instituted, in theory, as the basis of utility).
>
> (VE, 116–17)

"Pleasure", as it turns out, is a peculiar term for that which Bataille's wasteful acts are supposed to give.[4] Rather than denoting joy or lust, it is generated in "an act whereby being – existence – is bestowed upon an *unbearable* surpassing of being, an act no less unbearable than that of dying" (MM, 126). Eroticism is not necessarily tied to (genital) sexuality, as is shown by the striking fact that Bataille's texts on eroticism all reference accounts of mystic experience, as well as the texts of de Sade, when attempting to speak of this "violent pleasure".

> In speaking of their raptures, mystics wish to give the impression of a pleasure so great that the pleasure of human love does not compare. It is hard to assess the degree of intensity of states that may not be incommunicable, perhaps, but that can never be compared with any exactness, for lack of familiarity with other states than those we personally experience. But it does seem allowable to think that we may experience, in the related domains of eroticism and religious meditation, joys so great that we are led to consider them exceptional, unique, surpassing the bounds of any joy imaginable.
>
> (AS 2, 103)

By contrast, another term central to eroticism is much more communicable: desire. For Bataille, eroticism is not possible without desire, and desire is not possible without fear. The general thesis that we can only experience the sacred when the stakes are high once more serves as the operative principle behind this equation. First of all, the object of desire has to be unattainable. This object is later more precisely qualified as another desire – we desire the desire of our partner in eroticism, even when this object cannot be known from outside: "Without doubt, the intellect remains behind and, looking at things from the outside, distinguishes two solitary desires that are basically ignorant of one another. We only know our own sensations, not those of the other" (AS 2, 113). This idea owes a great deal to the influential theory of desire as the origin of self-consciousness that Alexandre Kojève had presented from 1933 to 1939 to a prestigious audience (including, besides Bataille, Jean-Paul Sartre, Jacques Lacan and Maurice Merleau-Ponty among others) (cf. Kojève, 1980).

Rather perplexingly, Bataille continues to postulate the ultimate object of erotic desire as the prostitute. Two questions arise in the face of this claim: (1) Does the prostitute not turn eroticism into a commodity, thereby profaning it? (2) Bataille established earlier that the object of desire is first and foremost the other's desire. But can we assume any desire at all in the prostitute *per se*? It may be there – or it may just be faked, a means to an end. Bataille acknowledges and responds to the former objection, yet leaves the latter unaddressed. Generally, Bataille here refers to the sacred prostitutes who accepted luxurious gifts for their services, whereas his elaborations on the subject in

Eroticism subdivide prostitution into religious and "low" prostitution. Low prostitution itself is not classified as eroticism, since the prostitute is completely shameless (and does not even feign shame), and therefore does not generate awareness of the prohibition she transgresses. Moreover, she lacks the means and the ambition to embellish herself. This embellishment, however, is vital for eroticism as it accentuates the specific kind of beauty suitable to attract erotic desire; a sovereign beauty that can only be such when it cannot be subjected to the laws of utility.

> [...] women subjected to a factory job have a roughness that disappoints desire, and it's often the same with the crispness of businesswomen, or even with all those women whose dryness and sharpness of traits conflict with the profound indolence without which a beauty is not entirely feminine.
>
> (AS 2, 147)

These reflections on the ideal erotic object provide insight into a – not exactly highly original – male fantasy: "[...] passivity is in itself a response to desire's insistence. The object of desire must in fact restrict itself to being nothing more than this response; that is, it must no longer exist for itself but for the other's desire" (AS 2, 143). By confining his theory of desire to the most stereotypical and rigid grid of gender roles, Bataille runs the risk of contaminating it with cliché. An alternative, more favorable reading would reverse the order and see in Bataille's attempt to make the prostitute personify his vision of the sacred not an endorsement of existing gender roles, but rather their subversion. The prostitute, then, would be the paradigm of a sexual difference that would not be thought on the basis of a model of equal and mutual ownership. Her desire is desirable not in spite of, but because of its categorical unattainability. She is indeed sacred, but in the sense of her being quintessentially untouchable. Here we might find the theoretical framework in which the literary apotheosis of the whore Madame Edwarda takes place: the whore who calls herself "God".

Eroticism and knowledge

Bataille began to negotiate his methodology with regard to the discussion of eroticism in his "History of Eroticism". Criticizing scientific approaches which attempt to speak of the sexual domain – psychoanalysis among them – Bataille imagines a "procedure [...] in which [...] eroticism and thought would no longer form separate worlds", a particular challenge since thought is inherently "asexual [...], antithetical to sovereignty" (AS 2, 23). *Eroticism* adds some new elements to meet this challenge. The question of method arises in a rather pragmatic context in a chapter of the book dedicated to the Kinsey reports, an early version of which was first published in Bataille's journal *Critique* in 1948. Bataille here clarifies his position vis-à-vis the books *Sexual Behaviour in the Human Male* and *Sexual Behaviour in the Human Female* that were published to great public response in 1948 and 1953 respectively. The books present the results of an extended series of interviews conducted by sexologists in which the participants gave detailed accounts of their sex lives. The essential critique Bataille voices in the face of these statistics is that they take an objectifying view of eroticism, assuming that man can be studied like a thing. In contrast, Bataille insists that where animals can be treated like objects, humans cannot, as they exceed all biological and cognitive classification: "[O]nly a serious lack of understanding would confuse something different in kind, something sacred, with a mere thing" (E, 155).

Examining modern sexuality was the task of Foucault's 1976 *The Will to Knowledge*. His essential argument consists in a refutation of what he called the "repressive hypothesis", which holds that modern sexuality is characterized chiefly by its repression, and thus implies that power relations are mainly to be understood negatively. If the prohibitions and restrictions concerning sexuality were lifted, so the hypothesis goes, our free, positive sexuality could be uninhibitedly acted out without sanction or censorship. As is well known, Foucault, on the contrary, posits power in a Nietzschean vein as positive and all-encompassing; there is no "beyond", "outside", or "against" which would lay bare our natural sexuality. The imagined liberation from repression is advanced by a "*scientia sexualis*", a discursification of sex that offers the uncovering of the "secrets" of sexuality through confession and via incessant discussion of them. While sexuality has always been discursively integrated, Foucault finds the assumption that there is an underlying, historically uncorrupted sex to be equally flawed. While the repressive hypothesis is the principal assumption of many discourses about the relation between society and sexuality among Bataille's contemporaries on the left, Bataille, nonetheless, I would argue, cannot easily be aligned with such writers.[5] When he underscores the affinities of religious and erotic experience, he refers mostly to ancient cults and non-European religions. The banning of eroticism from the sphere of the sacred then is Christianity's offence – to this extent, Bataille seems to agree with the repressive hypothesis. Yet – and this is Bataille's recourse to transgression – any prohibitions Christianity imposes on us ultimately increase the potential for a deeper pleasure. Even if Christianity does not acknowledge the ambiguous meaning of the sacred, Bataille takes it to be preserved in the sovereign moments of life (cf. AS 2, 132–4). The question is thus whether Bataille criticizes the repressive hypothesis or whether he just points to the fact that all knowledge purportedly gained from a scientific examination of human sexuality is inherently dubious and deficient. Unlike Foucault, Bataille seems not overly concerned with the possibilities of regulation and power that the practice of a "*scientia sexualis*", such as the Kinsey reports, generates. Instead, he points out the ridiculous tone the study assumes, thereby invalidating its impact. Bataille hardly feels threatened by the reports since he finds them marked by a certain "impotence" (E, 153). Yet most importantly, Bataille claims that there is an outside of discourse that cannot be approached by science, an "abyss [that] yawned beneath the facts they report" (E, 155). He thus attempts to reverse the "great process of transforming sex into discourse" (1978, 22) that is identified and condemned by Foucault. "What man means to us transcends details of this sort"; thus "true knowledge of man's sexual life" (E, 154) is not to be gained through the scientific reports. For Bataille, such "true knowledge" does exist and he avidly seeks for ways to access it for "nothing interests us more than forcing out the secrets of eroticism" (AC 2, 17). However, Bataille's is a particular "will to knowledge".

Madame Edwarda's demand that the first-person-narrator take a close look at her genitals – "you've got to see, look…" (MM, 135) – is emblematic for Bataille's fundamental drive to gain knowledge about inaccessible realities. This impossible desire shifts through different objects in the course of Bataille's life and writing: from the gazing at the blinding sun in "The Jesuve" (VE, 73–8) and in *The Story of the Eye* to the staring at the photograph of the tortured Chinese man in *Inner Experience* and *Guilty*. These attempts are exemplary for the transgression at the core of Bataille's project: the point at which experience and knowledge are no longer separated. "I think like a girl takes off her dress. At its most extreme, thought is immodesty, obscenity itself" (IE, 175) – pleasure and knowledge, thought and obscenity coincide in Bataille's writing. Even though the experimental, self-conscious style of the *Summa Atheologica* is dismissed in favor of a more systematic approach in his later writings, the aporetic endeavor of "thinking that which exceeds thought's possibility" (MM, 126–7) is never abandoned:

> Our minds' operations as well never reach their final culmination save in excess. What, leaving aside the representation of excess, what does truth signify if we do not see that which exceeds sight's

possibilities, that which is unbearable to see as, in ecstasy, it is unbearable to know pleasure? What, if we do not think that which exceeds thought's possibilities?

(MM, 126–7)

It should be noted that Foucault, too, presents a possible counterpart to the confession on which the *scientia sexualis* relies: the *"ars erotica"*, as practiced in many eastern societies, is a tradition that revolves around the truth of and the achievement of pleasure. I would argue that if we follow Foucault's reconstruction of a pre-modern *ars erotica* as opposed to the modern *scientia sexualis*, Bataille's approaches to eroticism, even at their most systematic, stand in the tradition of the former. Bataille's quest for the knowledge of eroticism is focused on the truth of pleasure itself. As in the *ars erotica*, the secrets of eroticism cannot be confessed but only experienced. The modern addition to this practice is Bataille's consciousness of the prohibition, which he perversely employs to add to his pleasure. "You are in the power of desire, spreading your legs, exhibiting your forbidden parts. If you ceased to experience this position as prohibited, desire would die at once, and with it, the possibility of pleasure" (G, 133 trans. mod.). This "formula" for pleasure is an especially blatant reminder of the Christian heritage insofar as it mirrors or mimics Paul's letter to the Romans: "What shall we say then? Is the law sin? God forbid. Nay, I had not known sin, but by the law: for I had not known lust, except the law had said, Do not covet" (Romans 7:7 KJB). Foucault, somewhat enigmatically, concludes his book on modern sexuality with this demand: "The rallying point for the counterattack against the deployment of sexuality ought not to be sex-desire, but bodies and pleasures" (Foucault 1978, 157). And the *forte* of Bataille's writing was not, as I have tried to show, analyzing desire but rather remaining respectful to the truth that is the secret of a multi-layered pleasure: "And there would be no knowing what is happening if one were to know nothing of the extremest pleasure, if one knew nothing of extremest pain" (MM, 125).

Notes

1 Shorter texts of Bataille's, such as "The Solar Anus" and "The Language of Flowers" may be regarded as more experimental precursors to those theoretical works. Both texts sketch the idea of a parodic universe in which the obscene appearance of the genitals is mirrored in the forms of nature – in the cosmological movements of the planets in the first, and in particular flowers, in the second.

2 In *Literature and Evil*, Bataille adds another pair of attributes to this series: "feeble" as opposed to "powerful communication".

3 In "The History of Eroticism" as well as in *Eroticism*, Bataille fails to stay true to this distinction, using the alternating terms "sex", "sexuality", and "eroticism". I try to avoid confusion by sticking to Bataille's original categorization when possible.

4 Jacques Lacan came to describe a specific form of pleasure which he named "*jouissance*", which he defined as that which "serves no purpose" (Lacan 1998, 3), an inane form of enjoyment without any regard for the avoidance of pain, that is, without any regard for self-preservation. It seems very closely related to Bataille's "violent pleasure" and his "stubborn defiance of impossibility", more so than Freud's pleasure (*Lust*) would be. For more on the relation between Georges Bataille and psychoanalysis see: Roudinesco (1995) and Botting (1994).

5 It is most prominently proposed in the Freudo-Marxism of Wilhelm Reich, Herbert Marcuse and Norman O. Brown.

References

Botting, Fred. 1994. "Relations of the Real in Lacan, Bataille and Blanchot." *SubStance* 23/1, Issue 73, 24–40.

Foucault, Michel. 1977. "Preface to Transgression" in *Language, Counter-Memory, Practice: Selected Essays and Interviews*. Edited & translated by Donald F. Bouchard. New York: Cornell University Press.

Foucault, Michel. 1978. *The History of Sexuality. Volume 1: An Introduction*. Translated by Robert Hurley. New York: Pantheon Books.

The Holy Bible, King James Version. Cambridge Edition: 1769; *King James Bible Online*, 2015. http://www.kingjamesbibleonline.org/

Kendall, Stuart. 2007. *Georges Bataille*. London: Reaktion Books.

Kojève, Alexandre. 1980. *Introduction to the Reading of Hegel: Lectures on the Phenomenology of the Spirit*. Translated by James H. Nichols. New York: Cornell University Press.

Kristeva, Julia. 1982. *Powers of Horror. An Essay on Abjection*. Translated by Leon S. Roudiez. New York: Columbia University Press.

Lacan, Jacques. 1998. *On Feminine Sexuality: The Limits of Love and Knowledge*. Translated by Bruce Fink. New York & London: Norton & Company.

Roudinesco, Élisabeth. 1995. "Bataille entre Freud et Lacan: une expérience cachée" in *Georges Bataille après tout*, edited by Denis Hollier, 191–212. Paris: Belin.

Surya, Michel. 2002. *Georges Bataille: An Intellectual Biography*. Translated by Krzysztof Fijalkowski. New York: Verso.

11 Art

Michèle Richman

Sovereignty is the recurrent keyword when Bataille writes about art because, like sacrifice, art removes an object from the realm of *things*. As such, it is evidence of the human desire to be free from an exclusive subordination to work, production, and accumulation. Bataille's anthropology never disputes the primacy of tools and reasoning for the successful transition from animal to human life. But he also argues that irrespective of their level of material riches, cultures in all times and places have responded to the sovereign urge by diverting resources toward non-productive goals. Isolated in a world of thing-ness, where the horrors of death and destruction are repressed, individuals seek to transmute their anguish into the exaltation of a sovereign experience. Bataille's notion of sovereignty has little to do with material objects. Eroticism, poetic élan, cries, tears, spit, silence and laughter simulate sacrifice through a radical modification of the subject. Can the same be said of art?

A 1928 review of pre-Columbian art suggests the connection between art and sacrifice that would remain a constant of Bataille's thought. The introduction to Aztec society reinforced his understanding of sacrifice as contrary to the utilitarian premise that an offering is made in view of some ultimate recompense, including salvation. Instead, Bataille agrees with the interpretation proposed by Henri Hubert and Marcel Mauss (1981, first published in French in 1899), where the spectator identifies with the sacrificed object. Projected into the realm of death and non-being, the sacrificial victim mediates the collectivity's encounter with the menacing forces segregated by religion as sacred. Violence is liberated and the discontinuity separating individuals momentarily overcome. Because sovereignty is never an end point but an interminable process, it is impossible to predict when it will erupt in an artwork. Bataille's approach was to view art as a cultural and experiential phenomenon that trumps formal considerations. The

Lascaux study (1955), for instance, favors technically inferior figures because they communicate sovereignty. At the same time, he notes that their effect relies on some degree of artistic virtuosity. He readily acknowledges that his big questions were not a substitute for specialized scholarship. But it would also be wrong to conclude that Bataille's art publications simply provide legitimation for quirky predilections or an appealing venue for his heady mix of eroticism and recondite subject matter. Discussion of art and artworks is scattered throughout his sprawling work and frequently embedded in review essays; there are also two high-profile monographs in the prestigious Skira series, one on the painter Manet and one on the prehistoric art of the caves at Lascaux. In these writings, he reveals a deep-seated concern with the historical context of artistic production and reception.

A final testament to the centrality of art for Bataille's thought was exhumed from his unpublished notes. Despite a debilitating illness, he envisioned an *exalted universal history of art's glory in all times and places* (OC X, 1987, 729, n. 1).[1] How to understand such a project is the question for today's student. What did he mean by universal history and why is it coupled with art? Can we extrapolate from his published work the lineaments of a project to be fulfilled by future generations? These issues resonate in recent theories about art's social and political dimensions, just as they spur controversies about the place of global art in contemporary museum practices. Bataille's unorthodox answer is that humanity has always recorded its inner life in signs of revolt. Prehistoric rock paintings or Abyssinian children's graffiti may not yield a literal message. But by proposing an alternative to the tools used for work, art's various media bear the potential to communicate sovereignty.

Documenting sovereignty

Art does not provide obvious guidelines within the labyrinth of Bataille's writings. Few artists are discussed in any sustained way other than Édouard Manet, about whom Bataille wrote a commissioned monograph in 1955. But already in his early writings, one sees the importance of the problematic status of art in his thinking: in these texts, he argues that, even if individual artists offer local examples of rebellion, the place of art in Western culture is more accurately assessed by architecture's role in monumentalizing the principles of domination and authority. His indictment encompasses all manifestations of *construction* – whether evidenced in physiognomy, dress, music, or painting – as testaments to the moral straitjacket of idealism. Thus,

Documents, the eclectic review he edited between 1929 and 1930, leveled an iconoclastic and subtly subversive assault on the hierarchy within the arts in Western society (Bischof, 1984). Assisted by fellow excommunicants from the surrealist movement, Bataille contributed texts whose impact was bolstered by their symbiosis with the photographs of Eli Lotar and Boiffard. *Documents*, as Michel Leiris noted, was an *impossible* undertaking – a glossy journal of art in the minds of its backers, at odds with Bataille's determination to explore the impossible underside of bourgeois civilization. Bataille was responsible for a critical dictionary, whose entries apply scholarly references to seemingly banal or everyday objects which, when isolated and juxtaposed with esoteric figures, create an effect that critics have compared to the sensation of the uncanny (Fer, 1995, 167); or, for its de-familiarization, to an ethnographic surrealism (Clifford, 1988). Roland Barthes admired Bataille's ability to reinterpret icons of industrial civilization and even the body – one thinks of the big toe as well as the factory chimney – in affective terms that resist both the psychoanalytic police and the temptation to aestheticize.

Propelling art history toward the extremes of both cave painting and cubist modernism, *Documents* provided the platform for what is undoubtedly Bataille's most *exorbitant* claim about art. In his reading, archaic African rock painting points to

> a stupefying *negation of man*. Far from seeking to affirm humanity against nature, man, born of nature, here voluntarily appears as a kind of waste. [...] The blatant heterogeneity of our being in relation to the world that gave birth to it, which we have become incapable of proving through tangible experience, seems to have been for those among us who have lived in nature, the basis of all representation.
>
> (CH, 46)

To the extent art reveals anything, it is an awareness of humanity's violent *otherness* in relation to nature. This rupture is also manifested in prehistoric cave art's "shocking duality" (CH, 40), where rare outlines of human figures contrast with the abundant, masterfully rendered animals. Because there is no technical explanation for the disparity, Bataille interprets it as the archaic psyche's sense of inferiority to animals and confusion as to what it means to be human.

Prior to the discovery of the Lascaux painted cave in 1940, Bataille had already extracted from prehistoric sources his virulently anti-mimetic and anti-idealistic theory of art (CH, 35–44). Rather than in the iconic bisons of the Altamira cave paintings, he found the origin of art in the "formless" doodling that early humans left in their wake. Aurignacian palimpsests offer a dizzying puzzle of imbricated figures overlapping and intruding within a shared space. Their disregard for spatial boundaries sparked associations, he writes, with his own aggressive, libidinal childhood impulse to dabble ink on the pupil in front of him. If imitation was responsible for the birth of art, then it would have been a matter of humans following the example of bear scratches on cave walls. The unleashing of universal sadistic impulses leads to the destruction and alterations enacted by art, and it is through this process of "monstration" that humans discover themselves (Nancy, 1994, 70). Whereas such markings can eventually produce recognizable forms, that is not their primary intention. The emphasis here is on the process of repeated destruction and re-construction. Prehistory's sovereign scribbles are mirrored in the transgressive graffiti of Abyssinian schoolchildren, who deface the lower level of church columns despite the threat of punishment.

Bataille completed his early detour into prehistory with a return to modern art. An obvious rejoinder to those who would accuse him of anti-modernism, *Documents* was a prime outlet for the most radical artists of the first decades of the twentieth century. His admiration for Picasso's de-formations of the canonical human figure of western classicism explains their frequent appearance in the review. Bataille had wondered whether modern art would be capable of replacing archaic rituals and staging the encounter with the disruptive forces of death and sexuality. His answer appears in his description of modern art's impact on the conventional expectations of the viewer, when he compares its alterations to "a transformation that rather abruptly displayed a process of decomposition and destruction that was no less painful to a lot of people than the sight of the decomposition and destruction of a corpse" (CH, 43). *Alterations* is arguably one of the Bataillian keywords to which greater attention must be paid. Bataille would complete his discussion of the body's cycle by insisting on its alterations from an object of desire to a repugnant site of putrefaction to the sanctity of purified bones. A visual correlative was featured in *Documents'* photos of Catholic ossuaries filled with neatly stacked skulls, not unlike the earliest repositories of bear skulls on which Bataille would later comment.

When Bataille's position at *Documents* was terminated after two years and fifteen issues, his ambitions for a universal approach to art history were stymied. At first glance, *Documents'* eclecticism should have appealed to its sophisticated financial backers. But where the collector's eye is trained on market as well as aesthetic considerations, Bataille wanted to display "the most irritating, unclassified works of art and certain heterogeneous productions neglected until now, which will be the object of studies that promise to be as rigorous and as scientific as those of archaeologists" (quoted in Surya, 1987, 127). Both promises were fulfilled as the review challenged sacrosanct assumptions regarding the origins of Western civilization in Greek classical art, metaphysics, and cultural values. Scholars of Sumerian, Scythian, Chinese and Japanese art and archaeology showed how the myth of the Greek miracle relied on academic as well as popular versions of a widespread Orientalism Bataille was determined to undermine (Miller, 2006, 48). Almost a century after *Documents* was isolated by the interwar's reactionary classicism, its dialogue between the archaic and the modernist avant-garde animates current research (Chi and Azara, 2015).

Bataille would subsequently clarify that a universal history must encompass prehistory, a conviction that set the agenda for much of his final research. The term "universal" also connotes a totality distinct from the sum of its parts. The irreducible excess is generated by the alternation between prohibitions and their transgression, a social and psychic structure inherent to humans. Among those interdictions, the taboo surrounding death is the most prominent. Universal history therefore begins with Neanderthal burial sites, where human skeletons are intentionally placed along an east/west axis next to tools and animal bones, attesting to humanity's earliest reckoning with its own mortality. Although the conventional starting point for world art history is cave-painting, these rudimentary graves deliver a greater psychic charge according to Bataille. At a spatial remove from daily life, carved into the earth, they delineate the domain of the sacred from that of the profane.

Art communicates the sovereign play of transgression, thereby completing the meaning of prohibitions. Bataille never confuses the two realms of experience. Yet in 1943, Jean-Paul Sartre reproached *Inner Experience* for its overvaluation of the sovereign instant by reminding Bataille that he too must eat, sleep, and work at the Bibliothèque Nationale. Bataille's subsequent writings would take a more guarded approach to sacrifice in relation to sovereignty by directing caveats against the temptation to memorialize the instant of expenditure. Art would be an obvious culprit. The following section's heading – *The sovereign work of art* – suggests the dual duty of *work* as both noun and verb, in order to appreciate Bataille's revision of those key terms.

The sovereign work of art

Sovereignty traditionally refers to a position of political authority placed outside of legal jurisdiction. Most pressing for Bataille, however, was the exemption from work that sovereignty conferred on a privileged few. "Nothing," he noted, "is more anguishing than the concern to free the human spirit from the necessity dictated by work" (OC X, 713). But this echo of Marx's utopian thinking leads to a strikingly opposed conclusion: rather than a tantalizing future realm liberated from the constraints of necessity, Bataille insists that work is inevitable and therefore incumbent upon everyone. At issue is how sovereign moments can be envisioned without appearing to foist each individual's responsibility to work onto others. From the vantage of aesthetic concerns, is it possible to insist on the sovereign instant's apartness as a reminder of the need for revolt without falling into romantic clichés? Irreducible to a decorative framework for homogeneous exchanges, art must jolt the individual into a *continuum* among humans by creating an exhilarating sense of intimacy that work cannot provide.

The democratization of sovereignty would remain at the forefront of Bataille's post-war concerns while resisting any one political or ideological label. Acutely aware of art's traditional role in the religious consecration or political and social promotion of a sovereign few, his studies of Goya and Manet would turn on the politics of modern art's emancipation from the dictates of the *ancien régime*. But how would the art of the newly liberated individual displace the church and monarchy's crushing majesty, so effective in uniting the majority under its tyrannical sway (M, 25)? A 1949 review of Goya and the *democratic tradition* called for a methodological shift:

> *Few intellectual undertakings are of greater interest than the sociological analysis of art works.* Whether it is a matter of literature, plastic arts or architecture, traditional criticism has had little regard for the social or economic conditions or the class conflicts in effect at the time of a work's elaboration.
>
> (OC XI, 550, emphasis added)

Bataille's critique resonates with the discontent elicited by traditional art criticism in the post-war period (Rancière, 2002). Under the purview of philosophy since the end of the eighteenth century, its quasi-theological and moral posture had become anathema to the modern human sciences. A sociologically-inflected alternative, he argued, need not hew to a strict economic base/superstructure determinism. Correlations between rank and taste need to accommodate the vagaries of social and political history.

In his studies of Goya and Manet, the artist emerges as an allegorical figure of sovereign struggle, at once dependent on the system he is sapping from within (more so in the case of Goya since Manet was financially independent), while proposing a new aesthetic idiom. Sovereignty thwarts existing expectations, often incurring the derision of the very public for whom it should be most relevant. Why are republicans so conservative when it comes to art, Manet queried. Equally thorny is the question of history: Bataille reminds us that modern art's rupture with pre-revolutionary forms is evidenced in its absence of narrative. Manet's sovereign *indifference to the subject* relinquishes a story line, whether as a readily identifiable narrative or in a more literal allusion to a historical figure or event.[2] Just when Bataille's own discourse feels detached from the paintings themselves, it suddenly directs us to the dark intensity of Berthe Morisot's sovereign gaze in the famous *Le Balcon* scene, projecting beyond the confines of the balcony/barrier into the unknown.

Bataille's review of Goya illustrates his ability to extrapolate major historical movements from a single painting. It also provides welcome insights into how Bataille addressed his own aporias regarding sovereignty by means of another medium. Indeed, with his portraits of the *majo*, Goya recorded how a feudal version of sovereignty was espoused by a colorful figure of late eighteenth-century Madrid street life. Where their European counterparts were slavishly imitating the upper classes, the *majo* and his female companion set a sartorial standard for all of Spanish society, including the aristocracy, who would adopt their outlandish costumes during their own festivities. Politically, their way of dressing signaled antipathy to the French styles favored by a liberal faction of the Spanish ruling elites. Especially in the post-Napoleonic period, reactionary nationalist sentiment united traditionalists from every social rank. As exemplar of "the true nature of old Castille," the *majo* stood for a sovereign indifference to economic and social realities. The poor man's Dandy became the embodiment of a contradiction at odds with political, social and economic progress for centuries. Unsparingly critical of bourgeois cultural values, Bataille nonetheless concurred with Marx that capitalist accumulation is a precondition for economic and social modernization. With a bourgeoisie too close to the populace – especially when the latter was bound to an aristocratic persona of a generosity that belied its impoverished reality – Spain lacked a social group sufficiently "patient" to shore up the necessary resources for an investment in its future.

Within the Spanish showcase of social cross-dressing and inverted political allegiances, Goya displayed a remarkable double life, not unlike Bataille's own Janus-like existence. Grateful for his affluent patrons, courageously representing imperiled workers, disturbed by popular magic and religious fanaticism, *incomparable*, as Bataille says, in the depictions of madness, cruelty and violence he often kept from public view, Goya secured a place of distinction in Bataille's artistic pantheon. For his aesthetic translation of the insoluble contradictions roiling his culture of origin (in protest and frustration, he sought refuge in France for the last part of his life), Bataille concluded that Goya was the painter of the *impossible.*

Readers of Bataille will recognize "the impossible" as one of his key terms. Goya was the painter of the impossible for having expanded the sovereign instant to the point of death. Yet his allegorical value for sovereignty is limited. A hasty factura in many of his works reflects the same impatience noted above among his countrymen. It signals Goya's relative isolation due to total deafness and/or circumstances that did not foster the collective work needed to ensure the passage to modernity his work announces. By way of contrast, the daily intensity of friendship between Manet and the poet Stéphane Mallarmé consecrated their shared aesthetics of indifference to the bourgeois subjugation of art to narrow moral or social ends.

Art's sovereign communities

Bataille endorsed surrealism's imperative that art be produced by all, not one. He was vitally concerned with the moments of collective effervescence that the sociologist Emile Durkheim credited with the genesis of major cultural and religious forms, and he continued to seek the possibility of such moments under modern conditions. Bataille's numerous collective enterprises underline his conviction that aesthetic transitions occur within a broad network of social relations. Thus, the post-war studies of Lascaux and Manet show how the possibility for community was translated into the affinity experienced for certain artworks or artists. Social mediation through beauty was placed under the sign of friendship. It encompassed intimate collaborations with the artists André Masson and Jean Fautrier, or is evoked through the sovereign presence of the famous stick figure in Lascaux, discovered at the base of a shaft hidden deep within the cave's recesses. Suspended in a possibly trance-like state, this "formless" representative of humanity faces a raging, wounded bison emptying its entrails. The viewer is moved by its bird-head, a symbolic defiance of death according to Bataille. The conjunction between death and the figure's penile erection illustrates the French expression for orgasm, "*la petite mort*" or little death. Friendship is sparked by the exultation of the artist who confronted his own animality and death-fearing self, thereby attaining the sovereign majesty of the beautifully rendered animals throughout the major parts of the cave.

Bataille and Maurice Blanchot forged their friendship in pursuit of an aesthetics of sovereign silence. Bataille's 1955 study of Lascaux proclaimed that sovereignty was instantiated by the superb animals depicted. Their apparent indifference to language or work struck him as a rebuke to mankind's hard-won progress through subservience to prohibitions, and to what Blanchot characterized as the machine of language. Despite being tethered to the apparatus of linguistic production, both writers extolled the pure happiness in the face of death they discovered through sovereign silence. Bataille drew inspiration from fantastical, archaic animal/human figures, whose animal masks he interpreted as a sign of humanity's *shame* at having to work. Decades of researching composite figures, such as the *archontes* in *Documents* or the famous so-called Horned-god of the Trois-Frères cave, indicate Bataille's preoccupation with his own animality (Agamben, 2004). Two of his preferred icons of sovereign silence complete this brief survey. One, the celebrated prehistoric statue of a headless bear from the Montespan cave, dating from 20–30,000 years ago, is considered the oldest human clay sculpture on record. The other, the 1936 a-cephalic figure designed by André Masson for the review and secret society Bataille convoked under the title Acéphale. Between them lies the oft-cited Siberian legend of the bear "who could speak if he wanted," but whose "willed silence" is a sign of superiority over man (CH, 31). In the proverbial contest pitting words against images, these figures – animal-like, headless and wilfully silent – gesture toward the third way of Bataillian sovereignty.

Art as festival/festival as art

It is in his study of Lascaux that Bataille first crystallizes his controversial theory that art coincides with the festival, the moment at which the worker that *homo sapiens* first was, and still is, threw down the tools by which it was possible to transform nature. In so doing, early humans demonstrated their capacity to break the rules or prohibitions they had instituted in order to keep the disorder of death and sexuality at bay. Transgression marks the moment when necessity is transformed into abundance, and the products of human labor are sacrificed. Bataille hypothesized that interdictions on sexuality were also complemented by moments when erotic pleasure knows no end other than its own. In this moment of sovereign abandon, play prevails over purposeful activity. This view of prohibitions as an enabling structure is undoubtedly one of the most challenging moments of Bataille's anthropology:

> We may propose as fairly certain that, in the strongest sense, transgression only begins to exist when art itself becomes manifest, and that the birth of art fairly closely coincided, in the Reindeer Age, with the tumultuous outbreak of play and festival announced by these cave-painting figures, vying with one another in energy and exuberance that attain fullest expression in the game of birth and death played on stone.
>
> (LBA, 38)

Art emerges when the thing-ness of an object is sacrificed, its utilitarian significance annulled, and communication in the strong sense of sovereignty is realized. By attributing to art the status of a transgression, Bataille envisaged it as an instantiation of Nietzsche's hyper-morality beyond good and evil, beauty and ugliness.

Bataille's legacy

More than a half-century has elapsed since Bataille's death in 1962, when André Malraux banned his last book, *The Tears of Eros* (1961). Its visual orgy of eroticism and violence documents Bataille's final epiphany: art is the privileged site for an encounter between *divine ecstasy* and its opposite, *extreme horror* (TE, 207). While exploring the relation of art to cruelty, earlier essays had warned against the aestheticization of extreme situations intended to provoke a sense of sacred terror. The stated goal of *The Tears of Eros* was to expand a conscious awareness of such possibilities without aspiring to liberation from their obsessive effects. Rather than aesthetic criteria, the basis for inclusion compares with the typology proposed for literary texts – those to which their authors had been *constrained*. Bataille's recurrent illustration is his own necrophilia – including arousal by his mother's dead body. The Bataillian aesthetic's shock quotient is thus intensified by its willingness, as well as ability, to depict states of being that escape volition, but to which the subject bears witness.

By the mid-1970s, the Bataillian reworking of certain categories and notions in relation to excess – whether sovereignty and heterogeneity, or expenditure and the accursed share – pervaded the critical discourse of disciplines committed to deconstructing their foundational basis. The repercussions for art criticism of his anti-architecture were equally wide-ranging, proposing nothing less than a rebuttal to the Vitruvian premise that representative art originated with the reflection of Narcissus in the light of architectural verticality (Hollier, 1989). Lascaux offered an alternative mythological space, led by the charging bull in labyrinthine obscurity. Despite the increased availability of his work, however, references to Bataille in architecture and art criticism initially lagged in comparison with acknowledgments of his pre-eminent influence on contemporary continental philosophy. Some works have filled the lacunae in the United States (Krauss, 1986, 1993; Jay, 1993; Tschumi, 1994), where art historians had not been attentive "to how his alternative mythological practice ... unravels the neat categories of a too formulaic modernism" (Krauss, 1986, 153).

That Bataille was "passionate about images"(Bercé, 2006, 24) is evidenced in the profusion of commentaries, exhibitions – including his own drawings (*Underground Surrealism*, 2006) – and artistic practices inspired by some facet of his involvement with the visual arts. But recognition for the Bataillian aesthetic, whether reprised in terms of the "formless" (Krauss, 1986, Bois and Krauss, 1997), rending resemblance (Didi-Huberman, 1995), the sacrificial sacred (Biles, 2007) or the sovereign instant (Kennedy, 2014), is fraught with the risk of betraying its radical heterogeneity. Scholars therefore have proposed counter-histories of art and aesthetics (Didi-Huberman, 1995, 2000; Gauthier, 2006; Richman, 2007) by foregrounding the techniques of montage and anachronisms found in *Documents*. Arguably among his most influential writings, contributions to *Documents* have been singled out for translation. (*October*, 1992, *Encyclopedia Acephalica*, 1995). An outstanding recent monograph in English devoted entirely to sovereign aesthetics has bolstered scholarly recognition for this aspect of his thought (Kennedy 2014). Bataille himself would remind us that a sacrificial aesthetic commits art to an endless task, at once safeguarding sovereign indifference from appropriation, while subjecting it to a *ravishment without repose* (OC XI, 485).

Note

1 Unless indicated otherwise, translations from the French are my own.
2 Indifference is a keyword for Bataille. Because of its proximity to sovereignty, we have chosen to cite it without further discussion.

References

Agamben, Giorgio. 2004. "Acephalous". In *The Open: Man and Animal*, trans. Kevin Attell. Stanford, California: Stanford University Press.

Barthes, Roland. 1984. "Les sorties du texte". In *Le bruissement de la langue: Essais critiques IV*, 271–283. Paris: Les Editions du Seuil.

Bercé, Yves-Marie. 2006. "Bataille et l'histoire des mentalités". In *L'Histoire-Bataille. Ecriture de l'histoire dans l'oeuvre de Georges Bataille*, ed. Laurent Ferri and Christophe Gauthier, 21–26. Paris: Librairie Droz.

Biles, Jeremy. 2007. *Ecce Monstrum. Georges Bataille and the Sacrifice of Form*. New York: Fordham University Press.

Bischof, Rita. 1984. *Souveränität und Subversion: Georges Batailles Theorie der Moderne*. München: Matthes & Seitz.

Bois, Yve-Alain and Rosalind Krauss. 1997. *Formless: a user's guide*, New York and Cambridge, Mass.: MIT Press.

Chi, Jennifer and Pedro Azara, eds. 2015. *From Ancient to Modern: Archaeology and Aesthetics*, Princeton: Princeton University Press.

Clifford, James. 1988. "On Ethnographic Surrealism." In *The Predicament of Culture: Twentieth-Century Ethnography, Literature, and Art*, 117–151. Cambridge, Mass.: Harvard University Press.

Damisch, Hubert. 1995. "Du Mot à l'aspect. Paraphrase". In *Georges Bataille après tout*, ed. Denis Hollier. Paris: Belin.

Didi-Huberman, Georges. 1995. *La Ressemblance informe ou le Gai Savoir visuel selon Georges Bataille*. France: Editions Macula.

Didi-Huberman, Georges. 2000. *Devant le temps. Histoire de l'art et anachronisme des images*. Paris: Editions de Minuit.

Fer, Briony. 1995. "Poussière/Peinture: Bataille on Painting". In *Bataille: Writing the Sacred*, edited by Carolyn Bailey Gill, 154–171. London and New York: Routledge.

Gauthier, Christophe. 2006. "Documents: De l'usage érudit à l'image muette". In *L'Histoire-Bataille. Ecriture de l'histoire dans l'oeuvre de Georges Bataille*, ed. Laurent Ferri and Christophe Gauthier, 55–69. Paris: Droz.

Hollier, Denis. 1989. *Against Architecture: The Writings of Georges Bataille*, translated by Betsy Wing. Cambridge, MA: MIT Press.

Hollier, Denis. 1992. "A Documents Dossier," *October* 60: 25–29.

Hubert, Henri and Marcel Mauss. 1981. *Sacrifice: Its Nature and Function*, trans. W.D. Halls. Chicago: University of Chicago Press.

Jay, Martin. 1993. *Downcast Eyes: The Denigration of Vision in Twentieth-Century French Thought*. Berkeley: University of California Press.

Kennedy, Kevin. 2014. *Towards an Aesthetics of Sovereignty: Georges Bataille's Theory of Art and Literature*. Cambridge Station, Palo Alto: Academia Press.

Krauss, Rosalind E. 1986. "Antivision." *October* 36: 147–154.

Krauss, Rosalind E. 1993. *The Optical Unconscious*. Cambridge, MA: MIT Press.

Miller, C.F.B. 2006. "Archaeology" in *Undercover Surrealism. Georges Bataille and Documents*, eds. Dawn Ades and Simon Baker, 43–48. London and Cambridge: MIT Press.

Monod, Jean-Claude. 2006, "L'Art avant l'histoire, ou comment Bataille célèbre Lascaux." In *L'Histoire-Bataille. Ecriture de l'histoire dans l'oeuvre de Georges Bataille*, ed. Laurent Ferri and Christophe Gauthier, 107–121. Paris: Droz.

Nancy, Jean-Luc. 1994. *Muses*, trans. Peggy Kamuf. Stanford: Stanford University Press.

Rancière, Jacques. 2002. *Malaise dans l'esthétique*. Paris: Galilée.

Richman, Michèle. 2007. "Spitting Images in Montaigne and Bataille. For a Heterological Counterhistory of Sovereignty." *Diacritics*, vol. 35, no 3: 46–61.

Surya, Michel. 1987. *Georges Bataille: La mort à l'oeuvre*. Paris: Librairie Séguier/Frédéric Birr.

Tschumi, Bernard. 1994. *Architecture and Disjunction*. Cambridge, Mass.: MIT Press.

Warin, François. 1994. *Nietzsche et Bataille. La parodie à l'infini*. Paris: Presses Universitaires de France.

Wilson, Sarah. 1995. "Fêting the Wound: Georges Bataille and Jean Fautrier in the 1940s." In *Bataille: Writing the Sacred*, edited by Carolyn Bailey Gill, 172–192. London and New York: Routledge.

12 Religion

Mark Hewson

Bataille's thought takes on a new inflection in the 1930s after his short-lived engagement with the group Contre-Attaque. The political activities of this group were perceived by the members themselves, as well as by others, as having been unsuccessful. Bataille nonetheless at once re-directed his energies into the formation of Acéphale. There is no great rupture at the level of the ideas: the "Program (relative to Acéphale)", the first position statement of the group was originally written for Contre-Attaque. But the Acéphale group comes to define itself in opposition to the immediately political aspect of the preceding group's activities. Political conflict is now denounced as futile and depressing, but also, and more importantly, as tangential to the real crisis, and the group's own existence is referred to as "religious" in its meaning. The first issue of the journal of the group takes an epigraph from Kierkegaard: "What looks like politics and imagined itself to be political, will one day unmask itself as a religious movement" (VE, 179). At moments, Bataille will describe Acéphale as an attempt to found a religion. In a draft for a preface to *Guilty*, referring to this period, Bataille writes "I was resolved if not to found a religion, at least to move in that direction" – although he also writes that this was a "monstrous error" (OC VI, 369, 373). We will not enter here into the details of this strange history; but the thought of this time is invaluable for locating Bataille's thought in relation to its own social and political horizon. One still finds much, if not all, of the position represented by the texts written in connection with Acéphale in the post-war books such as the *Theory of Religion, The Accursed Share*, or *Eroticism*, even if these works present themselves with the detachment of philosophical and historical reflection. In particular, the Acéphale movement allows one to understand why religion is such a central topic in these books, even when it is apparently remote from the ostensible subject-matter.

One can give a rapid sketch of Bataille's thought at this time in referring to "The Sacred Conspiracy" (1936), published as the opening text of the first issue of the journal Acéphale. The text has the style of the avant-garde manifesto, and proclaims a war on civilization in its present-day form. European civilization, it is said, offers only a life that is "reasonable and learned, without attractions"; all that can be said for it is that it is "convenient". Life in society has been narrowed down to the pursuit of self-interest and the obligation to work. Above all, this society offers nothing to be loved – "as a man loves a woman":

> In the past world, it was possible to lose oneself in ecstasy, which is impossible in the world of mundane civilised man. The advantages of civilization are compensated for by the way that men make use of them. Present day men make use of it in becoming the most degraded beings of all those who have existed.
>
> (VE, 179)

The degradation is not attributed to any kind of moral decline or to deficiencies in the political institutions of the day, but precisely to the highest values of this society – to reason, logic and science. By identifying ourselves with Reason, we place ourselves in a condition of servitude, and more even, we impose this same servitude on all that there is: "The Earth, as long as it only gave rise to cataclysms, trees and birds, was a free universe; the fascination of freedom was tarnished when the Earth produced a being who demanded necessity as a law above the universe" (VE, 180). Freedom, then, – at every distance from the tradition of Kant and Hegel – is the freedom to exist without reason. "Acephale", the figure of man without a head, designed by André Masson for the journal, announces a humanity that has recovered the freedom of the Earth.

Already on the basis of this brief programmatic text, one can mark out two ways in which the conditions of Bataille's thought are given by the situation of religion. In the first place, the decline of established religion and the "death of God" announced by Nietzsche, the central philosophical reference of the Acéphale texts, is an essential condition of this discourse, since it alone makes possible a critical reflection on the *function* that the notion of God has served up until the present time. Now that we are no longer bound by them, we can recognize that the teachings of the Church have served to provide a rationale for the universe. This diagnosis goes together with Bataille's consistent interest in archaic forms of religion – invoked in "The Sacred Conspiracy" with the reference to the "past worlds" – which do not have such a rationalizing function. It is fundamental to Bataille's thought that the dominance of the Judaeo-Christian tradition in Western culture has distorted our understanding of religion: as it begins to lose its force, it becomes possible to re-situate this tradition as one element within a universal history of religion.

These theses are given their most comprehensive – if not necessarily their most accessible – form in the *Theory of Religion*. An attempt to give his philosophy of religion systematic exposition, this book was written in two months, in 1948, but then left unpublished by Bataille, despite its high degree of completion.[1] The book divides into two parts – the first proposing an interpretation of archaic religion, and the second giving a historical sketch of the steps by which religion came to assume its present-day form.

The theory of archaic religion begins with a reflection on the anthropogenesis, a question which is fundamental to Bataille's post-war writings. The principle that the transition from the animal to the human takes place with the use of tools is generally admitted in pre-history and archaeology, but as Bataille argues in his later writings, its significance for philosophical anthropology still remains to be fully exploited.[2] The use of tools is not simply an additional capacity possessed by humans, from which they gain an adaptive advantage, but results in a fundamentally new relation to the world. In the terminology of the *Theory of Religion*, work initiates a relation of "transcendence". It interrupts the situation of immediate participation in the elements of the world, experienced by animals, whose condition is designated by contrast as one of "immanence". "The tool brings exteriority into a world in which the subject has a part in the elements that it distinguishes [...]" (TR, 27–28). Bataille argues that the very emergence of objects as such, in the sense of stable and known entities, is dependent on this transition. It is only once things are worked upon, once they are transformed in view of an ulterior result, that they begin to be recognized as having their own independent existence and duration, beyond the sequence of "attractive or distressing phenomena" which he imagines to make up the animal experience (TR, 25).

Work does not only create the conditions under which objects can be perceived and known, but also locates objects within a definite horizon of meaning. To eat something, as an animal, is simply to annihilate it, but to work upon a thing is to change its very nature: it is to *subordinate* it to a purpose that is exterior to what it is. Human work constitutes what Bataille calls in this text "the order of things" (or sometimes "the real order"), a world of things defined in their very being by their usefulness in relation to our purposes. The entry into this order, he suggests, is always experienced at some level as a privation:

> Generally speaking, the world of things is perceived as a fallen world. It entails the alienation of the one who created it. This is a basic principle: to subordinate is not only to alter the subordinated element, but to be altered oneself. The tool changes nature and man at the same time: it subjugates nature to the man who makes the tool and who uses it, but it ties man to a subjugated nature. Nature becomes man's property, but it ceases to be immanent to him. It is his on condition that it is closed to him.
>
> (TR, 41)

The *Theory of Religion* thus both repeats and modifies the position of "The Sacred Conspiracy". It re-states the diagnosis of a fundamental alienation afflicting the human being; but this claim is no longer directed against Western humanity, with its cult of Reason and logic; instead, it is identified with the human mode of being as such, which originates with the rejection of its immediate participation in the world in the interest of assuring its preservation. Later in the text Bataille writes: "Man is the being that has lost, and even rejected, that which he obscurely is, an indistinct intimacy" (TR, 56).

Now, religion, Bataille proposes, is essentially "the search for the lost intimacy" (TR, 57). In other words, religion is the attempt to recover what is lost in the very transformation by which humanity as such comes into being.[3] This word "intimacy" is a central term for Bataille, especially in this work and in *The Accursed Share*. It creates difficulties for the translation of his texts, because the range of meaning in the French word *(intimité)* is wider than the English "intimacy". The metaphorical potential of amorous contact, the dominant sense of the English word, was utilized in "The Sacred Conspiracy", when it was said that modern civilization no longer offers its inhabitants a world that can be loved "as a man loves a woman". The term "intimacy" preserves this metaphor in the *Theory of Religion*; but it takes on a more precise terminological sense within the framework of the argument identifying the human mode of being with work. Intimacy is the contrary of alienation: it designates the relation to the world that is excluded by the intentional structure of work. To work is to have a distance, a reserve in relation to the world. "Intimacy", by contrast, signifies a giving of oneself to the world which, just like amorous intimacy is at once a risk to the self and also a satisfaction that is not to be had in the attitude of reserve, the holding-back demanded by work and by the operations of reason.

The material basis for Bataille's thesis comes from research in ethnography and the sociology of religion in the tradition of Durkheim and Mauss. An annotated bibliography attached to the *Theory of Religion* lists a number of works from this tradition.[4] Like many other texts of Bataille, this work gives a central place to the phenomenon of sacrifice. The interpretation advanced here is articulated in terms of the contrast – which we have seen at work in "The Sacred Conspiracy" – between the subordination that is imposed upon things by human reason and the freedom or the "caprice" of the earth: "Sacrifice destroys the bonds of real subordination of an object; it draws the victim out of the world of utility and restores it to the world of unintelligible caprice" (TR, 43). The defining trait of sacrifice is not killing, but giving away, abandoning:

> What is important is to pass from a lasting order, where all consumption of resources is subordinated to the need for duration, to the violence of an unconditional consumption; what is important is to leave a world of real things, whose reality derives from a long-term operation and never resides in the moment – a world that creates and conserves (that creates for the benefit of a lasting reality). Sacrifice is the antithesis of production, which is accomplished with a view to the future; it is consumption that is concerned only with the moment.
>
> (TR, 49)

The religious sense of sacrifice is encapsulated in the term "consumption" (*la consumation*) – a key word in Bataille: it was the title planned for the first volume of *The Accursed Share*, when this text was to reappear as part of a three-volume work. Here again there are difficulties for the translator, since the word is chosen for its difference from the normal sense of consumption (*la consommation*), a distinction which English effaces by folding both senses into one word. The relevant sense of the word here is that which the verb "consume" has in expressions such as "consumed by fire", or "consumed by passion".[5] Consumption, in this sense, is "violent", not because of the physical violence involved in the act of killing, which is, after all, an everyday affair in agricultural production, but because it is not governed by the imperative of self-preservation or the priority of the future good. "Paradoxically, intimacy is violence and it is destruction, because it is not compatible with the positing of the separate individual" (TR, 51). The separate individual, for Bataille, only comes to be in the order devoted to productive operations, in which the priority is given to the future. This fundamental reorientation is only possible under the condition of the suppression of the force of life, which dwells in the instant. The religious rites – the sacrifice and the festival – are structured in such a way as to allow for a controlled release (*déchainement*) of this force.

Since humanity has allowed itself to be constrained into a productive apparatus, its intimate life acquires a violent character in its release and manifests itself in destruction. The mixture of fear and fascination that characterizes anything that is considered to be sacred comes from this violence. For Bataille, the highly organized character of religious ritual is necessary, not in order to sacralize the place and the actions by purifying the profane elements (as Hubert and Mauss had argued in their study of sacrifice), but in order to protect the profane world from the contagion of the violence released within the limits set by the ritual. Religion is the annulling and the preservation of the order of things, Bataille reiterates at several points in this work: it interrupts work and accumulation, and allows for the reign of pure consumption, but it also limits this reversal by its restriction to the time and the space of the festival. In interrupting the productive character of everyday work, the religious festival also revokes the enclosure in the self of the individual. The sacrifice is the moment of a communication, a breaking of the barriers that are set up in the process of work, an opening on to what is common to all – and this common element for Bataille is precisely consumption, the intimate life that is suppressed in the order of work.

It is decisive for Bataille's presentation that what takes place here is not experienced in full consciousness. The festival and the sacrifice are given their meaning in relation to agricultural production, or the favour of the spirits that are invoked. Beyond these utilitarian meanings, they are also understood to affirm and consolidate the communal bond; but then a shift takes place in the understanding of community, which places it back in the horizon of self-preservation. The moment of "communication", when the individual dissolves into contagious consumption, the sacred intoxication, comes to be understood as the reaffirmation of the permanence of the group, the enacting of the social cohesion that makes possible collective work. "The basic problem of religion is given in this fatal misunderstanding of the festival" (TR, 56).

The second part of the *Theory of Religion* shows this misunderstanding at work in the historical process by which religion became what it is today. This history is certainly very schematic, proposing a sketch of universal history within a matter of 30 pages or so. It is evident that the concern is not to give an adequate representation of the actual historical process, but to identify the moments of a logical sequence, visible in the background of the realities, rather in the style of Hegelian history.

The archaic society centred on the sacrifice and the festival enters into a historical development with the emergence of what Bataille calls the military order. In archaic society, war has the same character of a "release" (*déchainement*) of violence as the sacrifice or the festival – except that the violence of war is directed outwards, at an opposing social group, rather than inwards, as in the sacrificial destruction of the property of the community or the transgression of the prohibitions by which it maintains itself (TR, 57–58). Unlike sacrifice, however, war has an inherent tendency to lead to acquisition. If this question becomes primary, and war is fought in the name of territorial gain and security, then it will lose the organized character, by which it resembles the games of the festival, and develop instead in the direction of the greatest effectiveness in the deployment of force. The shift goes together with a gradual decline in the importance of sacrificial practices. The society that is ordered around the military conquest and military rule preserves religious rituals inherited from archaic society, but it tends to moderate forms of ostentatious expenditure, as part of the drive for efficiency; at the very least, such practices are displaced from their position at the centre of social life, which is now located with the military authority (TR, 65–66).

The resulting transformation of society initiates a profound structure in the meaning of religion. Under the military order, religion is co-opted into the task of maintaining the internal order of society. In archaic society, social order was maintained by pre-moral prohibitions, based on emotional attractions and repulsions. The military order takes over these prohibitions as the basis for its own laws, but it chooses among them, preferring those more suited to its purpose, and understanding them as *serving* this purpose, rather than being simply given (TR, 70). The division of the sacred and the profane is reorganized as part of the rational and purposive ordering of society that is introduced with the ambition for conquest. The sacred sphere of archaic religion includes both benevolent spirits (those associated with ancestors for example) and dangerous spirits, which need to be appeased; and Bataille underlines that it is always the latter that are invested with greater sacred charge. Under the military authority, however, the sacred comes to be associated with the pure and the good, and the dangerous spirits are relegated to a secondary and marginal place (like that of the devil, in Christianity). The divinity is now the moral God, who gives his authority to laws and customs regulating moral conduct in the world.

In making the good divinity into the locus of the sacred, and in giving it a law-preserving function, the moral religion of the empire can no longer serve the same need as the archaic religions. It can no longer restore the "intimacy" that is lost with the entry into the "order of things". This can only be recovered in the violence that rejects or suspends this order, and not in conforming to moral principles ordained by the exigencies of production and military expansion. Bataille sees the religious reforms that have marked Western history as inspired by the renewal of the desire for "intimacy". Let us here very briefly sketch out the principal moments of this itinerary:

1   In general terms, the new religious structure of the military state is dualist, since it opposes the divinity, as the principle of the good, to the profane world that it governs. In its radical formulations, however, Bataille argues, the positing of a transcendent sphere "has the same intention as the archaic sacrifice" (TR, 76). In Plato, and more generally, in the religions of transcendence, the turn towards the "beyond" is accompanied by the rejection of the profane world of things. The violence of this gesture is comparable to that of the sacrifice; in each case, there is a resolute turning away from the exigencies of conservation that govern everyday life. Bataille can thus suggest that the turn towards transcendence represents an awakening of the desire for "intimacy", which is no longer satisfied once the sacrifice and the festival become routinized (TR, 77). Ultimately, however, the desire for intimacy cannot be satisfied by the contemplation or the reminiscence of the Ideas. The negation of the sensible world is "at once too complete and impotent" (TR, 76) and so the religion of transcendence relapses into the "sleeping position" of a dualism internal to the world, in which reason and morality are opposed to passion and self-interest with a view to the conservation of the order of things (TR, 77).[6]

2   In the crucifixion, which preserves elements of the archaic sacrifice, the Christ-narrative re-introduces the "violence" that is missing from the state religion. For this reason, Bataille argues, the figure of Christ offers the believer an intimate communication that is not possible with a benign moral God. Christianity is not explicit about its reliance on the source of its religious power, however. The crucifixion of Jesus is narrated and imagined as a crime. Christianity draws its intensity from the schema of the sacrifice, but it also projects the responsibility on to another (the Romans or the Jews), and condemns the act (TR, 82–84).

3   The Reformation rejects the principle of good works (charity, pilgrimages, etc.) by which the Catholic Church allowed one to "earn" salvation, in essentially the same manner as one carried out any other kind of activity in the world (TR, 87–88). In locating the

possibility of salvation solely with faith and with the grace of God, Protestant theology re-establishes the radical distinction between the divine order and the world of work, and thus marks a separation between the real meaning of religion and the order-preserving function that it can fulfil. However, although salvation is now dependent upon the gift of grace, and not on conformity to a series of prescriptions, it still implies the priority of the future over the present. In principle, however, Bataille argues, the return to intimacy – the essential impulse at the origin of religion – "can only be given in the instant, and in the immanence of the here-below" (TR, 88 trans. mod.). At one level, the Catholic Church had satisfied this criterion, since it gave a place to unproductive expenditure with its festivals and its cathedrals, even if it ultimately functioned as a moral authority, serving the conservation and the reproduction of the order of things.

The Reformation also had an additional and unintended consequence. Bataille here draws upon the analyses of Max Weber, who is discussed in more detail in *The Accursed Share.* In contesting the value of "works", the Reformation disallows economic activity any direct part in the religious life. But in purifying the religious sphere in confining it to the inner spiritual life and to divine election, it effectively grants autonomy to the economic sphere. Material life can in principle be freed from religious supervision from the moment that it is denied religious meaning. The conditions were thereby created for industrial capitalism, in which production and trade are subject to the sole imperative of accumulation. With the rise of this economic and social form, human life is integrated entirely into the production process, and the theological pre-conditions become progressively less important: "the millenial quest for the lost intimacy was abandoned by productive humanity" (TR, 92). The result is the institutionalization of alienation: modern man is "more estranged from himself than ever before" (TR, 93).

By a dialectical transition, however, Bataille argues that the atrophy of religion also creates the conditions for definitively resolving the reduction of human to the world of things – the problem to which, by his theory, religion has always proposed itself as the solution. The abdication of religion favours the development of what Bataille refers to as the "clear consciousness" (i.e. modern critical and scientific thought). This consciousness reduces all that is to the profane world, denying the existence of a separate sacred sphere, and critiquing the hybrid character of any understanding of this world which continues to be marked by mythic determinations (such as theological assumptions about the creation and the nature of the world). It carries this same practice of critique into the social domain, moreover, rejecting traditional and sacrosanct authority, and opening up the prospect of a more rational form of social organization.

For Bataille, however, the deficiencies of industrial capitalism cannot be resolved purely on the level of the distribution of tasks and resources, as is suggested by Marxism. The need for such a re-organization is not in question; but it can only be the precondition for a recovery of the human being from its instrumentalization and reification. What is necessary, Bataille argues, is to turn the light of science, which has illuminated the natural and the social world, on to the sphere of religious experience, on to "intimacy" (TR, 97). Certainly, here, the progress of the clear consciousness encounters a limit. As we have seen, "intimacy" is defined as the immediate participation that is lost in the constitution of the objective world, and so it cannot be given, as a thing within the world, among others. Consciousness is compelled to recognize "the obscure nature" of intimacy, "the night that it opens to discursive knowledge" (TR, 98). What is possible, however, is to critique the "equivocations" of the institutions of religion:

> The weakness of traditional understandings of the intimate order resides in the fact that they have always involved it in the operation; they have either attributed operative quality to it, or they have sought to attain it by way of the operation
>
> (TR, 99)

The "operation" here is a term for any kind of activity carried out within "the order of things", within "the real order". The sacrificial ritual has been given operative quality in that it is seen as bringing about a desired result (as in the sacrifice linked to agricultural production, for example); salvation has been sought "by way of the operation" in that it is seen as dependent on the performance of certain prescribed actions.

It is inevitable, Bataille states, that there should be some link between intimacy and the sphere of activity, since humanity has "placed its essence in the operation": it made itself what it is in its commitment to work. What has happened, however, with the institution of religion is that intimacy has been reduced to the operation: it has been given its sense within a sequence of actions, extended over a temporal axis. The critique of mythology and religion, effected by the modern consciousness, enables us to recognize this reduction, since the operationalization of religion is always effected by mythology – or to put it another way, the operational value of religion is essentially imaginary. Having recognized this principle, it is now possible to proceed to "the reduction of the reduction" (TR, 99). Instead of subjecting intimacy to the reality principle, instead of giving religious activities an operational value, it is possible rather to reduce operations to intimacy. This possibility can be grasped in terms of the most prosaic reality. In principle, it is already in action when the worker, manual or intellectual, puts aside the tools and takes a glass of alcohol, making the transition from a mode of being oriented towards the future good to a consumption that is absorbed in the instant (TR, 101–104). At this moment, consumption no longer takes place in order to make possible work and accumulation; rather that which has been acquired through conscientious work is consciously dissipated in the intimacy of consumption. "The real reduction of the real order brings a fundamental reversal into the economic order" (TR, 103).

In these concluding passages of the *Theory of Religion*, one sees the very close proximity of this work to the economic theories of *The Accursed Share*. Despite appearances, these two books do not really constitute two separate treatises, one concerned with religion and the other concerned with political economy. It would be more accurate to describe them as two approaches to the same central point, at which religion and economic activity cease to be distinct and independent domains of life. In the most general terms, the critical intervention of the *Theory of Religion* is to reduce and to relativize the element of moral authority and conservatism which plays so large a part in the ordinary understanding of religion. As we have seen, the law-giving and law-preserving function of religion is alleged to be the result of a shift in the social meaning of religion. For Bataille, historical and ethnographic research into archaic religions shows that these religions are essentially centred on the suspension of the profane order, which is the order of law, of self-preservation and of the individual. Religion then is originally identified with violence, desire and consumption: "Drunkenness defines in general the domain of religion", he writes in an essay from 1948, closely related to the *Theory of Religion* (OC XI, 325). This is no doubt a very provocative interpretation. But the claim is not primarily oriented towards an unmasking or a denunciation of the gravity of institutionalized religion, whose power of intimidation was in any case already much diminished. In the *Theory of Religion*, as in "The Sacred Conspiracy", the primary critical target is secular civilization, not the residual prestige of religion. Modern society has liberated itself from religious authority; but in the terms of the historical picture developed here, this emancipation only signifies that it no longer needs God, since "the order of things" is now preserved by the authority of the purely human good, given by instrumental reason. In his post-war texts, Bataille no longer proposes to found a religion, as at the moment of Acéphale, but his questioning of the modern economic and individualist order can still be located on the religious, rather than the political plane. Once religion is separated from the belief in God, as it is in this theory, it can serve to indicate the zone of obscurity at the origin of the theoretical and practical deficiencies of the society founded on the demise of this belief.

Notes

1   There are few indications as to why Bataille abandoned this tightly written little treatise when it was so close to completion. The notes to the *Oeuvres Complètes* reproduce a number of later plans for a multi-part work in which it is assigned a place, so it does not seem to signify a repudiation of the work. The text is very dense, and is perhaps not entirely intelligible without a reading of other texts of Bataille from the same period, especially *The Accursed Share*, published a year later, with which it stands in a very close relation. The section on the Aztecs in *The Accursed Share* re-states the analysis of archaic religion in the first part of the *Theory of Religion*; and section IV on the Reformation and the rise of capitalism works through much of the historical argument from the second part. The most detailed commentary of the *Theory of Religion* is Feher (1981), a general introduction to the later Bataille, built around a reconstruction of this work. Feher's excellent study elaborates Bataille's highly condensed analysis on many points.

2   See the concluding arguments of "Prehistoric Religion" (CH, 139 ff).

3   The structure of this argument is one of the points at which one can recognize the proximity of Bataille and Blanchot. This question of a relation that is eclipsed in the constitution of language and consciousness figures centrally in Blanchot's "Literature and the right to death" (Blanchot, 1949), and reappears in many subsequent texts. And it does not figure in Bataille's pre-war texts, prior to his encounter with Blanchot.

4   Much can be gained from considering Bataille in the light of this tradition, as has been shown by the recent studies of Michèle Richman (2002); Simonetta Falasca-Zamponi (2011); and Tiina Arppe (2014).

5   French has two verbs corresponding to these two meanings: *consommer*, by far the more common, corresponding to the ordinary meaning of consumption, where a useful purpose, such as nourishment, is understood to take place: on the other hand, *consumer* signifies the using up or destruction of a substance, without reference to any further use (as in "consumed by fire").

6   Here Bataille is drawing on *Le Dualisme dans l'Histoire de la Philosophie et des Religions* by Simone Petrément (a historian of philosophy and close friend, and later biographer, of Simone Weil) (Petrément, 1946). His 1947 review article of this work "Du rapport entre le divin et le mal" (OC XI, 198–207) develops arguments closely related to the position advanced in the *Theory of Religion*.

References

Arrpe, Tiina. 2014. *Affectivity and the Social Bond – Transcendence, Economy and Violence in French Social Theory.* London: Ashgate.

Blanchot, Maurice. 1949. *La Part du Feu.* Paris: Gallimard.

Falasca-Zamponi, Simonetta. 2011. *Rethinking the Political: the Sacred, Aesthetic Politics and the Collège de Sociologie.* Montréal: McGill-Queen's University Press.

Feher, Michel. 1981. *Conjurations de la Violence: Introduction à la Lecture de Bataille.* Paris: PUF.

Petrément, Simone. 1946. *Le Dualisme dans l'Histoire de la Philosophie et des Religions.* Paris: Gallimard.

Richman, Michèle. 2002. *Sacred Revolutions: Durkheim and the Collège de Sociologie.* Minneapolis: University of Minnesota Press.

13 Evil

Tiina Arppe

Bataille himself explicitly articulates the question of evil only in relation to modern literature (in *Literature and Evil*, 1957). Yet the theme is omnipresent in his texts: in the domain of economy his interest lies in the "accursed part" of the productive system; with regard to the sacred it is precisely the "impure" or "dark" side that fascinates him; instead of God, he is obsessed with blasphemy, and when examining eroticism he infallibly moves towards the question of sadism – not to speak of his notion of the social core which revolves around affective repulsion and is founded upon a crime. It does not seem like a gross exaggeration to characterise Bataille as the thinker of evil *par excellence* in 20th century French social theory. However, his conception of evil is of a particular sort, since it cannot be separated from his idea of "general economy" nor from his theory of sovereignty as the domain of the impossible, i.e. that which escapes representation. Of particular interest in this regard are thus not only his essays on literature, but also the connection of the Bataillean "morality" (if we can speak of such a thing) with his more general notions of economy and sovereignty.

Literature and Evil, written during the 1940s and 1950s, is in fact a collection of Bataille's essays from the revue *Critique* which he founded and directed from 1946 until his death. It poses the problem of evil in the framework of modern literature – along with de Sade and Genet, Bataille analyses the texts of Emily Brontë, Charles Baudelaire, Jules Michelet, William Blake, Marcel Proust and Franz Kafka. In the brief and enigmatic foreword of the book, Bataille claims an intimate connection between what he calls the "acute form of evil" – communication – and literature in its "essential" sense. The evil that he designates in this way has a "sovereign value" for man and demands not so much a morality as a "hypermorality" (the Nietzschean connotations of the formulation are hard to miss). It is precisely against this sort of sovereign evil, the necessary condition of the authenticity of any artistic enterprise, that

Bataille wants to reflect upon the literary project of Jean Genet. However, his argumentation is also intimately connected with Jean-Paul Sartre's reading of Genet's work, and more implicitly, with a larger debate with Sartre, started with the publication of Bataille's book *Inner Experience* (1943), of which Sartre wrote a rather bitter critique in the revue *Les Cahiers du Sud*, accusing Bataille of mysticism and latent Catholicism (Sartre 1947). The analysis of Jean Genet thus gives Bataille another chance to measure his differences with the leader of the existentialist school.

Jean Genet, certainly France's best known thief and homosexual in the 1950s, but also a reputed novelist, was greatly helped in his climb to literary fame by Jean-Paul Sartre, who wrote an epic seven-hundred-page psychological and philosophical treatise *Saint Genet: Actor and Martyr* (1952) as an "introduction" to the complete works of Genet. In this monumental and often merciless portrait Sartre proposes what could be called a "paradox of sovereign evil" which he claims characterises Genet's literary project. According to Sartre, Genet's work can be understood as a transformation of a curse coming from the outside (from society and the "decent people") into a vocation, an imperative value: they labelled me a thief, so a thief shall I be (sanctification of the evil). On one hand, Genet assumes evil as a divine nature, akin to a religious revelation; on the other hand, he wants it to be an act, assumed deliberately and consciously. Consequently, stealing becomes an act through which Genet both recreates his inner nature and sanctifies it as his eternal essence (Sartre 1952, 64–85).

However, Sartre notices an insurmountable paradox in Genet's attitude: in order for the evil will to be able to deny the good, it must first impose the good and want it; in other words, the evil will must not cease to hate its own evil deed and be horrified by it. But then the sovereign evil also presupposes that the evil-doer acts out of passion, i.e. for the evil itself, not for some other purpose exterior to it. Like the good, the evil demands to be its own reward, not a means to some other end. However, if the evil-doer is no longer horrified by his own deed, he turns it into a desirable thing, that is, into something good. Hence, concludes Sartre, sovereign evil is an impossible project (Sartre 1952, 174–193).

In Sartre's interpretation this fundamental paradox is also reflected in Genet's attempt to sanctify himself through words and in his ambivalent attitude towards his audience. Genet does not want to be a mere "thinking substance", but a demonic and sacred reality. This is why he transforms even the most cruel sufferings into signs of his own election, his chosenness into evil. Sacredness is transferred into words which become symbols of election. Genet is a poet who exalts his inner disgust in order to be able to bear it and who addresses his poems to a divine absence (to non-being or evil). But on the other hand, he also needs an audience with whom he has to be able to communicate in order to be read. The sanctification has to come from the others, the people he wants to shock and attract at the same time. According to Sartre, Genet in fact lures his readers to accept a universe which revolts them because of its moral ugliness, but which they are obliged to accept for its formal beauty. Although Sartre sees a certain optimism in Genet's work, because evil is presented as a result of freedom in the human being, his project is doomed to fail, because the recognition he gets is not granted to a criminal as it should be, but to a poet and novelist. He wants to be recognised as a person who has created himself, but his victory remains paradoxically on a purely verbal level.

These are the most important points which Bataille takes up in his own essay. He wants to emphasise Genet's fundamental aspiration to saintliness (*la sainté*) – which the latter nominates, by way of provocation, as the most beautiful word in the French language. However, Genet's saintliness only has one meaning, as Bataille points out: that of abjection – which makes repulsion the only way to reach it (LE, 177). Genet's saintliness is that of a jester, dressed and made up like a woman, delighted to be ridiculed. In the novel *Notre-Dame-des-Fleurs* (1944; trans. *Our Lady of the Flowers*) one of the characters (the one Genet himself largely identifies with), the gay prostitute and drag queen Divine, drops his coronet of false pearls which falls apart; all the "*tantouzes*" (faggots) of the cabaret are on their knees, trying to pick up the pearls, when Divine saves the situation with a gesture, in which comedy and tragedy, utter ridiculousness and sanctity intermingle: "She tears her bridge out of her open mouth, puts it on her skull and, with her heart in her throat, but victorious, she cries out in a changed voice, with her lips drawn back into her mouth: 'Dammit all, Ladies, I'll be queen anyhow!'" (Genet 2004, 66).

For Bataille, the aspiration to saintliness, and especially its horrifying, impure pole, is in Genet's case combined with an aspiration to sovereignty, but one that is paradoxically ridiculous. The exaggerated will to evil also reveals the fundamental signification of the sacred: the sacred is never stronger than when it is reversed (in Bataille's own texts "God" is often identified with obscene and vulgar realities – notably in *Madame Edwarda*). The horror is here mingled with ascetic vertigo: "Culafroy and Divine, with their delicate tastes, will always be forced to love what they loathe, and this constitutes something of their saintliness, for that is renunciation" (Genet 2004, 51). However, the fact that Genet associates his sovereign evil often with mundane, banal, or

even obscene things should not prevent us from seeing its ultimate –
and tragic – connection with punishment: Genet can only be sovereign
in evil, sovereignty itself is perhaps nothing else, and evil is never more
surely evil than when being punished. This is why of all crimes, murder
is for Genet the most magnificent: not only does it mean killing
another person, but it also entails the risk of being killed oneself in
punishment (LE, 179).

Unlike Sartre, who concentrates on the impossibility of sovereign
evil as a *project*, Bataille also insists on the revelation-like character of
Genet's sovereignty. It cannot be attained by conscious efforts, but
rather falls upon the subject like a divine grace. The beauty that Genet
is seeking in his books is always a transgression, an infraction against
the law, and this, according to Bataille, is also the essence of sovereignty:
sovereignty is the power (or ability) to rise, in the utmost indifference
towards death, above the laws guaranteeing the maintenance of life.
From this point of view, there is no fundamental difference between sovereignty and sacredness, since for Bataille (as for the whole Durkheimian
school before him) the sacred is essentially defined by the prohibition
(*l'interdit*) affecting it: the term "sacred" denotes that which is forbidden,
violent and dangerous, that with which the mere contact can bring
about destruction – in a word, it denotes evil. Genet's sacredness is of
the most authentic sort, since it transgresses the prohibition which
usually sets the accursed or forbidden apart, and protects it from any
mundane contact. His "morality" stems from the sentiment of a contact to the sacred – a sentiment generated by evil. Whereas classical
morality is linked to duration (being is that which endures or lasts),
sovereignty has its privilege or its excellence from its indifference
towards duration, even attraction to death (LE, 182).

The idea of transgression as an opening to sovereignty and sacredness
through evil is a pivotal element in Bataille's reading of Genet. Like
Sartre, Bataille notices the impasse into which Genet is driven when
trying to pursue evil consciously: when the aspect of horror is lacking,
evil is turned into an obligation. However, in Bataille's philosophical
anthropology, the transgression of the laws or symbolic prohibitions
which ensure the duration of being is elementally linked to human
existence. And this is precisely the blind spot of Sartre as far as Bataille is
concerned; Sartre sees the sacredness of Genet as a kind of vestige
from the primitive societies of consumption; for him it is an attitude
doomed to vanish in modernity. Although he sees Genet's poetry as
the most monumental attempt to salvage the sacred from the wreck of
the profane man, for Sartre this is but another form of self-deception, a
refusal to fully assume the consequences of one's own liberty

In this context Bataille attaches the notion of transgression directly to the ideas of morality and communication. In a debate on the concept of sin, organised in 1944, in which Sartre also participated, Bataille proposes the notion of a "moral summit" which he opposes to degeneration or decline.[1] The summit corresponds to excess and overabundance of forces, linked to an unlimited dissipation of energy – an idea which Bataille extends some years later to a cosmic scale in his notion of a "general economy", through which he understands the movements of energy on earth (AS 1). However, in this context, as in his pre-war writings more generally, the idea is linked rather to human affective economy, in which useless expenditure is integrally connected to a violation of the integrity and self-sufficiency of beings.[2] Thus, it is closer to evil than to good in the traditional sense of the term. "Decline", on the other hand, is linked with the exhaustion of forces and moments of fatigue. From this point of view, the overriding value which commands the everyday life is the enrichment and preservation of being. In the traditional sense, decline would thus define the moral good. Even though in Bataille's writings arguably the most important single difference between man and the other animals is the system of symbolic (cultural) prohibitions, paradoxically the communication between men entails the violation of these very same interdictions. This means that communication is only possible through the evil or crime – or as Bataille himself puts it, communication is love, and love taints those whom it unites (N, 18).

What must be emphasised in this context, however, is the distinction that Bataille makes between communication in a weak (traditional) sense of the term, and communication in a strong, demanding sense with which he himself is preoccupied. Usually communication is associated with the established universe of labour in which it is understood as conveying messages by means of the abstract notions of language. By contrast, the deeper communication which Bataille is after is at its strongest precisely where the barriers of language are transgressed. It does not refer to transmitting a message or meaning, but to the fleeting instant in which the boundaries of an isolated creature are being violated. "Communication" in this sense presupposes imperfection; it is linked to the idea that human existence is animated by a fundamental desire, the defining feature of which is to be insatiable, characterised by an essential lack. This conception was originally propagated by Alexandre Kojève in his lectures on Hegel, which postulate negation as the constitutive feature of human desire (Kojève 1947, 11–14). It can also be found in many of Bataille's contemporaries, Sartre and Lacan included (on this, see for instance Baugh 2003). The unsatisfiable nature of desire is due to the fact that its ultimate object is nothingness (*néant*).

The insatiable desire and the anguish it generates prompts human beings to reach out for what is beyond them. It is through this experience that the presence of the other being (*l'autre*) is revealed in Bataille's theory, but only insofar as the other also reaches out to the extreme limits of his/her nothingness. Communication can be described as the evanescent unification of wounds: it always requires this sort of mutual exposure, and can therefore occur only where existence is put at risk (N, 23–24; LE, 198–199).

The constitutive link between subjectivity, communication and useless expenditure is crystallised in Bataille's critique of the Sartrean notion of subjectivity. Bataille argues that Sartre places excessive emphasis put on the isolated, Cartesian subject. Whereas for Sartre the *cogito* is an inviolable and atemporal atom, the irreducible foundation of human existence, for Bataille it can be conceived only as a *relation*, the nodal point of real communications taking place in time. "Sartre reduces a book to the intentions of an author, the author. If, as it appears to me, a book is communication, the author is only a link among many different readings" (OC VI, 408). For Sartre this irreducible subjectivity of man is the domain *par excellence* of clarity and consciousness. Bataille, on the other hand, stresses its ultimately unfathomable and therefore scandalous character. Our consciousness is a scandal precisely because it is the consciousness *of another* consciousness, the desire *of another* desire; the momentary revelation of this fact is a scandal. By contrast, consciousness devoid of scandal is an alienated consciousness, exclusively directed towards clear and distinct, rational objects (LE, 200). In Bataille's view, it is precisely by posing the philosophy of consciousness as the irreducible starting point of his analysis that Sartre blinds himself from seeing communication as the foundation of *socius*, and hence is only able to grasp the relationship to others as an impenetrable opaqueness. For Bataille:

> [H]umanity is not composed of isolated beings but of communication between them. Never are we revealed, even to ourselves, other than in a network of communications with others. We bathe in communication, we are reduced to this incessant communication whose absence we feel, even in the depths of solitude, like the suggestion of multiple possibilities, like the expectation of the moment when it will solve itself in a cry heard by others.
>
> (LE, 198–199)

At the same time, however, man cannot escape his position as an isolated individual which in Bataille's theory is linked to the human consciousness of objects. The birth of the transcendental universe of objects gives rise to the fear of death, since the consciousness of time emerges simultaneously with the division of the world into subjects and objects. The isolated and, in this sense, object-like individual can only regain access to the immediacy of the world relation during those short instants in which the projective relationship (concern or anguish) to the future vanishes for a split second. This is the point where the useless expenditure steps into the picture: for Bataille expenditure is the channel through which the isolated beings communicate. In fact, all the Bataillean figures of expenditure (sacrifice, eroticism, authentic art, etc.) can be seen through this lens which amalgamates expenditure and communication: outflow of energy, transgression of the limits of the separated individual. Bataille wants to emphasise that the isolation of beings only pertains to the domain of the real, that is, the universe of objects:

> The *subject* leaves its own domain and subordinates itself to the *objects* of the real order as soon as it becomes concerned for the future. For the *subject* is consumption insofar as it is not tied down to work. If I am no longer concerned about "what will be" but about "what is," what reason do I have to keep anything in reserve? I can at once, in disorder, make an instantaneous consumption of all that I possess... If I thus consume immoderately, I reveal to my fellow beings that which I am intimately. Consumption is the way in which separate beings communicate. Everything shows through, everything is open and infinite between those who consume intensely.
>
> (AS 1, 58)

Man thus finds himself in a deeply ambivalent position. To refuse communication (to lock oneself away in an egoistic solitude) is obviously not acceptable. But on the other hand, communication cannot occur without violating and soiling those it involves, and so it is also impregnated with guilt. Paradoxically, men can only communicate with each other when stepping outside of themselves. And since they have to communicate, they also have to *will* the evil and the defilement which makes them *penetrable* to one another only by exposing their being, putting it at risk.

The link between communication, morality and evil is located at this point. In communication the object of desire is essentially the transgression of being, or the violation of its integrity. Evil, on the other hand, fundamentally abandons all concern for the future. It is precisely in this sense Bataille can claim that the aspiration to the summit, i.e.

the impulses toward evil, are the very basis of *morality* within us. Morality demands that we risk ourselves and reject any concern for the future – otherwise it is but a rule in the service of utility, devoid of any passion, or of authentic innocence (N, 27–28; LE, 186–187). Heroism, sanctity and evil thus spring from a common source: the possibility of breaking the rule, the frightening yet attractive infraction which is bound to exuberance and contempt for death.

The basic problem of Sartre's conception of morality, as Bataille sees it, is how to reconcile the idea of radical freedom with traditional, conventional morality, the ultimate foundation of which is utility.[3] Bataille points to Sartre's way of rejecting categorically the "ancient societies of consumption", whose feudal practices Genet tries to capitalise on, and to which Sartre opposes the useful and productive Soviet society. In other words, Sartre associates evil with the harmful and the good with the useful – useless expenditure is morally reprehensible. But how is this stance to be reconciled with his idea of radical freedom, defining man's being-in-the-world? Bataille claims that the freedom which Sartre is proclaiming is on the side of the devil without knowing it, insofar as good always signifies *submission* and obedience to firmly established rules, whereas freedom is revolt, violation of the rules and hence an opening to evil. Sartre himself hints at the connection between freedom and evil when he observes that Genet places himself above and beyond all essences by declaring his will and capacity to do what best pleases him (in other words, he is not limited by any essence). However, what Sartre does not see is that the useless expenditure that he so categorically condemns, is the opposite of production, in precisely the same way as the sovereign is the opposite of the subordinate or freedom that of slavery (LE, 196–198).

Bataille's "morality" (if we can speak of such a thing) which associates the moral summit with the abundance of energy and its unlimited consumption, has strong and explicit Nietzschean undertones. However, instead of "good" and "evil", Bataille proposes to talk about "summit" and "decline". In this sense his approach is devoid of the slightly contemptuous and superior tone Nietzsche often assumes, for instance when speaking about Christianity as a "slave morality". Morality in Bataille's writings is simply founded on economical reasoning, although one that defies any standard economistic thinking.[4] It should be noted that the "moral summit" he is advocating is essentially a place where life is in the end impossible. It can be approached only by wasting forces without calculation or limit. But human forces are not unlimited, as Bataille himself points out – hence the necessity of prohibitions on which the domain of labour and reserves is based. Human nature cannot reject the concern for the future, otherwise it would be at the mercy of its slightest desires. The states in which this concern no longer touches us are super- or sub-human (characteristic for the Nietzschean superman or a beast).

In Bataille's theory the ultimate foundation of sovereignty and evil is the never-ending play of prohibition and transgression. Evil always presupposes a common measure (prohibition, law), even though it is itself incommensurate (that is, accessible only in the transgression of the law). Therein lies also the problem of Jean Genet. In his striving for an unlimited evil, for the annihilation of all laws, he misses the essential. The attraction of sin is at the origin of his frenzy; but if he denies the legitimacy of any rule or law altogether, his action loses its motives. The will to nothingness, which does not accept any limits, is reduced to futile agitation. The evil-doer would be left with nothing, were it not for a literary trick that allowed him to present as worthy a thing, the worthlessness and falsehood of which he has himself already realised (LE, 187–188).

This observation is coupled with another critical remark that Bataille addresses to Genet. Genet does not strive to communicate with his readers; on the contrary, he denies the very idea of communication. This is why his works do not attain the stronger communication which poetry and literature are always striving to reach. The author struggles to abolish his/her own isolation in the work; he/she addresses the reader who reads in order to annul his/her separation, to reach something sovereign for a split second. Since Genet refuses communication, he never touches this sovereign instant – the moment when he would cease to reduce the world to his own actions as an isolated individual. He demands to be sanctified by the reader, but the very idea of communication presupposes the equality of those communicating. It is this fundamental affinity that Genet denies, however: he wants to be recognised by an audience that he himself refuses to recognise. From Bataille's point of view, herein lies his imposture: without the "authentic innocence", that is, the shared passion of being opened up and exposed, literature and poetry will lose their *raison d'être*. What is left is but the empty hubris of an isolated individual, the mask of a jester (LE, 189–192).

Jean Genet is seeking sovereignty in evil; it is evil that generates those moments of vertigo during which he feels able to escape the essence constricting him. But the will to surrender oneself to an *unlimited* evil paradoxically signifies the loss of sovereignty, because the evil that sovereignty presupposes is necessarily limited: *sovereignty itself constitutes its limit*. Sovereignty in the Bataillean sense thus demands that we position ourselves also above its own eventual "essence" – at the very same (empty) spot where Sartre situates freedom. It is precisely as communication that sovereignty also ranges itself against any attempt to subordinate it to serve an individual utility. "*In the instant* in which it occurs communication presupposes the sovereignty of the individuals communicating with each other, just as sovereignty presupposes communication" (LE, 201).

Genet's indifference to communication is the reason why the reader finds his stories interesting, but fails to engage passionately in them. Their seductive effect is subordinated to the interest of external success. However, it should be emphasised (and Bataille does not fail to do this) that we cannot speak about Genet's "lacking sovereignty" as if it could be juxtaposed with or opposed to some sort of "real" sovereignty, on which we could lean. Sovereignty, which man has never ceased to pursue, has never been within his reach and never will be. What Bataille advocates is a virtual sovereignty which has its basis in the human existence: every human being partakes in it, but it is not located in any of them and no one can own it (sovereignty is precisely the opposite of a thing). In his search for a royal dignity and sovereignty Genet commits a double misunderstanding by trying to *use* sovereignty for his *own* interests alone.

The same basic paradox supports Bataille's analysis of Marquis de Sade, whose work obsessed him from the beginning of the 1930s until his death. Sade is also examined in *Literature and Evil*, where Bataille focuses on the impossibility of the experience which he sees Sade as pursuing. For Bataille, this impossibility culminates in Sade's will to achieve clear consciousness of what outbursts of violence "normally" reach without acknowledging it, namely the suppression of the difference between the subject and the object (the age-old dream of philosophers, Bataille notes); this consciousness entails the modification, or rather, the annihilation of the object (LE, 115). In this sense the liberty that Sade is after, being the ultimate limit of all liberty, is in the end impossible – in the same way as is his will to reach the summit of sexual frenzy (*jouissance*) lucidly, in full and clear consciousness.

Of equal if not greater interest in this context are Bataille's two essays on de Sade published approximately at the same time (1957) in *Eroticism*. It is here that Bataille analyses what could be called the "paradox of apathy" which pertains to the attitude assumed by the protagonists of de Sade's fictions. Although the sadistic torturers seemingly get their pleasure from the sufferings of their victims, this excitement paradoxically presupposes a profound indifference concerning all feelings. The one who admits the value of the other, necessarily limits himself.

Therefore, brought to its logical end, the movement of excess entails the destruction of its object. This supreme moment of violence (and of *jouissance*) is what Sade calls "apathy". Apathy requires the annihilation of all "parasitic" sentiments, such as pity, gratitude, or love, the energy of which is by this way recuperated and redirected to other (superior) ends; but it also constitutes the opposite of any sort of spontaneity of passion or "sentimental effusion": in order for the passion to be transformed into energy, it has to be *contained*, mediated by a moment of insensibility. Paradoxically, the greatness of the truly great libertines is thus due to the fact that they have killed in themselves all capacity of pleasure – in the end, their cruelty is but the extreme form of negation of oneself, as Bataille points out (E, 170–173).

This unlimited form of pleasure, pushed to the borders of the (im) possible and unhesitatingly judged as evil by any average man, equates with the search for an impersonal sovereignty. However, this sort of sovereignty is only possible for fictional characters, devoid of any loyalty towards the subjects to whom they owe their power. The sovereign man of Sade becomes victim of his own sovereignty in the sense that he is *not free to depart* from his own extremity (for instance by subordinating himself to more mediocre forms of pleasure). At this point of negation (of oneself as well of the others), all personal pleasure loses its meaning – the only thing that counts is the crime pushed to its peak. And this requirement is, in a way, exterior to individuals; it is like an impersonal mechanism that, once set loose, is unable to stop or to change its course. Bataille also calls this paradoxical situation "impersonal egoism". In this respect, Sade in his moral solitude is much closer to the authentic sovereignty than Genet: not only does he *not* ask to be recognised by his audience, but he demands that even his name be forgotten, effaced from the memory of the living. What he communicates is the impossibility of communication, that which exceeds all that could be shared (E, 174–176).

In spite of these insurmountable paradoxes as well as the utterly monotonous character of the catalogues of tortures in Sade's fictions, Bataille claims that his impossible project still manages to capture a capital aspect of human existence. Sade's truth is precisely in the *revolt* and horror which he generates in the *average man* – this other that his fictions so systematically want to annihilate. The era of psycho-analysis has acknowledged the existence of these destructive impulses and classified them as pathological. Sade's fictions have contributed to the self-awareness of the modern man in showing that what most horrifies him is, in fact, *inside* of him. Those who slaughtered their fellow beings in Auschwitz or Treblinka were not monsters from outer space, but ordinary family men. This is what Bataille pointed out quite clearly already before the war in Acéphale: the monstrosity is not outside (in the "other"), but inside of us (VE, 181).

Yet, what distinguishes Sade from the slaughterers of the Nazi regime is not only his *solitude*, the fact that his violence is that of an individual giving free rein to his passions as opposed to the cold, calculated and disciplined violence of an organised state, where affectivity is *subjugated* to serve a legal power.[5] It is also the fact that the legitimate cruelty of the torturers appointed by the state is *mute*: it does not speak out its name, it does not use the language of violence but that of bureaucracy. Sade, by contrast, dwells on words: his torturers are given to monologues, never tiring of explaining their deeds. But in the end, as Bataille observes, it is Sade, the solitary victim in his prison cell, who speaks in their name – who addresses his fellow beings with this paradoxical and outrageous discourse defying the limits of all morality. In this sense, Sade also betrays the sovereign silence which characterises real violence. Language belongs to the moral or "normal" man whom he wants to defy and shock, but his own revolt can only happen through words (E, 186–190).

In the end, we cannot learn the lesson of Sade if we do not first comprehend its absurdity – this is why the modern admirers of the divine Marquis completely miss the point, as Bataille remarks, referring first and foremost to Breton and the surrealists. Sade's voice comes from another world, that of an *inaccessible solitude*, and cannot be heard unless the paradox and the impasse it involves is first grasped. What Sade wanted to bring into the domain of consciousness is precisely what revolts it the most. This paradoxical enterprise was only possible in a complete solitude – physical as well as moral, as Maurice Blanchot had already observed (Blanchot 1949, 220–221) – and under the guise of fiction. As it has been pertinently pointed out, in this sense, Sade's perversity is illuminating in a way which would not have been possible before the era of psychoanalytical and ethnographic self-understanding (Gifford 2006, 206).

> If normal man today is entering profoundly into an awareness of what transgression signifies for him, this is because de Sade opened up the way. Now normal man knows that his consciousness had to open itself to what had most violently revolted him: what revolts us most violently is within us.
>
> (E, 196)

The moral summit that Bataille seeks is reminiscent of Kafka's Castle: in the end, it is always out of reach. As Bataille himself puts it, it withdraws from us precisely as far as we remain human, that is, as far as we continue to *speak*. The summit posed as a goal or a good is no longer the summit. It is reduced to utility *by the sole fact of being talked about*. Since sovereignty belongs to the domain of silence, we betray it as soon as we open our mouths. Cutting at the limits of language, the stronger communication which Bataille posits as the foundation of poetry and literature, is ultimately the desire for the impossible, just like the sovereign evil of Genet and Sade. With one important difference, however: Bataille's communication presupposes *community*, the multiplicity of those communicating. The "misery of poetry" is what we are faced with when the author reduces his work to his personal obsessions as an isolated subject.

But this also means that authentic poetry in Bataille's sense must suppress the author's desire to endure. The authenticity of poetry and, more generally, of art, is tied to a paradoxical temporality which defies endurance. The "poetry of event" or of instant – a notion which Bataille elaborated during the 1940s – can again be seen in contrast with and as a response to the Sartrean "engagement", or the philosophy of the project: a dynamic, heterogeneous experience of qualitative intensities, challenging the always projective, anticipatory temporality of the Sartrean ego.[6] However, this instantaneous temporality also places the Bataillean sovereignty beyond the spheres or action and of history, where it has no power whatsoever: sovereignty can only exist in a constant revolt against any form of duration.[7] It is only as revolt that it can maintain the purity of passion which is the condition of the moral value in Bataille's sense – the very same revolt which also binds it to the infraction (transgression) of the law, that is, to evil (OC XI, 248–249; OC XII, 164). All in all, sovereignty which calls into question both the metaphysical mastery of the subject and the reign of historical time, is ultimately always out of reach, even if the singularity of human existence is constituted by its pursuit.

> Perhaps the desire to know has just one meaning: to serve as motive for the desire to question. No doubt knowledge is necessary for the autonomy that action – by which it transformed the world – procures for humanity. But beyond the conditions of *doing*, knowledge finally appears as a decoy, when faced with the interrogation that commands it. [...] If I knew how to respond to moral questions... I would distance myself decidedly from the summit. It is by leaving the interrogation open as an inner wound that I maintain chance, a possible access toward the summit [...]
> (E, 47)

Notes

1 In this debate, preceded by a presentation, Bataille elaborated his views, especially concerning the traditional concepts 'good' and 'evil' and, more generally, his views on morality; see US 26–76; on the discussion itself, its general context and participants, see also Surya 2010.
2 On the relationship between affectivity and economy in Bataille's writings, see Arppe 2014.
3 It must be noted that Bataille's analysis of Genet dates from 1957 (his first discussion on the subject is already from the beginning of the 1950s in the essay "Jean-Paul Sartre et l'impossible révolte de Jean Genet", published in the revue *Critique*), whereas Sartre's posthumous notes on the moral philosophy (*Cahiers pour une morale*) were not published until 1983.
4 On the relationship of Bataille's "general economy" to the main lines of the political economy, see also Sørensen 2012.
5 On the evil harnessed to the service of a legal power and the problems posed by the historicity of morals, see also Surya 1992, 523–535. The difference between the disciplined affectivity and the free rein of passions was already very much at the forefront in the dissent between Bataille and Roger Caillois in the Collège de Sociologie – on this, see also Arppe 2007.
6 On the Bataillean "poetry of event", see in particular Guerlac 2000, 89–90; on the difficulty of reconciling the ontology of the subject with the historico-political engagement in Sartre's own philosophy, see also Sichère 2006, 120–129.
7 On the problem of the relationship between sovereignty, revolt, action and history, see also Bataille's essays on Hegel and Camus: Bataille OC XII, 149–169; OC XI, 349–369.

References

Arppe, Tiina. 2007. "Sorcerer's Apprentices and the 'Will to Figuration' – the Ambiguous Heritage of the 'Collège de Sociologie'". *Theory, Culture and Society*, 26(4), 117–145.

Arppe, Tiina 2014. *Affectivity and the Social Bond – Transcendence, Economy and Violence in French Social Theory*. London: Ashgate.

Baugh, Bruce. 2003. *French Hegel – from Surrealism to Postmodernism*. New York & London: Routledge.

Blanchot, Maurice. 1949. *Lautréamont et Sade*. Paris: Minuit.

Genet, Jean. 2004. *Our Lady of the Flowers*. Paris: The Olympia Press (originally *Notre Dame des Fleurs*, Gallimard, 1951).

Gifford, Paul. 2006. *Love, Desire and Transcendence in French Literature: Deciphering Eros*. London: Ashgate.

Guerlac, Suzanne. 2000. *Literary Polemics: Bataille, Sartre, Valery, Breton*. Stanford: Stanford UP.

Kojève, Alexandre. 1947. *Introduction à la lecture de Hegel*. Paris: Gallimard.

Sartre, Jean-Paul. 1947. "Un nouveau mystique". In *Situations*, I, 173–213. Paris: Gallimard.

Sartre, Jean-Paul 1952. *Saint-Genet – comédien et martyr*. Paris: Gallimard.

Sichère, Bernard. 2006. *Pour Bataille*. Paris: Gallimard.

Sørensen, Asger. 2012. "On a universal scale: Economy in Bataille's general economy". *Philosophy and Social Criticism* 38(2), 169–197.

Surya, Michel. 1992. *Georges Bataille – la mort à l'œuvre*. Paris: Gallimard.

Surya, Michel 2010. "Présentation". In Bataille, Georges, *Discussion sur le péché*, 7–49. Paris: Lignes.

14 Bataille's Literary Writings

Patrick ffrench

Georges Bataille is the author of some of the most distinctly trans-gressive and singular fictional writings of the 20th century, although some of these were written under various pseudonyms – Lord Auch, Pierre Angélique, Louis Trente – and others long existed only as forgotten or unfinished drafts, belatedly or posthumously published. In keeping with his theoretical emphases on the continuity of the sacred and the abject, on the fundamental need for sacrificial or other forms of expenditure, and his consistent affirmation of extreme experience as the source of revelation and of truth, Bataille's fictional texts perform excess, both in terms of their themes and events, and in their form and shape. Often incomplete, punctuated by silence, fractured and frag-mented, they reveal in this very lack of closure and completion the limits of language, and in doing so provoke an abyssal vertigo in their readers.

The corpus of Bataille's fictional texts is not in itself extensive, con-sisting of six main narratives: *Story of the Eye*, by "Lord Auch" (1928, revised 1947), *Blue of Noon* (written in 1935 but not published until 1957, under the name Georges Bataille), *Madame Edwarda*, by "Pierre Angélique" published in 1941, *L'Abbé C*, published in 1950, by Georges Bataille, *My Mother*, posthumously published in 1966 and *The Dead Man*, a narrative in 28 "tableaux", written in the early 1940s, also incomplete texts, published posthumously. A further short narrative text, "Story of Rats" is included in the book *The Impossible*. Other unfinished projects such as *Charlotte d'Ingerville* and *La Maison brûlée* (*The Burnt House*), the latter consisting of narrative fragments for a potential feature film, never realized, would also, strictly speaking, come under the genre of literary fiction. However, Bataille's fictional writings, those texts which feature an independently existing world with imaginary agents endowed with some kind of psychology, are only separated by porous boundaries from other less generically identifiable texts such as parts of *Inner Experience* and *Guilty*. As we will show, the fictional texts are imbricated in the theoretical writings, and vice versa, to the extent that despite the undeniable autonomy of works such as *Story of the Eye, Blue of Noon* and *Madame Edwarda*, their writing springs from the same creative, transgressive impetus that produces the more pedagogically oriented texts such as *The Accursed Share* or *Eroticism*, or the subversive visions of *The Solar Anus* and *The Pineal Eye*.

Bataille conceives of fiction as something to which an author has been *driven*. Stories and novels, written in rage, and read "sometimes in a trance", reveal the excessive possibilities of life and in doing so enable us to discover the "manifold truth of life" (BN, 105). The 1957 preface to *Blue of Noon* establishes an implicit programme for fiction – to reveal the truth of life; insofar as, for Bataille, that truth lies in excess, fiction must chart the territory of extremity. Bataille thus conceives of fiction as fundamentally *realist*, not in the sense of mimesis – a re-presentation of the real, but as revelatory of the truth of life in emotive and affective intensity. Irrespective of the subject matter involved, only those stories which derive from or induce states of excessive intensity *count*; Bataille's "haphazard" list of what counted for him includes works by Emily Brontë, Kafka, Proust, Stendhal, Sade, Maurice Blanchot, Balzac and Dostoyevsky (BN, 105).

It is worth asking, however, if Bataille conceived of his own fictions as having lived up to this demand; do they accompany the list of "limit" texts Bataille highlights? In the preface cited above he confesses that the "freakish anomalies" of *Blue of Noon* emerged from a state of anxious intensity, that it was written "in the blaze of events" (BN, 106). But, he adds, the moment has passed, and he had "more or less forgotten" about the manuscript (BN, 106). He defers to the judgement of his friends who had urged him to publish the text. The 22-year gap between the writing of the main body of the narrative and the publication of the book is symptomatic of the troubled state of Bataille's authorship, when it comes to his fictional writings. Many if not all of his significant fictional texts appear somewhat displaced, as if they occupied a space slightly beside themselves, doubling and commenting on their status as literary fictions with a corrosive irony.

Bataille's narrative texts are, in this light, fictions of failure. They do not fail in the way that Beckett's texts fail, drawing on failure as the entropic force of their persistence, failing again and failing better. They fail in a much more radical manner, failing to cohere, to continue, to complete. In one dimension this is the failure of desire; it is desire that fails at the extreme point, the point of abjection, of exhaustion, of illness or drunkenness; at the extreme point of desire as such, desire fails.

Bataille writes the narrative of this fading, of impotence, of *aphanisis*, the disappearance of desire. Perhaps more than any other writer Bataille explores in his fiction the relations between writing and reading and desire, but not in terms of the desire for an object, that can be satisfied by the attainment of that object (despite the title of an early translation of *Madame Edwarda: A Tale of Satisfied Desire*), and not in terms of a desire for truth, for meaning, but desire at its extreme limit, a kind of desire which induces rage. Like the writers that he says are worth reading, one feels that Bataille wrote out of rage. This rage cannot, however, be sustained; it fails; it collapses. Unlike poetry, which could in Bataille's sense consume (destroy) meaning instantaneously in a "holocaust of words", in the explosion of the obscene word itself, in fiction, the intensity, the rage is sustained, but fails (IE, 137). It is sustained through the construction of a theme, a narrative, through the incidence of chapter headings, images, "characters", all the aspects of what usually constitutes fiction; but it fails to come to fruition, except as loss.

If Bataille's fictions fail to cohere as fictions, fail to complete and sustain themselves as self-sufficient independent worlds, this is also because they are punctured by the real, and because they constantly overflow and seep into the discursive reality of his other writings. They are highly unstable and corrosive objects. It is not an over-generalization to say that all of Bataille's fictional writings problematize their own fictional status, as well as their status as fictions by the "author" Georges Bataille. The narrative of *Story of the Eye*, the "first part" of the book published under that title, is followed by a "second part" in which the author considers the "reminiscences" or "coincidences" of his childhood and adult life which had, he realizes, determined the production of the "partly imaginary" tale (SE 69). The fictional narrative is doubled by a commentary which situates different elements of the narrative in relation to real historical events (such as the death of the bullfighter Granero in Madrid on 7 May 1923). But is this authorial intervention any less part of the fiction the "story" of the eye designated by the title? If we also consider that *Story of the Eye*, as its author tells us, was written in the context of a psychoanalytic "cure" (Bataille was seeing the analyst Adrien Borel), the boundaries between fiction and autobiographical "confession", between the imaginary and the real, are blurred further (SE 71). Our capacity to read the text according to the usual parameters that constitute literary fiction, or those that underpin autobiography, are disabled, troubled. Bataille's authorship, moreover, is not straightforward – the narrative originally "circulated" in 1928 under the name "Lord Auch", and was not formally associated with the name Georges Bataille until much later, in problematic circumstances. *Madame Edwarda*, similarly, was published in 1941 under the name Pierre Angélique, while a "Preface to Madame Edwarda" appears in *Eroticism*, by Georges Bataille, in 1957. *Blue of Noon* was written in 1935, but then forgotten, and not published until 1957. *My Mother*, written in the mid-1950s, was unfinished and published in 1966, four years after Bataille's death. Of Bataille's fictional publications, only *Blue of Noon*, "Story of Rats" included in *The Impossible*, and *L'Abbé C* appeared in his lifetime with the name of the author as "Georges Bataille". The two latter texts, moreover, consistently disturb the authority of the narrative voice, and the stability of their generic status. *The Impossible*, originally titled *The Hatred of Poetry*, is a book which comprises aphoristic essays on poetry, poems and the short narrative "Story of Rats", as if narrative here has to double and shadow the extreme reduction of Bataille's often monosyllabic "poems". *L'Abbé C* is framed by an editorial preface and postface, within which the two narratives of twin brothers oppose and subvert each other. The larger part of "Bataille's literary writings" are thus either pseudonymous, posthumous, or troubled internally, in their very structure.

Yet despite the apparent reluctance, on Bataille's part, to foreground narrative fiction as a major and significant aspect of his expressive voice, there is, in Bataille's work as a whole, a consistent affirmation of the absolute and excessive authority of literary fiction, its *sovereignty*. Literature has a sovereign value (a value not subservient to any higher authority) for Bataille; it is perhaps for this reason that its place in his *œuvre* is apart, displaced, isolated from the rationale of authorship, of genre, of theme. Bataille's fictions are sovereign and singular events, to some extent bound to the singular occurrence, the contingent encounter. Marguerite Duras said of Madame Edwarda and of Dirty, in *Blue of Noon*, that they shared the characteristic of being "there"; Bataille met them in the street one day (Duras 1984, 36). Fiction, for Bataille, is, paradoxically, a means of communicating the truth of such encounters, encounters with something, or with some feeling, which exceeds the bounds of orthodox social communication. This perhaps explains why narrative fiction occupies an important, but displaced, separated place within Bataille's *œuvre* as a whole, and why his fictional texts are deeply imbricated in his other writings. Doubled within themselves, Bataille's fictions are also folded into other texts: a version of the italicized "Part One" of *Blue of Noon* appears as a "chapter" of *Inner Experience*, synthesizing elements of an experience of "atrocious" enlightenment Bataille underwent in Italy in 1934, with his lover Colette Peignot (Laure). The "Preface to Madame Edwarda", ostensibly written by

Georges Bataille but referring to Pierre Angélique as the author of the narrative, is included as a chapter in *Eroticism*, alongside the other "case studies" of the second part, illustrating the anthropological theses of the first part. Theory constantly doubles fiction, and fiction inhabits theory, in Bataille's work.

One explanation for this is fairly straightforward: both fiction and theory have their generative matrix in experience, and the need to communicate experience, and to communicate experiences of excess, generates a form of writing for which generic distinctions carry little weight. From this point of view Bataille's writing appears as the undifferentiated expression of the same dimension of experience, and the generic and disciplinary distinctions – essay, novel, philosophy, economics, literature... – are simply convenient categorizations we impose on the writing after the event, betraying its radical heterogeneity. This explanation, however, belies the specific importance Bataille seemed to attach to fiction, writing, as we have seen, that stories "read sometimes in a trance, have the power to confront a person with his fate" (BN, 105), or devoting two significant review articles of the early 1930s to two key novels of the time – Malraux's *Man's Estate* and Céline's *Journey to the End of Night*, devoting a significant section of *Inner Experience* to poetry (Rimbaud) and to Proust's *In Search of Lost Time*, and many articles and essays to the work of figures such as Emily Brontë, Franz Kafka, Jean Genet, Maurice Blanchot, Samuel Beckett and other contemporaries.[1] Narrative fiction is a predominant theoretical concern for Bataille. I would suggest, again, that this is because it has a sovereign value for Bataille, and as such has a value that is inherently one of contestation, a radical suspension of the world. It is in order to emphasize this suspension and this sovereignty that Bataille situates his own fictions parenthetically within his own work, in order to give them some purchase in the world of the concept, without which they would simply float, in that place apart, suspended and independent from anthropology, economics, expenditure and sexuality, our everyday concerns.

A different way of putting this would be to say that Bataille struggles to conceptualize his own fictions, struggles to accommodate them. The suite of pseudonyms – Lord Auch, Pierre Angélique, Louis Trente, Dianus... – indicates a reluctance to "admit" to these works, as if it would betray them to comprise them under the "name of the author". The fact, however, that at one time Bataille retrospectively envisaged the re-publication of a series of three works "by Pierre Angélique" – *Madame Edwarda, My Mother,* and the incomplete *Charlotte d'Ingerville* – also suggests that there was an impetus towards endowing the fictions, after the event, with a consistency that they lacked, an absent continuity. But this reluctance to "admit" to the fictional texts, to promote them under the authority of the name of the author, of the father, also attests to a desire to maintain their "secrecy", to sustain the contestation which they embody, to resist their dialectical insertion into the body of "literature", or of "fiction", to resist even their recuperation under the heading "Georges Bataille".

If Bataille's fiction is consistently incomplete as fiction, this is in part because through an open window or wound, it seems to connect to the real, to events and their experience. Aside from in the sense proposed above, however, Bataille is neither a realist nor a "committed" (*engagé*) writer, and the landscape of his texts is only minimally historical. Works such as *Story of the Eye*, and *The Dead Man* occur in a fantasy space (albeit one geographically situated), which echoes the terrain of the Gothic. The space and period of *My Mother* and *L'Abbé C* is modern, but only thinly sketched: villages, resorts, churches, bell-towers, with the woods, where wild abandonment occurs, never far. In *Madame Edwarda* and *Blue of Noon*, however, place and event are rather more significant. The brothel *Les Glaces* (the Mirrors) existed, in Paris. The Porte St Denis, under whose arch Edwarda disappears, is real. This real architecture anchors the timeless erotic drama in the modern, and ties it to the precise historical circumstance and economy which now determine the erotic. The architecture of Paris in *Madame Edwarda* serves as the modern stage of what for Bataille is an anthropologically fundamental act of sacrifice, but after Hegel, and after Nietzsche; in other words after the death of God. The brothel is the stage upon which the prostitute Edwarda can come to embody God in the obscenity of her sex.

Blue of Noon, meanwhile, is the most overtly political of Bataille's fictional texts, set against the historical reality of pre-Civil war conflict in Barcelona, and Vienna, just after the assassination of Dolfuss. Bataille sets the drama of Troppmann's sexual drive against the backdrop of a Europe which is drifting inexorably towards fascism. Troppmann, despite his sympathies for the left, is not a Marxist hero. But his attraction for Dirty seems to embroil him in a dubious fascination with death and abjection, with the infinite loss of a fall upwards into the starry sky, implicitly postulated as the only possible counter to the Nazi parade, which elevates death into a phallic obscenity. Resonant in this with his political activity of the time, in such groupings as Contre-Attaque and Acéphale, Bataille's writing and thought risks association with fascism through the evident preference for images and experiences of excess and virulence over those of moderation and humanist consensus.

Blue of Noon nonetheless stakes out a position against the erection of power and the "upright posture" of the militarized regime, posing against it the fall, the collapse, the "fading" of desire into abjection and impotence.[2]

In this light one might assume that Bataille's fictional texts are politically irresponsible, obscene luxuries. Bataille would presumably agree, since for him, literature owes it to itself to plead guilty, and is not subject to moral judgement (it is sovereign, in the sense alluded to earlier). *Blue of Noon*, and in particular its final sequences, are perhaps the moment where the "hyperpolitics" of Bataille's fiction comes most acutely to the fore. It is a fiction which represents and performs sacrifice and loss, which performs the negative, without reserve, and which offers this performance as an acephalous counter to values and ideologies. In this it is a sovereign destruction.

Not in this dissimilar to narratives by Sade, Bataille's texts recurrently resolve into tableau-like erotic scenes – in *Story of the Eye* Sir Edmund strangles the priest Don Aminado while Simone fucks him and the narrator watches. In *Madame Edwarda* the narrator watches while Edwarda mounts and fucks their taxi driver on the back seat. In *The Dead Man* Pierrot masturbates the Count while Marie pisses onto him. In *L'Abbé C* Robert, the priest, looks up and opens his arms as Eponine's coat opens in the wind, revealing her nakedness. Bataille's scenarios often seem to move towards such tableaux, in which the juxtaposition of coincident elements, or various kinds of corporeal ejection make for instantaneous transgressive flashes or freeze frames, often accompanied in their original versions by visual representations of the scenes by some of the 20th century's most powerful artists – Jean Fautrier, Pierre Klossowski, André Masson, Balthus. However, it is not so much external events themselves, the litany of what bodies do to other bodies, that drive Bataille's texts, as the inner experiences to which they give rise. Bataille's fictions are less pornographic or obscene texts in the pure sense of these terms, and rather narratives of the anxiety, shame, abjection and fear caused by the physical fact, by the real of sex and desire. More than Sadean litanies or series of erotic tableaux, they are phenomenologies of shame, disgust and betrayal, all states consistent in their focus on the distance between the common measure, the orthodox appearance of things, the social norm, and the truth of transgression, the extremities of human desire and abjection. Thus in *Story of the Eye*, the persistent return, in the imagination of the narrator or of Simone, of a sense of being "haunted" by the secret associations or continuities between things normally poles apart – an eye and an egg, a bull's testicle, the moon in the sky and a urine stain on a white sheet; the appearance of things is rent by a sudden illumination like a lightning flash. This visual figure lends conceptual form to episodes in other texts – in *L'Abbé C*, Eponine's nakedness, revealed by the opening of her coat, suffices to ruin what remains of Robert's ostensible appurtenance to God, and drives him further into shame – to leave his excrement in the street beneath her window, for example. It is the inner state of anxiety, the anxiety which the Eye's narrator tells us "anything sexual" provoked in him, which more often than not dominates the narratives (SE, 9). It is the anxiety which measures the distance between the acts of the flesh and the social propriety which denies them or hides them. Thus in *Blue of Noon* the narrator Troppmann is driven to stab Xénie's naked thigh, beneath the table, in a drunken wish to break through the veneer of her social face. In his fictions Bataille seeks to reach that place where a being is undone; an animal at its throat, a woman under her dress.[3]

This recurrent state of anxiety and perplexity in relation to things and events makes of the individuals who populate Bataille's fictional worlds strangely anti-heroic figures, apt inhabitants of a world in which moral and political action is at best, redundant, and at worst, impotent. Seldom driven by any will towards action in the world they are, as Leo Bersani (1990) has pointed out, the inverse of Malraux's existential heroes; they are more often than not haunted by the contingent associations of things and figures in the world, driven out of shame or fear or an obscure and apolitical compulsion, to rupture the crust of things, to do what they do. In one of the jacket comments for *Blue of Noon* readers were told that the book was the hidden link between Breton's *Mad Love* and Sartre's *Nausea*.[4] This unexpected trajectory is enlightening, for it reveals the way that Bataille's fiction as a whole combines the disjunctive excesses of the (surrealist) imaginary with an anxious awareness of the radical contingency of human meaning and the moral and ethical indifference of the physical world, including that of sex. Bataille's protagonists are confronted by situations which they are unable to interpret, which leave them in a state of perplexity and affective unrest, much like the state of the reader who assents to open their pages. The recurrent emotion is like having the ground pulled from under your feet, a state of vertigo in which images fuse and seep into one another uncontrollably and somewhat arbitrarily: "Everything was alien to me, I had shriveled up, once and for all, I thought of the bubbles that form over the hole a butcher opens in a pig's throat" (BN, 82); "I stretched out in the grass, my skull on a large, flat rock and my eyes staring straight up at the Milky Way, that strange breach of astral sperm and heavenly urine across the cranial vault formed by the ring of constellations: that open crack at the summit of the sky, apparently made of ammoniacal vapours shining in the immensity (in empty space, where they burst forth absurdly like a rooster's crow in total silence), a broken egg, a broken eye, or my own dazzled skull weighing down upon the rock, bouncing symmetrical images back to infinity" (SE, 42).

Within Bataille's fiction, to a greater extent than in his non-fictional texts, there is a consistent recourse to a poetic device which installs something like an explosive rupture at the heart of the narrative frameworks. I will offer a number of examples of these strange reversals and metaphors which often strike the reader unawares, ruining reliance on a recognizable litany of tropes and images. The reader is in foreign territory, without landmarks. The first example comes towards the end of *Story of the Eye*: "Now I stood up and, while Simone lay on her side, I drew her thighs apart and found myself facing something I imagine I had been waiting for in the same way that a guillotine waits for a neck to slice" (SE, 67). The second comes from *My Mother*, from the episode in which Pierre's mother Hélène has just hinted, for the first time, at the depths of her abjection: "Then she brought out that smutty laugh, the sound of which has left me impaired like a cracked bell" (MM, 24). The third is from *Madame Edwarda*, just after the narrator has pressed his mouth between her legs: "Her bare thigh caressingly nudged my ear, I thought I heard a sound or roaring seasurge, it is the same sound you hear when you put your ear to a large conch shell. In the brothel's boisterous chaos and in the atmosphere of corroding absurdity I was breathing (it seemed to me that I was choking, I was flushed, I was sweating) I hung strangely suspended, quite as though at that same point we, Edwarda and I, were losing ourselves in a wind-freighted night, on the edge of the ocean" (MM, 135). A guillotine awaiting the neck it will slice, a self cracked like a bell, suspension in the night at the edge of the ocean... Bataille's images open up an abyss within the sequence of events, which barely sustain themselves. Such images do not ground their reader in reference, in mimesis, but expose them to the contingency of language, which, as Bataille proposed "can break the links of logic in us" (WS, 138). At a micro-level in Bataille's literary writings one finds a quasi-surrealist suspension of reference, and the vertiginous opening up of the possibility that language can say, and do anything, even hinting at the infinite void in the voicing of words such as "silence" or "God".

Despite appearances to the contrary Bataille's fictions are not oriented towards any specific sexual or erotic content. One might be tempted to suggest that it is the scatological element within them which distinguishes them from other varieties of erotic or transgressive literature. Indeed *The Solar Anus*, which establishes a poetics of anal, volcanic and solar eruption as the dynamic principle of the universe, appears as a programmatic text. The concentrated form of *Le Petit*, which opens with an act of defecation in the street, proferred as an act of love, also places the anus at the secret heart of things, as the inadmissible, unacceptable core. Bataille's writing certainly shares many characteristics with the Bakhtinian grotesque, and draws much power from scatology. However, it is not the substance itself which is affirmed, and neither is it materiality as such, the organ as such, which underpins the abject affect of Bataille's writing, so much as the distance between the high and the low, between the sacred and the profane, which the writing can cut through with a "disastrous rapidity" (ON, 183). The higher the sacred or noble postulate, the lower the element which brings it down low; Bataille's fiction operates a desublimation, putting into play the fundamental "human" need for elevation and the corresponding physical reality. One of the most emblematic scenes in this regard is that in *Madame Edwarda* when the eponymous heroine spreads her legs in front of the narrator and utters the words: "You see, I am GOD" (MM, 135). Profanation is indeed recurrent in Bataille's texts, not least in the final scenes of *Story of the Eye*, with the revelation of the priest's lubricity, his murder and enucleation, or in *L'Abbé C*, entirely structured around the hypocrisy of the supposedly chaste Robert. Robert's betrayal of his God is an operation not limited to the religious world, however; transgression in Bataille's world is betrayal, a travesty of things by their opposites, by what they are not. The heretical copula of *The Solar Anus*, whereby "It is clear that the world is purely parodic, in other words, that each thing seen is the parody of another, or is the same thing in a deceptive form" provides a logic of betrayal or travesty which generates the transgressive flashes of Bataille's fiction, and leads any one thing to collapse into another (VE, 5). Thus the reader encounters propositions such as these: "Madame Edwarda went on ahead of me, raised up into the very clouds... The room's noisy unheeding of her happiness, of the measured gravity of her step, was royal consecration and triumphal holiday: death itself was guest at the feast, was there in what whorehouse nudity terms the pig-sticker's stab" (MM, 135–6). The "royalty" of the sacrifice here is brought low by the profane abjection of the abattoir, as the anthropological scene of sacrifice is displaced into a modern, post-theological world, but one which is in turn haunted by this primal scene. The same operation takes place in *My Mother*, where incest measures the distance between an orthodox rule-bound society and the degradation into which Pierre is drawn.

All of Bataille's fictional writings, without exception, feature a heterosexual couple: the narrator and Simone, in *Story of the Eye*, Troppmann and Dirty, in *Blue of Noon*, the narrator and Madame Edwarda, Pierre and Hélène, in *My Mother*. However, it is a singular feature of Bataille's fictions that in all cases these couples are supplemented by others, by third parties, doubles, substitutes or stand-ins; in *Story of the Eye* Marcelle, who hangs herself part way through, is "doubled" by Don Aminado, whose eye uncannily reproduces her gaze, originating from Simone's vagina, in the final, strikingly poignant tableau of the tale. The narrator and Simone are, moreover, accompanied by Sir Edmund, an envoy of the Gothic tradition. In *Blue of Noon* the male narrator remains a single, linear viewpoint, but the female counterpart is split, as in a kaleidoscope, across different emanations of desire: Xénie, Lazare, Dirty. In *Madame Edwarda*, in a more concentrated form, the taxi driver, whose furious ecstasy with Edwarda the narrator observes, occupies the role of third party. These three texts feature a first-person narrator, which provides continuity across the text, although this viewpoint is itself framed, re-framed by the intervention of the "author", in various forms of preface and postface. But Bataille's tendency towards re-iterative re-framing of the same events, from different narrative viewpoints, is exacerbated in *My Mother* and in *L'Abbé C*. In the latter text, and in "Story of Rats" the narrative viewpoint is doubled, split between two antithetical positions, and fragmented, as if to propose that no single view can complete the picture, that even the tragic decadence of one protagonist can be reversed in the ironic cynicism of another. Bataille seems to practise the constant reversal, or perhaps "betrayal" of any principle of completion, whether tragic or comic. But this procedure, whereby a couple, for example, is supplemented, and viewed from a third perspective, or whereby one narrative is framed within another, also permits excess, sacrifice and loss to be represented, rather than simply experienced. Experienced alone, it would be lost for the reader, and, moreover, the subject of that experience would betray the experience itself in narrating it, in telling it. More often than not, Bataille's narrators are the witnesses of a sacrifice, a sexual or defamatory act, rather than the perpetrators of the act themselves. While in *Inner Experience* Bataille writes of his own failure to write "The Torment", the experience of sovereign loss, in the fictional texts, that experience of loss is performed, staged; there is an inherent tendency towards dramatization in Bataille's fiction. This is perhaps most clearly evident in *The Dead Man*, sole among Bataille's fictions to involve a third person, objective narration, and which, as has been noted, proceeds through "scenes" resembling the "tableaux" of Sade.

Bataille's literary texts are thus hybrid, difficult objects, which represent and dramatize excess but also fail to represent, to cohere. They are sovereign, autonomous entities, but they also seep into the real, and are haunted by it. They feature a ubiquitously male narrative viewpoint, but enact the loss of desire, castration. The experience of reading them is of a vertiginous loss of sense, as if, like Troppmann and Dirty, one were to fall upwards into the void of the sky. To this extent they may be truer to Bataille's vision than the more pedagogically oriented texts such as *Eroticism* or *The Accursed Share*, even while they continue to explore and perform the excess theorized in these texts.

Notes

1 See LE and the review articles contributed to the review *Critique*, founded by Bataille in 1946, collected in the *Œuvres complètes*, vols. XI and XII. For Bataille's reviews of Céline and Malraux, see *Œuvres complètes*, vol. I.
2 For Bataille's analysis of the "upright posture" of the military parade, see "The Psychological Structure of Fascism" in VE.
3 See "Method of Meditation" in *The Unfinished System of Non-Knowledge*.
4 See RR, 310.

References

Bersani, Leo. 1990. "Literature and History". In *The Culture of Redemption*, 102–133. Cambridge, Mass.: Harvard University Press.
Duras, Marguerite. 1984. "A propos de Georges Bataille". In *Outside*, 34–36. Paris: Gallimard.

Bibliography

Texts by Bataille

This bibliography is intended for the English reader and only includes French texts which are referred to in this volume, and for which no English translation is available.

L'Abbé C. 1983. Translated by Phillip A. Facey. London: Marion Boyars.
The Absence of Myth: Writings on Surrealism. 1994. Edited and Translated by Michael Richardson. Verso: London.
L'Apprenti sorcier: Du Cercle Communiste Démocratique à Acéphale. 1999. Edited and introduced by Marina Galletti. Paris: Editions de la Différence.
The Accursed Share: an Essay on General Economy. 3 vols. 1988–1991. Translated by Robert Hurley. New York: Zone Books.
The Bataille Reader. 1997. Edited by Fred Botting and Scott Wilson. Oxford: Blackwell.
Blue of Noon. 1986. Translated by Harry Matthews. London; New York: Marion Boyars.
Choix de Lettres (1917–1962). 1997. Edited by Michel Surya. Paris: Gallimard.
Correspondence: Georges Bataille Michel Leiris. 2008. Edited by Louis Yvert. Translated by Liz Heron. Oxford: Seagull Books.
The College of Sociology 1937–39. 1988. Edited by Denis Hollier. Minneapolis: University of Minnesota Press.
The Cradle of Humanity: Prehistoric Art and Culture. 2009. Translated by Stuart Kendall. Cambridge MA: Zone.
Documents: Doctrines, Archéologie, Beaux-Arts, Ethnographie. 1991. Reprint. Preface by Denis Hollier. 2 vols. Paris: Jean-Michel Place.
Encyclopedia Acephalica. 1995. Edited and introduced by Alistair Brotchie. Translated by Iain White. London: Atlas.
Georges Bataille: Essential Writings. 1998. Edited by Michael Richardson. London: Sage.
"Georges Bataille: Writings on Laughter, Sacrifice, Nietzsche, Un-Knowing". 1986. *October* 36, 3–106.

"Hegel, Death and Sacrifice". 1990. *Yale French Studies* 78: 9–28.
The Impossible. 2001. Translated by Robert Hurley. San Francisco: City Lights.
"Letter to René Char on the Incompatibilities of the Writer". 1990. Translated by Christopher Carsen. *Yale French Studies* 78: 31–43.
Literature and Evil. 1997. Translated by Alistair Hamilton. New York; London: Marion Boyars.
Manet. 1983. New York: Skira/Rizzoli.
My Mother, Madame Edwarda, The Dead Man. 2012. London; New York: Penguin Modern Classics.
Oeuvres Complètes. 1970–1988. 12 vols. Paris: Gallimard.
On Nietzsche. 1998. Translated by Bruce Boone. New York: Paragon.
"Reflections on the Executioner and the Victim". 1991. Translated by Elisabeth Rottenberg. *Yale French Studies* 79: 15–19.
Romans et récits. 2004. Edited by Jean-François Louette. Paris: Bibliothèque de la Pléiade, Gallimard.
La sociologie sacrée du monde contemporain. 2004. Edited and introduced by Simonetta Falasca-Zamponi. Paris: Lignes-Manifestes.
The Story of the Eye. 2001. Translated by Joachim Neugroschel. London: Penguin.
The Tears of Eros. 2001. Translated by Peter Connor. San Francisco: City Lights.
Theory of Religion. 1989. Translated by Robert Hurley. New York: Zone.
The Trial of Gilles de Rais. 1991. Translated by Richard Robinson. Los Angeles: Amok.
The Unfinished System of Non-Knowledge. 2004. Translated and edited by Stuart Kendall and Michelle Kendall. Minneapolis: University of Minnesota Press.
Visions of Excess. Selected Writings 1927–1939. 1985. Translated and edited by Allan Stoekl. Minneapolis: University of Minnesota Press.

Texts on Bataille

This bibliography primarily lists books in English on Bataille or on related subjects.

Ades, Dawn and Simon Baker, eds. 2006. *Undercover Surrealism. Georges Bataille and Documents.* London and Cambridge MA: MIT Press.
Arnould, Elisabeth. 1996. "The impossible sacrifice of poetry, Bataille and the Nancian critique of sacrifice." *Diacritics* 26, 2: 86–96.
Arppe, Tiina. 2007. "Sorcerer's Apprentices and the 'Will to Figuration' – the Ambiguous Heritage of the 'Collège de Sociologie'". *Theory, Culture and Society*, 26(4), 117–145.
Arppe, Tiina 2014. *Affectivity and the Social Bond – Transcendence, Economy and Violence in French Social Theory.* London: Ashgate.
Baudrillard, Jean. 1993. *Symbolic Exchange and Death.* Translated by Ian Hamilton. London and Thousand Oaks: Sage.
Baugh, Bruce. 2003. *French Hegel – from Surrealism to Postmodernism.* New York & London: Routledge.

Biles, Jeremy. 2007. *Ecce Monstrum: Georges Bataille and the Sacrifice of Form*. New York: Fordham University Press.

Bischof, Rita. 1984. *Souveränität und Subversion: Georges Batailles Theorie der Moderne*. München: Matthes & Seitz.

Bischof, Rita. 2010. *Tragische Lachen: die Geschichte von Acéphale*. Berlin: Matthes und Seitz.

Blanchot, Maurice. 1988. *The Unavowable Community*. Translated by Pierre Joris. Barrytown, NY: Station Hill.

Blanchot, Maurice. 1993. *The Infinite Conversation*. Translated by Susan Hanson. Minneapolis: University of Minnesota Press.

Blanchot, Maurice. 2001. *Faux Pas*. Translated by Charlotte Mandell. Stanford: Stanford University Press.

Bois, Yve-Alain and Rosalind Krauss. 1997. *Formless: A User's Guide*. New York and Cambridge, Mass.: MIT Press.

Boldt-Irons, Leslie-Anne. 1995. *Bataille: Critical Essays*. Albany, NY: SUNY Press.

Botting, Fred. 1994. "Relations of the Real in Lacan, Bataille and Blanchot." *SubStance* 23/1, Issue 73, 24–40.

Botting, Fred and Wilson, Scott. 1997. *Bataille: A Critical Reader*. Oxford: Blackwell.

Chi, Jennifer and Azara, Pedro, eds. 2015. *From Ancient to Modern: Archaeology and Aesthetics*. Princeton: Princeton University Press.

Clifford, James. 1988. "On Ethnographic Surrealism." In *The Predicament of Culture: Twentieth-Century Ethnography, Literature, and Art*, 117–151. Cambridge, Mass.: Harvard University Press.

Connor, Peter Tracey. 2000. *Georges Bataille and the Mysticism of Sin*. Baltimore/London: Johns Hopkins University Press.

Derrida, Jacques. 2005. *Writing and Difference*. Translated by A. Bass. London: Routledge.

Didi-Hubermann, Georges. 1995. *La Ressemblance Informe ou le gai savoir visuel selon Georges Bataille*. Paris: Macula.

Dorfman, Ben. 2002. "The Accursed Share: Bataille as Historical Thinker." *Critical Horizons* 3, 1: 37–71.

Falasca-Zamponi, Simonetta. 2011. *Rethinking the Political: the Sacred, Aesthetic Politics and the Collège de Sociologie*. Montréal: McGill-Queen's University Press.

Feher, Michel. 1981. *Conjurations de la Violence: Introduction à la Lecture de Bataille*. Paris: PUF.

ffrench, Patrick 1999. *The Cut: Reading Bataille's Histoire de l'Oeil*. Oxford: Oxford University Press.

ffrench, Patrick. 2007. *After Bataille, Sacrifice, Exposure, Community*. London: Legenda.

Foucault, Michel. 1977. "Preface to Transgression" in *Language, Counter-Memory, Practice: Selected Essays and Interviews*. Edited & translated by Donald F. Bouchard. New York: Cornell University Press.

Foucault, Michel. 1978. *The History of Sexuality. Volume 1: An Introduction.* Translated by Robert Hurley. New York: Pantheon Books.

Gasché, Rodolphe. 2012. *Georges Bataille. Phenomenology and Phantasmatology.* Translated by Roland Végsö. Foreword by David Farrell Krell. Stanford: Stanford University Press.

Gemerchak, Christopher. 2003. *The Sunday of the Negative: Reading Bataille Reading Hegel.* Albany: SUNY Press.

Geroulanos, Stefanos. 2010. *An Atheism that is not a Humanism Emerges in French Thought.* Stanford: Stanford University Press.

Gifford, Paul. 2005. *Love, Desire and Transcendence in French Literature: Deciphering Eros.* London: Ashgate.

Gill, Carolyn Bailey, ed. 1995. *Bataille: Writing the Sacred.* London and New York: Routledge.

Goux, Jean-Joseph. 1990. "General Economics and Postmodern Capitalism." *Yale French Studies* 78: 206–224.

Grindon, Gavin. 2010. "Alchemist of the Revolution: the Affective Materialism of Georges Bataille." *Third Text* 24, 3: 305–317.

Guerlac, Suzanne. 2000. *Literary Polemics: Bataille, Sartre, Valery, Breton.* Stanford: Stanford University Press.

Haar, Michel. 1996. *Nietzsche and Metaphysics.* Translated by Michael Gendre. Albany: SUNY Press.

Hegarty, Paul. 2000. *George Bataille: Core Cultural Theorist.* London: Sage.

Hollier, Denis. 1989. *Against Architecture: The Writings of Georges Bataille.* Translated by Betsy Wing. Cambridge, MA: MIT Press.

Hollier, Denis 1992. "The Use-Value of the Impossible." *October* 60: 1–25.

Hollywood, Amy. 2002. *Sexual Ecstasy: Mysticism, Sexual Difference and the Demands of History.* Chicago: University of Chicago Press.

Hubert, Henri and Mauss, Marcel. 1981. *Sacrifice: Its Nature and Function,* trans. W.D. Halls. Chicago: University of Chicago Press.

Hussey, Andrew, ed. 2000. *The Inner Scar. The Mysticism of Georges Bataille.* Amsterdam (Atlanta): Rodopi.

Hussey, Andrew, ed. 2006. *The Beast at Heaven's Gate, Georges Bataille and the Art of Transgression.* Amsterdam: Rodopi.

Irwin, Alexander. 2002. *Saints of the Impossible: Bataille, Weil and the Politics of the Impossible.* Minneapolis: University of Minnesota Press.

Kendall, Stuart. 2007. *Georges Bataille.* London: Reaktion Books.

Kennedy, Kevin 2014. *Towards an Aesthetics of Sovereignty: Georges Bataille's Theory of Art and Literature.* Cambridge Station, Palo Alto: Academia Press.

Klossowski, Pierre. 2007. *Such a Deathly Desire.* Translated by Russell Ford. Albany: SUNY Press.

Kojève, Alexandre. 1980. *Introduction to the Reading of Hegel: Lectures on the Phenomenology of the Spirit.* Translated by James H. Nichols. New York: Cornell University Press.

Krauss, Rosalind E. 1986. "Antivision." *October* 36: 147–154.

Kristeva, Julia. 1982. *Powers of Horror. An Essay on Abjection.* Translated by Leon S. Roudiez. New York: Columbia University Press.

Lacan, Jacques. 1998. *On Feminine Sexuality: The Limits of Love and Knowledge.* Translated by Bruce Fink. New York & London: Norton & Company.

Mitchell, Andrew and Winfree, Jason, eds. 2009. *The Obsessions of Georges Bataille: Community and Communication.* Albany: SUNY Press.

Nadeau, Maurice. 1978. *The History of Surrealism.* Translated by Richard Howard. London: Penguin.

Nancy, Jean-Luc. 1991a. *The Inoperative Community.* Edited and translated by Peter Connor. Minneapolis: University of Minnesota Press.

Nancy, Jean-Luc 1991b. "The Unsacrificeable." *Yale French Studies* 79: 20–38.

Noys, Benjamin. 2000. *Georges Bataille: A Critical Introduction.* London: Pluto.

Pawlett, William. 2013. *Violence, Society and Radical Theory: Bataille, Baudrillard and Contemporary Society.* London: Ashgate.

Plotnitsky, Arkady. 1993. *Reconfigurations: Critical Theory and General Economy.* Gainesville: University Press of Florida.

Richardson, Michael. 1994. *Georges Bataille.* London: Routledge.

Richardson, Michael and Fijalkowski, Krzystof, eds. 2001. *Surrealism against the Current: Tracts and Declarations.* London: Pluto.

Richman, Michèle. 1982. *Reading Georges Bataille: Beyond the Gift.* Baltimore: Johns Hopkins.

Richman, Michèle. 2002. *Sacred Revolutions: Durkheim and the Collège de Sociologie.* Minneapolis: University of Minnesota Press.

Richman, Michèle 2007. "Spitting Images in Montaigne and Bataille. For a Heterological Counterhistory of Sovereignty." *Diacritics*, 35, 3: 46–61.

Roudinesco, Élisabeth. 1995. "Bataille entre Freud et Lacan: une expérience cachée" in: *Georges Bataille après tout*, edited by Denis Hollier, 191–212. Paris: Belin.

Sartre, Jean-Paul. 2010. *Situations I.* Translated by Chris Turner. London: Seagull.

Sichère, Bernard. 2006. *Pour Bataille.* Paris: Gallimard.

Sørensen, Asger. 2012. "On a universal scale: economy in Bataille's general economy." *Philosophy and Social Criticism*, 38, 2: 169–197.

Stoekl, Allan 1985. *Politics, Writing, Mutilation: the Cases of Bataille, Blanchot, Roussel, Leiris.* Minneapolis: University of Minnesota Press.

Stoekl, Allan. 2007. *Bataille's Peak: Energy, Religion and Post-Sustainability.* Minneapolis: University of Minnesota Press.

Surya, Michel. 2010. *Georges Bataille: an Intellectual Biography.* Translated by Krzysztof Fijalkowski. New York: Verso.

Winnubst, Shannon, ed. 2007. *Reading Bataille Now.* Bloomington, IN: Indiana University Press.

Index

Printed in Great Britain
by Amazon

59667667R00127